THE CONTROVERSIAL THOMAS MORE

THE BEGINNING AND THE BEYOND OF POLITICS

Series editors: James R. Stoner and David Walsh

The series is in continuity with the grand tradition of political philosophy that was revitalized by the scholars who, after the Second World War, taught us to return to the past as a means of understanding the present. We are convinced that legal and constitutional issues cannot be addressed without acknowledging the metaphysical dimensions that underpin them. Questions of order arise within a cosmos that invites us to wonder about its beginning and its end, while drawing out the consequences for the way we order our lives together. God and man, world and society are the abiding partners within the community of being in which we find ourselves. Without limiting authors to any particular framework we welcome all who wish to investigate politics in the widest possible horizon.

THE CONTROVERSIAL THOMAS MORE

POLITICS, POLEMICS, AND PRISON WRITINGS

TRAVIS CURTRIGHT

University of Notre Dame Press
Notre Dame, Indiana

Copyright © 2025 by the University of Notre Dame
University of Notre Dame Press
Notre Dame, Indiana 46556
undpress.nd.edu

All Rights Reserved

Published in the United States of America

Library of Congress Control Number: 2024947141

ISBN: 978-0-268-20914-8 (Hardback)
ISBN: 978-0-268-20915-5 (Paperback)
ISBN: 978-0-268-20917-9 (WebPDF)
ISBN: 978-0-268-20916-2 (Epub3)

GPSR Compliance Inquiries:
Lightning Source France, 1 Av. Johannes Gutenberg, 78310 Maurepas, France
compliance@lightningsource.fr | Phone: +33 1 30 49 23 42

To Robert and Lorraine

CONTENTS

	Acknowledgments	ix
	Abbreviations	xi
	Author's Note	xiii
	Introduction: Speaking Out or Keeping Quiet?	1
ONE	The Creation of More's Tower Works	9
TWO	*A Treatise upon the Passion of Christ* Reconsidered, 1534	32
THREE	The (Auto)Biographical More and *A Dialogue of Comfort against Tribulation*, 1534–1535	59
FOUR	A Letter from Prison to Alice Alington, 1534	85
FIVE	The True Martyr in *De tristitia Christi*, ca. 1535	106
	Conclusion: The Case of Malicious or Merry More	135
	Appendix: Key Dates	143
	Notes	149
	Bibliography	213
	Index	231

ACKNOWLEDGMENTS

I would like to express my warmest thanks first to the editors of this series, James Stoner and David Walsh, for their interest in and cultivation of *The Controversial Thomas More*. Both immediately recognized that the conventional and long-standing depiction of an imprisoned More needed reexamination, and from the start they encouraged my work. I am also indebted to the three anonymous reviewers provided by the University of Notre Dame Press and especially to Megan Levine, Matthew Dowd, and Scott Barker for their editorial leadership and insight in shaping the final version of this book.

I am pleased to thank those who made the writing of this book possible. I learned much from Mark Rankin, Guido Latrè, Martha Driver, and Alexandra Walshingham, who led a National Endowment for the Humanities Summer Seminar, "Printing and the Book during the Reformation, 1450–1650," at the Rare Books and Manuscripts Library at Ohio State University. Eric Johnson, head of the Thompson Special Collections at Ohio State, was unfailingly helpful and offered me hands-on work with early modern texts and, in particular, *The Works of Sir Thomas More* (1557).

Special thanks are due to the Center for Thomas More Studies for its conferences, speakers, and seminars, and especially to founding director Gerard Wegemer, whose comments and review of my entire manuscript proved to be invaluable. Among other colleagues at the Center, I am grateful to Seymour House, Stephen Smith, Marie-Claire Phèlippeau, David Oakley, Louis Karlin, Veronica Brooks, Emily Ransom, Joshua Avery, and Matthew Mehan. The Center's senior advisors, Elizabeth McCutcheon and the late Clarence H. Miller (1930–2019), shared their knowledge of the person and period of More with kindness and generosity in many valuable conversations.

I am pleased to acknowledge Frances Affleck, managing production editor for *Moreana: Thomas More and Renaissance Studies* at Edinburgh University Press, and Kathryn Wehr, managing editor of *Logos: A Journal of Catholic Thought* at the University of St. Thomas, for their permissions to use previously published materials that appear in chapters 4 and 5.

The Controversial Thomas More also owes a debt to students, colleagues, and family. I thank my students for their ongoing interest in More and in his writings. For friendship and good counsel, I am grateful to Michael Dauphinais, Bradley Ritter, and Michael Timmis. To my wife, Mary, and to my children, I offer thanks for their encouragement, and to my daughter, Marina, for my bibliography. This book is dedicated to my parents, Robert and Lorraine, and in loving memory of my father.

ABBREVIATIONS

CCTM	*The Cambridge Companion to Thomas More*, ed. George M. Logan (Cambridge: Cambridge University Press, 2011).
Corr.	*The Correspondence of Sir Thomas More*, ed. Elizabeth Frances Rogers (Princeton, NJ: Princeton University Press, 1947).
CW	*The Complete Works of St. Thomas More*, 15 vols. (New Haven, CT: Yale University Press, 1963–97).
EW	*The Works of Sir Thomas More, Knight, Sometime Lord Chancellor of England, Written by him in the English Tongue*, 2 vols., ed. William Rastell, (London: Scholar Press, 1978). Originally published in London by John Cawod, John Waly, and Richard Tottell in 1557.
Harpsfield	Nicholas Harpsfield, *The Life and Death of Sir Thomas More, Knight*, ed. Elsie Vaughan Hitchcock (London: Early English Text Society, 1932; repr. 1963).
LL	*The Last Letters of Thomas More*, ed. Alvaro de Silva (Grand Rapids, MI: Eerdmans, 2000).
L&P	*Letters and Papers, Foreign and Domestic, of the Reign of Henry VIII*, 21 vols., ed. J. S. Brewer, J. Gairdner, and R. S. Brodie (London: Longman, Green, Longman and Roberts, 1862–1932).
ODNB	*Oxford Dictionary of National Biography*
OED	*Oxford English Dictionary*

Roper	William Roper, *The Life of Sir Thomas More*, ed. Richard S. Sylvester and David P. Harding, in *Two Early Tudor Lives: The Life and Death of Cardinal Wolsey and The Life of Sir Thomas More* (New Haven, CT: Yale University Press, 1962), 195–254.
SL	*St. Thomas More: Selected Letters*, ed. Elizabeth Frances Rogers (New Haven, CT: Yale University Press, 1961).
Stapleton	Thomas Stapleton, *The Life and Illustrious Martyrdom of Sir Thomas More*, trans. Philip E. Hallet, ed. E. E. Reynolds (New York: Benziger Brothers, 1928). Originally published in Latin and as Part III of *Tres Thomae*, printed at Donai in 1588.
Statutes of the Realm	*The Statutes of the Realm*, 11 vols., ed. T. E. Tomlins et al. (London: Dawsons, 1810–1828; repr. 1963).
TMSB	*A Thomas More Source Book*, ed. Gerard Wegemer and Steven Smith (Washington, DC: Catholic University of America Press, 2004. I cite Margaret Roper's letter to Alice Alington (August 1534) from this edition and refer to it as the *Letter to Alington*.

AUTHOR'S NOTE

Unless otherwise indicated in the notes, I have modernized all citations from early modern English-language texts. Original spelling appears only for block quotations from More's writings or Rastell's paratexts in the notes. There, the letters *u*, *v*, *i*, and *j* are regularized according to modern usage and standard contractions or abbreviations are silently expanded.

Introduction

Speaking Out or Keeping Quiet?

On 16 May 1532, Sir Thomas More (1478–1535) returned the white leather bag with the great seal of England inside of it to King Henry VIII (1491–1547) and so resigned as lord chancellor. The Submission of the Clergy, which passed the day before, gave the king authority over Church law in England. It also meant that More could no longer serve Henry in good conscience.[1] More's time in government was over, but not his public career as a controversialist.[2]

Over the course of the next year and as a private citizen in Chelsea, More opposed royal propaganda and defended himself in *The Apology of Sir Thomas More*, *The Answer to a Poisoned Book*, and *The Debellation of Salem and Bizance*.[3] The first and last were vigorous defenses of the Church's traditional prerogatives in law and written in direct reply to Henry's own print campaign justifying schism.[4] For More's labors, he was identified and pursued throughout the spring of 1534 as a traitor. When More was given a summons to appear before a council of lords to swear an oath to the Act of Succession on 12 April, the most conspicuous and driven defender of orthodoxy at that time in England retired again, leaving the field of apologetics for good, and sought legal refuge in keeping silent.

Or did he? Of course, More rejected the oath offered him, and he refused to tell his interrogators his reasons for doing so, but after he was sent to the Tower of London, More continued to do what any prolific author of polemical literature does. He wrote. In the chapters that follow, I will examine More's prison writings, commonly now called the "Tower Works," as they have been collected and handed down since the original edition of *The Works of Sir Thomas More, Knight, Sometime Lord Chancellor of England, Written by him in the English Tongue* (1557), and edited by his nephew William Rastell (1508–65).[5] In the process, I will present a picture never before argued of More's opposition to his king. Contrary to the traditional understanding of More, he remained an apologist for the ancient Christian Church and its historical continuity and unity of belief, or what he called "Christ's true Catholic faith," or the "Catholic Church," which alone was instructed by "the spirit of God."[6] This was the Church of a united Christendom but one under threat of schism in England.[7] More never abandoned his defense of "the very common known Catholic Church" during the years of 1534 and 1535, the last ones of his life.[8] In short, he spoke out by writing.

Silent More is a manufactured image. Chapter 1 demonstrates that historians and biographers have emphasized More's final phase of life and canon to reveal a new man: More's incarceration significantly changed his outlook and caused him to look heavenward rather than ponder the state of England. According to this view, the Tower Works "contain no trace of More the humanist, More the lawyer, More the king's counsellor, or More the persecutor of heretics, but only of the More who had wished, long ago, to spend his life in a Carthusian monastery." In prison, More found a "merciful God," and "he became serenely human."[9] As a result, "devotional More," author of the Tower Works, is sharply distinguished from "controversial More," the author of apologetics, and both from an earlier "humanist More," known for *Utopia*.

Seen in this light, More's last works "become essential to the trajectory of English Catholicism in the next century," but they were not part of an ongoing personal campaign to rebut royal propaganda about Henry's claim to supremacy, or even an attempt to address the political and theological controversies of the day.[10] By extension, More's own witness on the scaffold spurred later nostalgic political dreams of English Catholics, which would be realized under Queen Mary I (1516–58, r. 1553–58), a brief reign that nevertheless produced a revival of More's writings.[11] In sum, the Tower Works point to More's religious prayers and reflections while imprisoned, a period read in anticipation of his trial and death, and his death as a moment when Henry's adversaries momentarily gain "cultural traction."[12]

Such a critical tradition stems from Rastell's *The Works of Sir Thomas More*, published at the expense of John Cawod (1514–72), John Waly (1546–86), and Richard Tottell (ca. 1528–93). Rastell set 1533 as the last year of More's apologetical writings, a marker unquestioned by most scholars, but I will prove that the *Treatise upon the Passion* extended his polemical phase into 1534 and show how More's other major Tower Works may also be read as controversial literature.[13]

As a result, my findings will challenge previous depictions of More's so-called polemical phase where "the real Thomas More" was advanced by an entire school of critics.[14] In these readings, "controversial More" turns out to be the "real More" and a highly unappealing human being. Were we to accept this view, right up until the last days of 1533 More was an unbalanced and troubled reactionary, even "schizophrenic," and "fueled by a mixture of fear, paranoia, hatred, and a zealous desire to defend the faith." In accordance with Rastell's division of More's canon, these same studies contrast such a figure with a "devotional More," who was "charitable" and found his "calm regained" after his turn from writing against heresy to *A Treatise upon the Passion*.[15] More, however, didn't become a completely different person after his arrest or even before it when he wrote his *Treatise* in the spring of 1534.[16] What becomes evident in examination of when and why More wrote his final works is that both the "polemical phase" and the "devotional phase" of his canon too easily lapse into biographical fictions or critical exaggerations tailored to fit Rastell's folio.

Indeed, there would be no genre of Tower Works, as we now understand it, without Rastell. The consensus view of this magisterial edition is that it remains "a valuable resource" because it includes "material that would otherwise have been lost."[17] Titles published by Rastell for the first time include the ninth book of the *The Confutation of Tyndale's Answer* (1533), *A Treatise upon the Passion* (1534), an English translation of *De tristitia Christi* (ca. 1535), and More's most important prison letters.[18] The last three are grouped together as Tower Works, and a fourth, *A Dialogue of Comfort against Tribulation* (1534–35), is included in the 1557 edition by way of a much-improved version of its original printing in 1553.[19]

So, too, modern scholarly editions of More's Tower Works rely upon Rastell's folio. The Yale editors of *The Complete Works of St. Thomas More*, today's most authoritative critical editions, are no exception. Gary Haupt, editor of the *Treatise upon the Passion*, explains: "We have every reason to believe that Rastell was a good editor, and although we cannot know what minor changes he may have made, it seems clear that his major changes were editorial liberties for which he no doubt felt (I believe correctly) that he had More's license. I have therefore chosen 1557 as copy text because it doubtless reflects More's intentions and because it is the text which has already entered into literary tradition."[20] Though Haupt himself was an excellent editor, we may not have every reason to believe that Rastell was just as good.[21] At least, Haupt's assurance that Rastell's "editorial liberties" had "More's license" raises a question. The Yale editors often assume that we know "More's intentions." How do they know? They infer them from Rastell's presentation of texts, which in turn validates his 1557 edition, and the subsequent Yale editions based upon the same.

Of course, Rastell's editing skills are often praised, and sometimes for good reason.[22] He was a publisher and editor of More works and modernized his uncle's spelling, eliminated virgules, and in some cases created printed texts superior to their originals.[23] He polished More's earlier versions by correcting biblical quotations according to the Vulgate and supplied marginal glosses.[24] Two-thirds of More's works had been published before the 1557 folio, but "Rastell's achievement is to have organized so unwieldy a bulk of materials into a single book."[25] This "achievement" wasn't merely editorial. After More's death, Rastell carefully preserved his uncle's books and manuscripts in London and during a period of exile in Louvain (1549–53).[26] Rastell is admired by some More scholars, in other words, not only for his printing but also for his loyalty or devotion to his uncle.[27]

Yet Rastell's treatment of the Tower Works is curious. Previously unpublished material by More now includes a biographical narrative that headnotes and paratexts develop. Thus, the arrangement and commentary for the Tower Works differs from the organizing principle

Rastell followed at the start. The case in point would be the inclusion of an English translation by Mary Basset (ca. 1523–72) of a Latin work by More in a collection otherwise dedicated to his English prose. Basset was More's granddaughter, but her translation wasn't a work "written by him in the English tongue." For reasons such as these, Dale B. Billingsley finds some "pious cunning" at work in Rastell's editorial art. The Tower section of Rastell's folio "seems designed to lead us to an understanding of More the martyr as we follow him on his way to the scaffold, not through the political processes that led to his death."[28] Billingsley's comment is richly suggestive not only for its reflection upon Rastell's legacy but also because it points toward the "political processes" underway while More wrote from prison.

Indeed, the reliance of scholars upon Rastell contributes to the conflation of More, the martyr-saint of England in 1557, with the prisoner in the Tower, who writes in 1534–35.[29] Thus, More's intentions under the reign of Henry reemerge undiluted and unchanged under Queen Mary I. Or, perhaps more accurately, the 1557 presentation of the Tower Works more than twenty years after their original composition remains the best account available of its author. But if so, readers of the Tower Works will follow the editorial design of Rastell, including his curated narrative of spiritual development and reflections, and without sufficient attention to the "political processes" that led to its author's execution.

This book interrogates More's purposes and Rastell's presentation of them. Chapter 1 documents Rastell's distortions and legacy with an emphasis upon how More's long-standing support of papal primacy came to be diminished by scholars today. Chapters 2 through 5 address More's major Tower Works in what I consider their probable chronological sequence of composition, a task that proved to be difficult. Rastell printed all the Tower Works as written in the year of 1534 and, in the process, erected an editorial barrier around More's actual dates of composition, which ranged across a fifteen-month period and well into 1535.[30]

Some dates may be established easier than others. Contrary to Rastell's proposition, I present, in chapter 1, *A Treatise upon the Passion* as an unfinished composition from the spring of 1534. Though critics continue to refer to More's *Treatise* as a Tower Work, I show that it was written before his arrest, and, in chapter 2, I argue that More wrote it to address the Eucharistic controversies derived from the previous year.[31] If we date the Tower Works from the time of More's imprisonment, beginning on 17 April, they open with *A Dialogue of Comfort*. I show in chapter 3 that a letter from Margaret More Roper (1505–44) in May 1534 inspired More's *Dialogue*, the longest of the Tower Works. Chapter 4's focus is on the *Letter to Alington*, which the consensus view dates accurately to August 1534. Finally, the unfinished *De tristitia Christi*, whose commencement remains difficult to pinpoint behind the label of 1534, I will show to have been written primarily during 1535 in the months leading up to More's trial and execution.

Such a chronological sequence allows me to revisit the circumstances of More's composition anew. In the case of the Tower Works, what scholars consider to be "devotional literature" is written during an intense period of religious and political strife in England, to which More responded. The discourse of Christian comfort and emphasis upon heavenly salvation strikes many as different in kind from arguments spoken in Parliament or the verbal wrangling over an oath in More's interrogations. In contrast, I present the political and religious controversies that were contemporaneous with the composition of the Tower Works as influential upon them. More's last writings reveal how he adjusts and augments his own conservative positions during a time of crisis; he wrote his way through the religious and political events in 1534–35, and he desired to convey his thinking on these matters to others before his death. Essentially, every one of the Tower Works responds to a perceived threat presented by the English Reformation.[32]

Rather than a work in illustration of More's transition from public disputes to private prayers, the *Treatise upon the Passion* is an attack upon Sacramentarian heresy. The *Treatise* addresses all of salvation history, but More's predominate concern is to educate readers about the real presence in the sacrament of the Eucharist.[33] He does so because this sacrament stands for unity of faith among Catholics and therefore obliquely criticizes Henry's movement away from Rome. To shape public opinion on this matter, More even leaves instructions for readers. His text is to be read aloud by "learned readers" to other less educated Londoners.[34] In this way, catechesis may involve those who could explain the doctrine behind the Eucharist, and the texts More presents in support of it.

More's *Dialogue of Comfort*, despite its status as martyr literature, is an assault upon Henrician schism.[35] The climax of the book identifies the significance of the "midday devil" and his ministers as those who forcibly convert others away from Catholicism. Instead of an avuncular author in More and a meandering conversation between the *Dialogue*'s central characters, More presents the "Turk" as a figure for all those in power, including Henry VIII, who persecute or imprison, torture, or kill others for their orthodox faith. The *Dialogue* shows More's defiance and how his rhetorical strategies aim at convincing others to join his cause.[36]

The *Letter to Alington* goes a step further. Rastell's suggestion that More may have contributed to what the 1557 edition printed as a letter from Margaret Roper to Alice Alington (1501–63), I will validate on stylistic grounds.[37] The letter's forensic design belongs to More. In the *Letter to Alington*, More provides a robust self-defense and an explanation of why others changed their position about the king's claims of supremacy. More's apologia defends his refusal to the take the oath and makes a counterargument against those that swore.

In *De tristitia*, finally, More rewrites martyr literature to emphasize papal authority and attacks the Church in England, especially its bishops.[38] Not only a private reflection upon the scriptures, More's last work counters royal propaganda in England and abroad on the theory and justification of the king's supremacy.[39] He does so by defining true martyrs as those who die for the sake of Christ and his Catholic Church, just as More plans to do in defiance of his king. Anne Dillon has recently shown that the Church rested upon "the foundational truth" of papal authority, but no martyrs had been put to death for maintaining that the pope was the visible and effective head of the universal Catholic Church until the Reformation made this kind of martyrdom possible. More's death gave witness to the belief that the pope was the true head of the universal Church, or "the belief that was denied by the reformers, the consequence of which repudiation was the Reformation." By anticipating his death and writing about the nature of martyrdom in terms of it, More himself provided and shaped a construction of "a new form of martyrdom."[40] Rather than a tepid supporter of papal primacy, More was adamant in his defense of Church unity, and unity predicated upon obedience to Rome. For this cause, he climbed the scaffold on 6 July 1535.[41]

Thus, More's Tower Works comment upon the ramifications of Henrician schism in ways that resemble and develop his earlier polemical approaches. More emerges as a man fully engaged in the events of 1534–35. He is known for his silence and for offering no explanation as to why he refused the oath presented to him, but his major Tower Works, traditionally considered, comprise three books and letters full of powerful pathos, and each addressed his current state and questions of religious and political consequence. Before turning to these works of controversial literature, however, we must first see how Rastell misrepresented them.

ONE

The Creation of More's Tower Works

One of the most notable achievements of William Rastell has been to provide Tudor historians with the illusion that More ceased writing as a Catholic controversialist in 1533. Any attempt to understand More's final polemical and political purposes, therefore, entails that we first survey how Rastell presented his imprisoned uncle. I will show in this chapter that Rastell fashioned a historically inaccurate image of More as an author of devotional literature alongside an authoritative edition of his uncle's final writings, and this portrait of "devotional More" persists in criticism and biographies.[1] Rastell's classification of *A Treatise upon the Passion* as a Tower Work instead of a polemical tract, in particular, meant that scholars not only misdated but also misread a "devotional phase" into More's writing career during the spring of 1534.[2] But the dating and arrangement of the entire Tower Works section remains a source of critical confusion about More's authorial tone and neglect of his apologetical aims.

Let us begin with Rastell's own agenda and whose edition of More's writings was occasioned by the allure of pleasing a new queen. "I trust this book shall be most acceptable," he writes in his dedication to Queen Mary, "both for that (I think) that it being read of many, as it is likely to be, shall much help forward your Majesty's most godly purpose in purging this your realm of all wicked heresies."[3] More's English works were first collected and published in celebration of Mary's rule (1553–58) with the goal of re-Catholicizing England under her reign. Both More's writings and his martyrdom would aid the queen's "mostly godly purpose." Martyrdom had augmented the reputation of More, and so Rastell remained confident of a large readership that would, in turn, discover More's antiheretical tracts, and these would refute the Reformed theology that had advanced under King Edward VI (r. 1547–53).[4]

At the same time of the folio's publication and with a shared purpose, Nicholas Harpsfield (1519–75) presented a biography of More in manuscript form to William Roper (1496–1578), More's son-in-law, as a New Year's gift in 1557.[5] Roper had commissioned Harpsfield to write *The Life and Death of Sir Thomas More, Knight*, and Roper himself contributed financially to the publication of Rastell's *The Works of Sir Thomas More*. The timing of Rastell's edition alongside a fresh biography was not by coincidence. "The composition of Harpsfield's life of More and the issuing of More's English works formed an ambitious double project," Eamon Duffy states, a "double project" that was meant "to refashion More's image as a paradigm of lay orthodoxy and true martyrdom, and to make available his antiheretical and martyrological writings in English."[6] Indeed, Harpsfield's prefatory letter to Roper sounded a similar note to Rastell's own dedication to Mary with regard to combating heresy. Harpsfield writes that More was Roper's "spiritual father" because by More's "good counsel and advice" and his "devout prayers to God" Roper had recovered his "lost soul" from "the deadly, dreadful depth of horrible heresies."[7] Since More was instrumental in Roper's conversion, More's "good counsel and advice" would extend to others who might learn from his antiheretical tracts.

Crucial to the success of this initiative was the depiction of More's prison writings as martyr literature. To do so, Rastell's folio arranged More's Tower Works into a single period, from the date of More's imprisonment (17 April 1534) to the day his books were removed from the Tower (12 June 1535), and less than a month before his execution.[8] Rastell dated every text from this period to the year of 1534 with the single exception of More's last "devout prayer," which was thought to have been composed after More was condemned to die but before his execution; a time period that must fall between 1 and 6 July 1535. Thus, More's fifteen months in the Tower became the single year of 1534.

THE FICTION OF MORE'S RETIREMENT

Rastell's arrangement of texts also meant that *A Dialogue of Comfort* (1534–35) inaugurated the Tower Works as a whole. In the 1557 edition, Rastell heightened the moment of More's turn from a polemical and public-minded author to a private man of peace by inserting the *Dialogue* at page 1139 just after More's *The Answer to a Poisoned Book* (1533), which encompassed pages 1035–1138. The latter was written in response to *The Supper of the Lord* (1533), an anonymous attack upon the Eucharist, and the last of More's works published during his lifetime. Rastell's editorial comment and headnote to the *Answer* reads: "By Sir Thomas More knight" in the year of 1533 "after he had given over the office of Lord Chancellor of England."[9] It was the same headnote and year specified in two antecedent works to the *Answer*, where Rastell placed *The Apology of Sir Thomas More, Knight* (1533) and *The Debellation of Salem and Bizance* (1533). Altogether, the 1533 works spanned pages 845 to 1138 and marked the ostensible end of More's canon and career as a polemicist.

Rastell's concluding note at the end of the *Answer* further stipulated that "after Sir Thomas More had caused to be printed this last book"—that is, the last book published in his lifetime—More wrote a final message "to the Christian reader," which Rastell printed in his 1557 edition to distinguish More's polemical works in 1533 from the devotional ones of 1534. In More's postscript, he corrected himself for "misremembering" a "word" of his adversary, Christopher St. German (ca. 1460–1540). The particulars of More's debate with St. German aren't relevant here, but what follows More's admission is important for grasping how Rastell illustrated More's transition to the Tower. More says of his mistake that he would "in no wise see it unreformed," and he then declares, "Nor never purpose while I live, wheresoever I may perceive, either mine adversary to say well, or myself to have said otherwise, to let for us both indifferently to declare and say the truth. And surely if they would use the selfsame honest plain truth toward me, you should soon see, good readers, all our contentions ended."[10] On the very next page, Rastell placed the title page from *A Dialogue of Comfort*, "made in the year of our Lord, 1534" and written by Sir Thomas More "while he was prisoner in the tower of London." With such an arrangement, Rastell gave the false impression that the polemical phase of More's writing career ended in 1533 with a petition for honest and plain truth from all parties. The plea for both sides of the debate to declare indifferently the truth confirmed the idea of a charitable farewell and withdrawal from religious and political disputes.

Of course, Rastell's presentation agreed with the depiction of More found in Roper's own biography of his father-in-law, *The Life of Sir Thomas More* (ca. 1556), an account Harpsfield incorporated into his own.[11] Roper wrote of a heavenly minded More as if it were a matter of fact. He comments: "after Sir Thomas More had given over his office and all other worldly doings therewith, *to the intent he might from thenceforth the more quietly settle himself to the service of God*, then made he conveyance for the disposition of all his lands, reserving to himself an estate thereof only for term of his own life."[12] Both More's office and "all other worldly doings" are abandoned with the express purpose of settling "himself to the service of God." More's decision is proved by the legal record, what Roper presents as a dramatic bequeathal of More's goods.

In Roper's *Life*, too, we find More speaking in words that would resound in Harpsfield's biography and comport with Rastell's editorial decisions. After More remained in the Tower just more than a month, Margaret More Roper, More's daughter and Roper's own wife, "got leave to go to him." During her visit, More says to her:

> I believe, Meg, that they that have put me here ween [suppose] they have done me a high displeasure. But I assure thee, on my faith, my own good daughter, if it had not been for my wife and you that be my children, whom I accompt the chief part of my charge, I would not have failed long ere this to have closed myself in as strait a room—and straighter, too.... I find no cause, I thank God, Meg, to reckon myself in worse case here than in my own house. For me thinketh God maketh me a wanton [pampered pet], and setteth me on His lap and dandleth me.[13]

Harpsfield repeated More's words verbatim from Roper, and Rastell's division of More's texts from polemical works in 1533 and devotional ones in 1534 validated the depiction of a pious but no longer political More. The earlier apologetical sections of Rastell's collection would serve to combat heresy, but the last section of the folio would provide Catholic England its martyr and saint. The Tower section of the *Works* (pages 1139–1458) documented More's status as a martyr-icon and created the impression of the book as a reliquary. Thus, the creation of the Tower Works and its author with his mind on heaven alone.

MARIAN MARTYROLOGY

Within this framework, Rastell's edition of More's *Treatise upon the Passion* was the first to be printed and subsequently considered to be authoritative, including its editorial commentary. In the *Works*, however, the *Treatise* appeared with the following note at its conclusion: "Sir Thomas More wrote no more in English of this treatise of the passion of Christ. But he (still prisoner in the tower of London) wrote more thereof in Latin whereof here followeth."[14] Next, *De tristitia Christi* was presented in English translation under this description: "A treatise upon the passion of Christ (unfinished) made in the year of our Lord 1534 by Sir Thomas More knight (while he was prisoner in the tower of London) and translated into English, by mistress Mary Bassset, one of the gentlewomen of the Queen's majesty privy chamber, and niece to the said Sir Thomas More."[15] Thus, the English translation of *De tristitia* became a continuation of the *Treatise*. Indeed, "A treatise upon the passion" appeared as the running title throughout Basset's translation of *De tristitia*.[16] Two distinct books written in two different languages were now a single work in English.

Rastell's blending of the *Treatise* and *De tristitia* amounted to a new genre and also a biographical study of More. At the end of Rastell's conflation of these texts, he added, "Sir Thomas More wrote no more of this work: for when he had written this far, he was in prison kept so straight, that all his books and pen and ink and paper was taken from him, and soon after was he put to death."[17] But just before this editorial note, Rastell printed the last words of Basset's translation of *De tristitia*, "and after all the apostles were fled away, and finally after the young man whom they were not able to keep (as sure hold as they had of him) was escaped stoutly (naked as he was) from them, that then after all this, did they first lay hands upon Jesus."[18] To compare Rastell's presentation with More's own signed holograph reveals that More planned to continue *De tristitia* beyond the point where it ended in the 1557 edition.[19] But the placement of Rastell's note suggested to readers such as Thomas Stapleton (1535–98), one of More's first biographers, that More's own captivity participated in the Passion narrative from the Gospels. According to Stapleton, More's text ended when a large crowd did "first lay hands upon Jesus" because "at that point" in writing the narrative "hands were laid" upon More himself, who then, "by the increased strictness of confinement," lost "all further opportunity of writing" in the Tower.[20]

What about the "young man" alluded to at the end of Basset's translation? More could be associated with the character described in Mark 14:51–52 too: "But a certain young man was following Him, having only a linen cloth wrapped about his naked body, and throwing it off he fled from them naked." Who was this youth, More himself asks, who follows Christ even after his "Lord" was arrested?[21] More answers that the youth is a figure for any person who cannot conceal his love for Christ:

> But Lord, how hard a matter is it to love, and not disclose it! This young man, for all he was [left], amongst the thickest of them that mortally maligned Christ, yet by his pace & other [in] his demeanor so betrayed he himself that they all might well perceive that he, when all the rest had forsaken him, thus followed Christ still, not to hurt him, but meaning to do him service. Whereupon they, espying at length that all the remnant of Christ's company were fled away, upon this young man in a great fury began they to take hold, whom they saw all alone so boldly following him.[22]

With these words and in retrospective contemplation of More's martyrdom, Rastell's readers could identify More as such a lover of Christ and see that More's own understanding of the youth from the Gospel account applied to More himself. In *De tristitia*, More treats nakedness as a sign of the virtue of detachment, and the casting off garments, ultimately, includes the garment of the body.[23] If we patiently endure the loss of the body for the love of God, More posits, then we shall "become fresh and young again, and so be shortly carried up into heaven, where shall never wax old after."[24] The implication of Rastell's blending of texts and arrangement of notes for hagiographical readings of More's life becomes apparent in the case of the young man, who boldly followed Christ, and lost his garment, or practiced the virtue of detachment. More was seized and brought to Tower Hill for beheading, but his execution meant escape from his body and flight to heaven.

To situate such a depiction of More within the Tower Works as a whole, even though the *Treatise upon the Passion* was written before *A Dialogue of Comfort against Tribulation*, Rastell reversed their order. The last book of the *Dialogue* includes exhortations to meditate upon the passion of Christ, which the *Treatise* does, and so both were arranged to culminate in *De tristitia*. In this way, the Tower Works emerge as continuous sequels to one another such that they reveal More's increasing piety as he approached execution. At the same time, More's writings on the Passion are not to be distinguished from his person because, according to Rastell's mind, they are evidence of More's own sanctity.[25]

WHAT IS A TOWER WORK?

I will return to Rastell's edition in the following chapters, but here I wish to note how the Tower Works, as a genre, were his creation, and a creation in service of constructing More's martyrdom for Marian audiences. He did so with a sleight of hand regarding chronology. We can date More's composition of the *Treatise* to the early months of 1534 with confidence. The Act of Succession was passed in March 1534, and by the end of the month all members of Parliament had taken it. In response, More went on pilgrimage to Our Lady of Wilsdon in the first week of April 1534.[26] From there, he wrote to his secretary, John Harris (d. 1565), with final corrections to the *Treatise*.[27] More signed his letter from Wilsdon, today known as Willesden, a parish northwest of County London, and this evidence alone makes it impossible for More to have sent his revisions from the Tower.[28] Because More sent these corrections before his summons to take the oath, he most likely wrote his *Treatise* sometime after the publication of his *Answer* in December 1533 but before being called to Lambeth on 12 April 1534.[29] If Tower Works are to be defined by the fact that an author composed them while in prison, then the *Treatise* would not qualify.

Rastell also wove together the pre-Tower *Treatise* with the later *De tristitia* into a single work. His own editorial notes, though, betrayed his combination of 1534–35 audiences with those in 1557, or the difference in More's authorial purpose with the agenda behind the 1557 edition. To see the difference, we need only begin with the title. Mary Basset, Margaret Roper's second daughter, accurately rendered More's own title into English as *Of the sorrow, weariness, fear, and prayer of Christ before his taking, as it is written in the 26th Chapter of Saint Matthew, the 14th of Saint Mark, and the 22nd of Saint Luke, and the 17th of Saint John.*[30] In Rastell's edition, however, Basset's title appears like a chapter heading and the editorial description receives pride of place. There, Rastell claimed that the continuation of the *Treatise* was "an exposition of a part of the passion of our savior Jesus Christ, made in Latin by Sir Thomas More knight (while he was prisoner in the tower of London) and translated into English by mistress Mary Basset."[31] Rastell also put the first six words of his description in large, bold type, and thus More's original could be and was reduced to *Expositio passionis Domini*, or *History of the Passion*, in subsequent editions.[32] From Rastell's edition in 1557 to the time of Miller's critical edition in 1976, More's work was known as *An Exposition of the Passion*.

The audience More wrote for in 1534–35 ought to have been distinguished from those who read *De tristitia* in English translation, but Rastell claimed otherwise. In the note, "The printer to the gentle reader," which followed Rastell's description of *De tristitia*, we discover the case for printing the work in English: "This work in Latin hath been by sundry great clerks read and weighed, and very well liked, and is again so set out in our tongue, and goeth so near Sir Thomas More's own English phrase that the gentlewoman (who for her pastime translated it) is no nearer to him in kindred, virtue and literature, than in his English tongue."[33] Here we learn that the Latin text was studied and acclaimed, but Rastell uses this fact to vindicate not the Latin original but an English translation of it. Basset's translation is so close to More's thought, the note continues, that it appears as if the English version was written by "More's own pen."[34] In Rastell's presentation, the translation rather than the original returns us to an imagined ideal of direct engagement with the author.

Rastell knew that an English translation could expand readership of the *Works* and potentially increase sales in England. *De tristitia* would complement the discussion of martyrdom in More's *Dialogue* and in his last letters; it could also be appropriated as a continuation of the *Treatise* with an English translation. Nearness to More's own thought and style could also be substantiated because of the connection between author and translator.[35] Basset, we learn in the same description, was "one of the gentlewomen of the Queen's Majesty's privy chamber" and also near to "sir Thomas More" through familial connection. The connection to the queen's chamber and to More himself would add cachet.

The attention Rastell lavishes on *De tristitia* through such paratexts indicates his excitement over its publication. Basset had translated More's original from a copy that had already sorted out insertions and cancellations marked in her grandfather's original, a manuscript that Basset inherited from her mother, Margaret More Roper.[36] Margaret had smuggled her father's *De tristitia* from the Tower sometime before his books were confiscated. After her death, the holograph fell to the capable hands of Basset, who was expert, like her mother, in translating classical languages.[37] Such a reception history intertwined with More's own descendants in a way that Rastell found to be an object lesson in God's beneficent providence.

Indeed, "the matter is so good," Rastell writes of Basset's translation, that it should be "read of all folks," but what did he mean by "all folks"? Of course, Rastell refers to a Marian audience. In part, too, his words are a good example of early modern marketing in 1557 and of, at that time, the only printed edition of More's text. Rastell's note alludes to this: "And some there were that fain would have had it set forth in print alone because the matter is so well handled that it were to be wished it might be read of all folks, which more would buy, set out alone, than with so many other of his works."[38] A separate edition in English would have been more cheaply produced than in a larger folio such as the *Works* and, thus, "all folks" refers to a London audience in 1557.

But the same paratext in relation to Basset hints at an earlier purpose that belonged to More. She was reluctant to publish her work for a telling reason. According to Rastell, Basset was "nothing willing to have it go abroad, for that (she says), it was first turned into English, but for her own pastime and exercise, and so reputeth it far too simple to come to many hands."[39] This was no modesty topos. *De tristitia* was translated into English as a "pastime and exercise" because More had wished for the Latin version to "go abroad" after his death.[40] The very act of committing *De tristitia* to writing and in Latin, the care with which More edited the Valencia holograph, and smuggling this text out of the Tower establishes More's wish for the text to be disseminated.[41] Basset made a translation into English as a "pastime" because she thought or hoped to one day honor her grandfather's original wish.

"All folks" in 1557 entails a distinction between the implied readership of *De tristitia* in 1535 versus the one in Basset's subsequent translation published more than twenty years later. More's Latin original was written for educated though not theologically expert readers. His audience, Clarence Miller says, wasn't "exclusively or even primarily clerical."[42] If not exclusively clerical, though, then lay readers, but if lay, then a group of scholars, aristocrats, gentry in general and among the merchant class, extending to Henry's own lay ambassadors.[43] The *Dialogue of Comfort* was written for English readers, but *De tristitia* was meant for readers, both lay and clerical, in England and throughout Europe. We shall see in chapters 3 and 5 that both were written in support of Catholicism and in defiance of Henrician reforms, but More's choice to write *De tristitia* in Latin suggests that he planned to contradict royal propaganda abroad.

PAPAL PRIMACY

Rastell's presentation of More's Tower Works also played a critical if inadvertent role in shaping our current understanding of how More viewed the papacy. Because of how Rastell sharply distinguished between polemical writings in 1533 and devotional ones in 1534, scholars mistakenly view More as a tepid supporter of papal primacy at the end of his life. To take an example from a leading Tudor historian, John Guy claims of More that "his final views on the papacy are unknown. The topic is a complete blank. He did not mention the Pope's authority in his later letters to his daughter, and there is no reference to his opinion of the papal supremacy at his trial beyond what Roper reports."⁴⁴ Yet the topic isn't blank. More's Tower writings touch often upon the question of Henrician schism, but his earlier arguments left no doubt how he would understand any claim for the king to be head of the Church in England.⁴⁵

Consider that as early as 1523 More made clear his position in his *Responsio ad Lutherum* (*Response to Luther*)—a work that Rastell did not include or have translated into English—in a way that echoed Henry's own earlier belief. In 1521, Henry VIII wrote to Martin Luther (1483–1546):

> I have no intention of insulting the pope by discussing his prerogative as though it were a matter of doubt.... Luther can hardly deny that all the churches accept and revere the holy Roman see as mother and ruler of the faithful as long as they are not cut off from her by distance or dangers.... He forgets the warning in Deuteronomy that whoever arrogantly refuses obedience to the priest who ministers to the Lord his God must be condemned to death. How much more deserving of death is someone who will not obey the highest priest of all and the supreme judge on earth!⁴⁶

Likewise, More not only defends papal primacy but feels moved to do so. In More's *Responsio*, he rebuked Luther on the same point. On the primacy of the pope and the Roman see, More wrote:

> I am moved to obedient submission to this See by all those arguments which learned and holy men have assembled in support of this point; moreover, I am indeed moved not least by a fact which we have so often noticed; that not only has no one been hostile to the Christian faith without at the same time declaring war on that See, but also there has never been anyone who declared himself an enemy of that See without shortly afterwards declaring himself also a notorious and foremost enemy and traitor both to Christ and to our religion.⁴⁷

Both Henry and More would continue in a similar vein, but More adds here "as regards to the pope" that "God who put him in charge of His church knew what an evil it would have been to have lacked a pope."

The "Christian world" would suffer greatly without its ruler and, thus, all of Christendom should desire popes who would benefit the "Christian commonwealth."[48]

By the time of More's *Confutation* (1532), More's position remained unchanged.[49] "If Tyndale bring in question whether the pope be of all those Christians countries the chief spiritual head under god and general vicar of Christ," More asks, "this question will not help him." For More, Church history and tradition already settled the point. When the Greek Church "confirmed" itself to "the see of Rome" they "finally confirmed themselves to the Latins and to the see apostolic."[50] As he did in the *Response to Luther*, More refers to the Council of Florence, convened between 1431 and 1449, which acknowledged "the Roman pontiff as vicar of Christ, head of the entire church, and father and teacher of all Christians."[51] The decree of Florence, which spelled out papal authority, was signed by delegates of the Greek Church on 5 July 1439.[52]

More referred to the same council again in his *Treatise upon the Passion* from 1534. His allusion is to be found in the dispute over whether the Last Supper aligned with or anticipated the first day of the Jewish Feast of Unleavened Bread. Of note, this is the same subject of More's letter to his secretary, John Harris. We have seen already how More sent Harris corrections to his *Treatise* in the spring of 1534 and before he was sent to the Tower, but now we can recognize why this otherwise complex theological question about the Last Supper was so important to More.

In More's letter, he supplies two sections of argument to justify the Roman liturgical tradition of "Maundy Thursday" against the teaching of the Greek Orthodox Church. Between these additions, More writes to Harris: "I put you in remembrance of this because I have mistaken it in the paper that you have, and have said the Greeks held that Christ kept his maundy on Tenebrae Wednesday: I pray you gentle John Harris amend that fault of mine."[53] More had misattributed to the Greek Church the belief that the Last Supper was on Wednesday, but that wasn't the main reason why this error required urgent attention.

Earlier in the *Treatise*, More used the disagreement over dating the Last Supper, the paschal feast of Christ, to demonstrate the teaching authority of the Roman Church. He warns his readers: "I would not good readers stick so long upon the declaration of this point, (as a thing wherein some shall peradventure take little savor) saving that I thought it not a time all lost, to let you know that upon the scripture in this point mistaken, the church of Greece fell from the church of the Latins in a point or two."[54] More's additions and corrections, in other words, are an attempt to illustrate why the Greek Church should have followed the Roman.

Central to More's case is which tradition rightly interprets scripture. "Maundy" Thursday was so called because, in Roman Catholic teaching, Christ issued his new commandment—or the *mandatum novum*, which was a new law for his disciples to love one another—at the Last Supper *and* on the evening of Passover. The Greek Church, however, maintained that Christ did not "eat his Paschal lamb in the day appointed by the law" but *anticipated* it. In contrast to or against anticipation of the lawful feast day, More cites Christ's words: "I am not come to break the law but to fulfill it."[55] For More, the Greek Church labeled Good Friday as the first day of the Feast of Unleavened Bread, but falsely taught that Christ celebrated it in anticipation the night before. Jewish custom, More reasoned, marked days from sunset to sunset such that Passover and the Feast of Unleavened Bread became interchangeable titles.[56] Good Friday, or the first day of Unleavened Bread, a feast spread out over several days, began on Maundy Thursday. Though the dispute may have seemed needlessly complex to some of More's readers, he belabored it for a reason.

In teaching that Christ anticipated the feast, the Greek Church used John to correct the Synoptic Gospels, creating a scandal by way of hermeneutics. The point of scripture under dispute revolves around John 13:1, which More gives in an abbreviated translation: "Before the holy day of the Paschal, Jesus, knowing that his time was come that he should go out of this world unto his father and so forth."[57] At first glance, the Last Supper occurs before but not on "the holy day of the Paschal." John's account therefore appears to contradict the ones found in Matthew 26:17, Mark 14:12, and Luke 22:7, which indicate that the Passover meal was prepared on the first day of Unleavened Bread. For More, the Greek teaching that only John's account is truthful renders the other three false. To maintain, though, that "any of the four Evangelists should in the story write anything false" should give "Christian men more than shame" to speak.[58] For, which account may one trust, More reasoned, when all are deemed inspired? Thus, the controversy over John 13:1 illustrates the need for an authoritative and unified interpretation among Christians.

Under these polemical circumstances, More refers to the Council of Florence as a "general council" of Christendom against schism, a position that hearkens back to his earlier defense of papal primacy and Roman Catholicism.[59] At the end of More's discussion over John 13:1 in the *Treatise*, More distinguishes between the old doctors of the Church in Greece, such as John Chrysostom, and their "posteriors," those who followed them. The latter category falls into two subdivisions: the Church of Greece in schismatic rupture from Rome; and the Church of Greece that "reformed in general councils," such as Florence.[60] More writes of the mistaken teachings of those in rebellion from Rome: "But surely the church of Greece was far overseen [mistaken] in this point [about Christ's last supper] and divers others, in which they partly acknowledged their errors after and were reformed in general councils, and yet returned of forwardness to their errors again, and in conclusion we see whereto they have come."[61] More's position in 1534 thus conforms to the one he supported and cited in 1523 from the king's own earlier defense of the papacy:

> Certainly, if anyone reads the records of history he will find that long ago, just after peace was established in the world, almost all the churches of the Christian world obeyed the Roman church. In fact, although the imperial power passed to the Greeks, yet we will find that in what pertained to the primacy of the Church, except for the time that Greece labored under schism, it submitted to the Roman church. Indeed, blessed Jerome clearly showed how much he thought men should defer to the Roman See by openly confessing, though he was not himself a Roman, that whoever else disapproved of his faith it was enough for him if the pope of Rome approved it.[62]

In the passage above, the example of Jerome amplifies More's overall point. The Greek Church fell into false teaching when it broke from Rome. In this way, the case of the Greek Church becomes a lesson in how it went astray. For More, problems arise when Christians "fall to an opinion contrary to the Church by construing the scripture after a few folk's fantasies."[63] After correction and out of rebelliousness, they return to their errors. As he does in earlier passages that address papal primacy, More means that the Greek Church should follow the teachings of either the Roman See or the Latin Church over which the vicar of Rome presides.[64]

Much in these same passages from the *Treatise* could be construed as an attack upon the king. By 1534, Henry's claims to be head of the Church of England already qualified as a schismatic rupture from Rome, but his earlier arguments on behalf of divorcing Queen Katherine of Aragon (1485–1536) offered parallels. Like the example of the Greek Church and its exegesis of John 13:1, Henry's case for divorce was developed from his isolation and elevation of two scriptures that served his point of view. Katherine had married Arthur, Prince of Wales (1486–1502), and Henry read Leviticus 18:16 and 20:21 as an absolute prohibition against taking a deceased brother's wife. Yet Henry glossed away Deuteronomy 25:5, which commanded a brother to marry a deceased brother's wife in the case of marriage without children so that the family line would continue. In the Church's traditional practice and in its canon laws, Leviticus could be dispensed to follow the mandate of Deuteronomy and protect family inheritances and lines of descent. In 1503, when Pope Julius II (1443–1513) gave then Prince Henry a dispensation to marry Katherine, the pope acted in line with Church precedent and law.[65] Both Henry's early defiance of Pope Clement VIII (1478–1534) and later claims to supremacy paralleled the "posterior Greeks" because schism, by More's definition, meant falling "to an opinion contrary to the Church."[66] So More amplified this same point in condemning anyone who would "after his own fantasy" interpret scripture instead of following "that interpretation that is received and allowed by the universal church." No man should "boldly frame himself a conscience" with "a gloss of his own making" because doing so "leads unto hell."[67]

Though More's attacks against schism occur in one of his last major works, scholars have failed to notice it or to advance its significance. Rastell himself didn't direct attention to it in his marginalia and, instead, misplaced the *Treatise* as part of *De tristitia*.[68] This single conflated work, in turn, testified to what has become conventionally known as "the devotional phase" of More's canon, a distinct writing period from his earlier polemical one. Today's canonical distinction between controversial and devotional writings remains Rastell's creation, but it fails to acknowledge More's adherence to papal primacy during his last years.

More's support of Rome deserves amplification at the outset of my study because scholars diminish or dismiss it as anachronistic special pleading by Roper. We have seen already why Roper should be handled with care as a source, but his report of More's trial corresponds with More's letter to Thomas Cromwell (1485–1540), Henry's chief minister at that time, from March 1534. At his trial, according to Roper, More asserted the "supreme government" of the Church "may no temporal prince presume by any law to take upon him" because that authority "belongs to the See of Rome, a spiritual pre-eminence by the mouth of Our Savior himself" and granted "only to Saint Peter and his successors, Bishops of the same See, by special prerogative granted."[69] But this position echoed and agreed with More's earlier one. He wrote to Cromwell in support of papal primacy: "For that primacy is at the leastwise instituted by the corps of Christendom and for a great urgent cause in avoiding of schisms and corroborate by continual successions more than the space of a thousand year at the least, for there are passed almost a thousand year since the time of holy Saint Gregory."[70] In the same letter, More claims to have learned the above lesson from the king himself:

> But surely after that I had read his Grace's book therein [*Assertion of the Seven Sacraments*], and so many other things I have seen in that point by this continuance of these ten year since and more have found in effect the substance of all the holy doctors from Saint Ignatius, disciple to Saint John the Evangelist, unto our own days both Latins and Greeks so consonant and agreeing in that point, and the thing by such general councils so confirmed also, that in good faith I never neither read nor heard anything of such effect on the other side that ever could lead me to think that my conscience were well discharged, but rather in right great peril if I should follow the other side and deny the primacy to be provided by God.[71]

I will return to the significance of More's long-standing endorsement of papal primacy for reading his prison writings as polemical theology, but we can see already that historians need not doubt More's trail speech solely because Roper wrote during the reign of Mary and after the pope's authority had been restored.[72] Guy reasons that "Roper's attributed speech is almost certainly a fiction. It is not what More said, it is what he ought to have said."⁷³ But More's stance in favor of papal primacy was what he had already said. "Since all Christendom is one corps," More wrote to Cromwell, the very man who would marshal the case against him in the months to come, "I cannot perceive how any member thereof may without the common assent of the body depart from the common head."⁷⁴ It was Henry's schismatic claim to be head of the Church of England that troubled More's conscience long before his trial. In short, More died in defiance of his king and for the sake of a united Christendom.⁷⁵

Once More was jailed, he was accused of persuading the king to write in defense of the papacy by "subtle sinister slights," but More rejoined that the king would never make that charge against him. Henry "right well knoweth" that More never "procured" Henry's opinion on papal primacy.⁷⁶ In fact, Henry didn't pursue that charge, and More's own confidence on this point stemmed from a living memory of Henry's own previous beliefs and actions. Henry's *Assertio septem sacramentorum* (*Assertion of the Seven Sacraments*) (1521) was not only a sensation during its time but also a sign of how his regime mobilized in defense of the papacy against Lutheranism.⁷⁷ Bishop John Fisher (1469–1535) put to print in English his sermon on how the pope was "the head of the universal church of Christ" in what was regarded as popular refutation that paralleled Henry's own in 1521.⁷⁸ Fisher's sermon drew upon Article XXV of his Latin *Confutation* of Luther, published for more educated audiences, and his sermon was part of the public burning of Luther's books organized by Cardinal Wolsey (ca. 1475–1530) and with papal and royal approval.⁷⁹

Henry again addressed the issue of primacy as late as 1526 in a published letter against Luther. Of the pope's "highness" Henry writes, "Surely Luther, albeit ye have taken yourself always for so great a man in your own conceit that ye have in writing openly professed yourself that ye were and ever would be both alive and dead, a perpetual enemy to the pope (*to whose highness I well know how far the estate of a king is inferior*), yet never made I so great accompt of you that ever I would vouchsafe to reckon myself for your enemy, albeit I am to your heresies as great an enemy as any man."⁸⁰ Elsewhere in the same letter, Henry condemns Luther for failure to "stand to any man's judgment" especially "the judgment of the pope and the church of Rome." Luther regarded Henry as a "papist," and the title, at one time, was deserved.⁸¹

In contrast to Henry's very public and drastic shift on the papacy, More's own letter from March 1534 seems measured.[82] After stating his opposition to schism and belief in papal primacy, More states, "Yet never thought I the Pope above the general council nor never have in any book of mine, put forth among the King's subjects in our vulgar tongue, advanced greatly the Pope's authority."[83] Here More "did not pose pope against council," writes John M. Headley, "but simply recognized that the church possessed and needed both these authorities."[84] But even so, More never "advanced greatly the Pope's authority" in his published English writings because before Henry changed his mind about the See of Rome there was no need to do so.[85]

RASTELL'S LEGACY UPON CONTEMPORARY CRITICISM

I want to conclude this chapter by documenting Rastell's general influence upon our current understanding of More's last years. Because my argument will redescribe More's motivations and prison writings as works written in direct reply to the theological controversies of 1533–35, it is best to provide a brief synopsis of Rastell's ongoing and pervasive influence on criticism here. Rastell is a rich and often accurate resource, but he should not have been trusted as much as he has been in the case of the Tower Works.

There is no better place to begin than with the editors of the most authoritative and scholarly editions of More's prison writings found in *The Complete Works of St. Thomas More*, published by Yale University Press. There, the editors accept and enlarge upon Rastell's presentation of the Tower Works as a unified genre, but the original emphasis upon re-Catholicizing England is excised. "The most profoundly moving literary achievements of Thomas More," writes Gary Haupt, editor of the *Treatise*, "belong to a group of his writings called the Tower works," by which Haupt means the *Dialogue of Comfort*, letters written from the Tower, the *Treatise*, *De tristitia*, and even More's prayers and instructions for reception of the Eucharist; all together, a group of texts that range from the spring of 1534 to the summer of 1535. Here "profoundly moving literary achievements" are other words for how More's example and language should inspire emulation or appreciation in readers. For this reason, Haupt writes that though "the *Treatise* was partly if not entirely composed before More entered the Tower, one is still more than justified to set it within the biographical framework of More's meditation on the Passion in his later years and group it with the 'Tower Works.'"[86] Haupt thus dated the *Treatise* outside of More's time in the Tower, but nevertheless claimed the *Treatise* as a Tower Work.

Subsequent editors do the same. Volumes 12, 13, and 14 of the Yale *The Complete Works of St. Thomas More* include Haupt's *Treatise*, Louis L. Martz and Frank Manley's *A Dialogue of Comfort against Tribulation*, and Clarence Miller's *De tristitia Christi*. All three volumes are devoted, the editors inform us, "to those writings of More that have come to be called 'The Tower Works' as printed in Rastell's folio."[87] Each editor reinforced Haupt's paradox of Tower Works composed outside of the Tower. Miller acknowledged that "Rastell and those who helped him produce the 1557 *English Workes* were not always scrupulously accurate in dating More's tower works," but then cited Haupt's introduction, already quoted above, on "the date of *A Treatise upon the Passion*."[88] Martz and Frank also noted Rastell's chronological errors, but they advanced Rastell's suggestion that the Latin treatise is "a continuation, yes, a sequel" to the English treatise, albeit "transposed, in the musical sense, into another key."[89] Martz and Frank went further: "These three great treatises are tied together inseparably: the *Dialogue of Comfort*, the English treatise on the Passion, including as its end the treatise on receiving the sacrament, and finally, the Latin treatise. The first two works converge upon and prepare the way for the meditative action of the Latin work."[90] Like Miller, Martz and Manley defer to and cite Haupt's introduction to More's *Treatise*. Because these editions remain scholarly standards in More studies, its editors set the critical paradigm for all recent studies of the *Treatise*.

The influence of Rastell's sixteenth-century *Works* over the twentieth-century Yale critical editions, however, isn't difficult to discover. Consider that Haupt's emphasis upon the "literary achievements" of More expands 1534 to 1535 under the auspices of devotional writing, and this genre under the purview of biography, or what Haupt refers to as "literary tradition."[91] This same tradition, Haupt informs us, derives from More's earliest biographers—not only Harpsfield, but also Stapleton—who followed Rastell's dating.[92]

The circular thinking of these biographers with Rastell's presentation is undeniable. Harpsfield's *Life of More* was commissioned, in part, as an advertisement for Rastell's *Works*. Harpsfield made extensive use of the *Works* and added that "we trust shortly to have all his [More's] English works ... wherein Master Sergeant Rastell doth now diligently travail."[93] Harpsfield therefore reinforced rather than investigated the date and circumstances of More's original composition of the *Treatise*. Harpsfield wrote: "Now have we beside other excellent and fruitful books of his which he made being prisoner in the tower, as his three books of comfort against tribulation, a Treatise to receive the Blessed Sacrament sacramentally and virtually both, A Treatise upon the passion, with notable introductions to the same. He wrote also many other godly and devout instructions and prayers."[94] Written after Harpsfield but published before him, Stapleton followed the biographical portrait of More as presented in Rastell's folio. Stapleton wrote in his *Tres Thomae* (1588):

> In prison he wrote *A Dialogue of Comfort against Tribulation*, in three books—a work of great beauty, full of piety and learning, which hardly has an equal amongst works of this kind. There, too, he wrote *A Treatise Historical containing the Bitter Passion of our Saviour Christ*, according to the four Evangelists, beginning at the text "The feast of unleavened bread was at hand" and continuing as far as the words "They laid hands upon Jesus." *At that point hands were laid upon him* [i.e., upon More], by the increased strictness of his confinement, so that all further opportunity of writing was denied him. This lengthy treatise is written with careful detail and is full of the deepest piety.[95]

Thus, Stapleton's account repackages Rastell's editorial notes and conflation of the *Treatise* and *De tristitia*, but these biographies formed the "tradition" to which the Yale editors deferred.

So did modern biographers of More. Apart from the Yale editors, if we consider only a handful of well-known biographies from the last hundred years, the magnitude of Rastell's original edition becomes clear. R. W. Chambers wrote in the most popular biography of the twentieth century, first published in 1935, that "it was therefore natural that when

More had finished his *Dialogue of Comfort* he wrote the *Treatise on the Passion*, preparing himself for the end which he saw to be inevitable."⁹⁶ Yet More wrote the *Treatise* before the *Dialogue of Comfort* and his arrest, and so what strikes Chambers as only a "natural" progression of More's thought is an effect of Rastell's sequencing of texts. About twenty-years later in another milestone biography, E. E. Reynolds concurred about the order of the texts, but noted of the *Treatise*: "More did not altogether avoid controversial matters in this treatise; indeed that would have been impossible in a book on a such a subject."⁹⁷ Like Chambers, Reynolds prioritized Rastell's printed order against the contents of the *Treatise*, which More wrote not in avoidance of controversial matters but in address of them. Even Richard Marius, who sought to undermine the saintly depiction of More in 1983, followed Rastell in calling *De tristitia* a work that "takes up the story of the passion of Christ at about the place where More's *Treatise upon the Passion* breaks off."⁹⁸ Others, such as archival historian John Guy, whose 2008 biography of More and Margaret More Roper included a chapter on the formation of the English *Works*, failed to question the inclusion of the *Treatise* as a Tower Work.⁹⁹ And where biographers such as Peter Ackroyd admit to the fact that More finished the *Treatise* before he was arrested, they nevertheless assume More's authorial purposes are personal rather than polemical.¹⁰⁰ More, in other words, writes in anticipation of his circumstances in 1535 instead of responding to his present circumstances in 1534.

Likewise, modern accounts of More, just as Rastell intended for early modern readers, suggest an author of devotional literature. This familiar line of argument has become so conventional that More's political theology and apologetics are ignored. In fact, many of the same influential biographers we reviewed above also reveal the pervasive portrait of "devotional More" still predicated on Rastell's division of his uncle's canon.

Chambers, for instance, remarked how "it has not been sufficiently realized" how More's previous "harsh words" against heresy altogether "cease" once More writes from the Tower, a change marked first in the *Dialogue of Comfort*, where More "is no longer defending this dogma or that" but "defining the right of the individual soul, against the command of the civil power, to hold any dogma at all." Yet Chambers fails to recognize how his biographical assessment of More contradicts this reading of the *Dialogue*. "Even the most stupid," Chambers asserts, "could not fail to see that most of what More wrote concerning the proper bearing of Catholics under the Turkish tyranny had the most intimate reference to his own case; and it involved a parallel between Henry and the Turk."[101] But if so, then More defends Roman Catholic dogma rather than individual conscience in support of any dogma. Chambers, in other words, confused the serene and disengaged More from Rastell's and Roper's depiction with parallels between "Henry and the Turk" from his own reading of the *Dialogue*.

In another prominent instance, E. E. Reynolds begins his account of More in the Tower with the *Dialogue* but imagines that its tale of a woman who "came into a prison to visit of her charity a poor prisoner there, whom she found in a chamber, to say the truth, to be meetly fair" was an accurate description of More's own cell. According to Reynolds, the woman who goes to see a "poor prisoner" is an account of Lady Alice's visit to see her husband. Frustrated by More's refusal to take the oath, Alice asks why he would remain "in this close, filthy prison, and be content thus to be shut up amongst mice and rats." More replies, "Is not this house as nigh heaven as my own?" The story of Alice's visit comes from Roper's biography and, thus, Reynolds weaves together the "meetly fair" cell of More's description from the *Dialogue* with the "filthy prison" from Roper's account.[102] Despite the contradiction, the central point about More's fixation upon a heavenly home, derived from Rastell and Roper, remains intact.[103]

More recent historians have done likewise and sometimes make strange bedfellows. Longtime critic of More, Sir Geoffrey Elton, echoes Roper's depiction of More: "The Tower liberated him because here, at last, he had reached his only possible cloister, out of the world." Elton goes on in words that recall Roper's account of Margaret's meeting with her father: "What others thought of as a good man's prison was to him his monk's cell. He had found the tonsure in the Tower."[104] Elton was an iconoclast who dedicated his career to elevating Thomas Cromwell and diminishing More.[105] Yet this same Tudor historian found himself in complete agreement with the very hagiographical tradition he otherwise sought to undermine.[106]

Marius and Ackroyd, finally, argue for the significance of More's *Dialogue*, but focus upon More's artistic craft and interior life. Marius calls the *Dialogue* "the greatest of More's Tower works and, to some, the finest thing he ever wrote"; Ackroyd remarks upon the "private and self-communing, almost brooding, quality which distinguishes it from its predecessors."[107] Instead of "almost brooding," Marius finds More in a state of "serene confidence that God has His own purposes and that Christians must yield themselves to those purposes in trust and hope." Meanwhile, Ackroyd discovers the "weariness of a man who now looked to death" in a dialogue that shows More invoking "the protection of God."[108] Both accounts, like that of Elton, are imaginative extrapolations of a politically disengaged More.

More should not have been depicted as he was by his earliest biographers and Rastell and, somewhat surprisingly, by recent historians and biographers. In opposition to these readings, I will show how his Tower Works are an extension of previous polemical and political aims and that these last writings remain inseparably tied to his sense of religious devotion. As we shall see in the chapters that follow, More wrote in a personal *and* political context about his plight and on publicly significant matters. The biographical, spiritual, and political import of his Tower Works cannot be separated from one another, but careful attention to More's personal circumstances can reveal much about his purposes.

TWO

A Treatise upon the Passion of Christ Reconsidered, 1534

During Thomas More's interrogation on 7 May 1535, he declared that his "whole study should be upon the passion of Christ" and his "own passage out of the world."[1] His words alluded to his ongoing composition of *De tristitia Christi* (*On the Sadness of Christ*) but not to the earlier and unfinished *A Treatise upon the Passion of Christ*. The latter was written along with instructions for receiving the Eucharist and composed before More's arrest on 17 April 1534.[2] More's personal focus on his "passage out of this world" and his study of "the passion of Christ"—howsoever closely these two came to be related after his arrest—should be distinguished from one another in the time before More's arrival to the Tower. The reason for this distinction arises because More wrote two books on the Passion rather than one, and that the first of these, the *Treatise*, was More's last planned defense of Christ's real presence in the Eucharist.

Ignored or confused for centuries with More's *De tristitia Christi*, More's original *Treatise* deserves critical reevaluation as a separate and independent work.[3] We saw in chapter 1 that the conflation of the two books into one was the work of William Rastell, More's nephew and editor of the folio edition of *The Works of Sir Thomas More* (1557).[4] There, Rastell presented an English translation of *De tristitia* as a continuation of the *Treatise*. He did so by manufacturing the chronology of More's composition of texts. In making *De tristitia* a sequel, the *Treatise* was postdated as a Tower Work.

In contrast, I will show that More carefully prepared his *Treatise* not only for Latin and English readers but also for communal and apologetical reading aloud to London commoners. The *Treatise*, long regarded as a Tower Work, was written outside of the Tower and without reference to it but, instead, marked the last of More's "pre-Tower eucharistic works."[5] Rather than devotional literature, these refer to a battle of books that begins with *A Christian Sentence* (1532) by John Frith (1503–33) and ends in a final rejoinder in *The Subversion of More's False Foundation* (1534) by George Joye (ca. 1495–1553). More's pre-Tower Eucharistic writings include his replies to both Frith and his *The Answer to a Poisoned Book* (1533), which was More's response to *The Supper of the Lord* (1533), an anonymous text that John Foxe (1516–87) attributed to William Tyndale (ca. 1494–1536).[6] Of important note, More wrote his final installment in this group of texts under increasing scrutiny from the government but before Henry was able to have him jailed.

Historians of the book remind us that if the *Treatise* is a distinct work from *De tristitia*, then it carries its own "expressive form" shaped by the intellectual and political conditions of its time.[7] Under the conditions of a religious propaganda war in 1534, More envisioned that readers of the *Treatise* would use his text as a resource for learning and spreading Catholic teaching on the Eucharist.[8] Once More's circumstances of composition are understood and the genre in which he wrote identified accurately, his authorial purposes may be grasped and compared with Rastell's later presentation of them under new critical auspices.[9]

CIRCUMSTANCES OF COMPOSITION

If More didn't produce his *Treatise* from the Tower, under what circumstances did he write it? We have seen how the *Treatise* was written after More published his *Answer* but before his arrest. At that time in early 1534, More thought he could continue writing in refutation of heresy so long as his *Treatise* would appear like devotional literature. More's polemical purpose remained unchanged, but he adjusted his terms of engagement because he fell under the regime's suspicion during a crisis point in the controversy surrounding Elizabeth Barton (ca. 1506–34), the "Nun of Canterbury," or the "Holy Maid of Kent."[10] In fact, More composed his defense of Church teaching while Henry VIII campaigned against him. Instead of a devotional author, what will become evident is how he adapted his apologetics under increasingly dangerous circumstances.

The composition of the *Treatise*, after all, coincided with a turn for the worse in More's fortunes that began in January 1534. Cromwell had summoned Rastell and accused him of publishing a book by More that had responded to the *Articles devised by the whole consent of the King's Council, etc.*[11] The contents of these articles suggest the ramifications of critiquing them. Printed at the end of 1533, the *Articles* asserted the bishop of Rome (no longer referred to as "pope") was subject to a general council and further denounced Pope Clement VIII (1478–1534) as a heretic and bastard.[12] This was the regime's response to Clement's earlier and conditional excommunication of Henry in July 1533.[13] The pope threatened the full and final measure if Henry were to remain obstinate in his second marriage, which Henry did.[14] The *Articles* were an escalation in the conflict.

In particular, the seventh and last entries would have concerned More. The seventh boldly condemned the pope's sentence of excommunication and commanded, instead, loyalty to the king: "Wherefore in this let us all show ourselves like true and obedient subjects, not esteeming or hanging upon any living creature, save only our prince and king, according to an old proverb in England, of old time past, much wont to be set by, and oft times rehearsed, which is one God and one king, minding thereby that all other folks' doings should be despised."[15] In conjunction with the above, the last article commended England to "Christ's law in which is all sweetness and truth, adjoining with it the laws of this realm" and severed ties with Rome, "which is nothing else but pomp, pride, ambition."[16] England was on the verge of a permanent schismatic break.[17]

Indeed, statements such as these were an advance upon the Act in Restraint of Appeals from April 1533. There, the supreme court of spiritual appeal, which had the power to address "causes of matrimony and divorce," would no longer belong to Rome; all such "causes" would be "determined within the king's jurisdiction and authority and not elsewhere," for England was an empire.[18] An extension of these points, the *Articles* were a policy statement before the Act of Supremacy in November 1534, which declared England—its king, council, and citizens—separated from the papacy but united under "one God and one king."

Meanwhile, More's awareness of the regime's pursuit of him grew. He wrote to Cromwell on 1 February, informing him that he did not write any reply to the *Articles*. More had put to sale his *Letter against Frith* and *The Answer to a Poisoned Book* together at the end of 1533, but Rastell had misdated the book to 1534, and so it only appeared like a timely rejoinder.[19] Despite the printer's error, both More's *Letter* and *Answer* attacked the Zwinglian view of the Eucharist put forward by English Reformers; neither of these texts addressed the king's policies, nor could they have done so. More had published before the *Articles* appeared.

More went still further in placating his king. "For many things which in that book be touched, in some I know not the law, and in some I know not the fact," More wrote to Cromwell. Since the *Articles* were published by the king and "his honorable council," More trusts that Cromwell knows "it were a thing far unlikely" that any response would come from him. At the same time, however, it must have dawned on More that his *Treatise*—especially its discussion of the Greek Church and denunciation of schism—might appear like a reply to the *Articles*, particularly its disavowal of Rome. In light of Henry's excommunication and his truculent reply to it, More's own letter reads like his description of it, a long and inelegant plea to his "good master and friend," Cromwell.[20]

The contents of the *Answer* and More's *Letter against Frith* were evidence of More's innocence, but a second attempt against him couldn't be addressed by pointing to a public record of already published books. In January, Cromwell had drafted a bill of attainder, condemning Bishop John Fisher and More, among others, for collusion with Barton. More was accused of conspiring with her to denounce Henry, a crime that amounted to treason and penalty by death. The bill came before Parliament on 21 February 1534 and specified that those attainted had asserted that Barton received a message from God, no less than a warning from heaven, "that in case his Highness proceeded to the accomplishment of the said divorce and married another, that then his Majesty should not be king of this Realm by the space of one month after, and in the reputation of God should not be king one day nor one hour."[21] By the time the bill of attainder was introduced, Henry had married Anne Boleyn (ca. 1500–1536), on 25 January 1533, despite Barton's message sanctioning rebellion against him if he were to do so. In the case of marriage with Anne, though, Barton had maintained that Henry's reign was no longer ordained by God, and he "should not be king one day nor one hour." Her prophecies therefore implicated Henry's reign as unholy during the same spring of 1533 when he was at odds with the papacy and looking for ways of legitimizing his new queen.

The indictment in 1534 also suggests how much public opinion mattered to Henry. His concern for his reputation may be illustrated against the background of what he had accomplished. By the time the act against Barton passed Parliament, Henry had everything else in hand: he married Anne in January 1533; by March of that same year, Henry had convinced Pope Clement to appoint Thomas Cranmer (1489–1556) archbishop of Canterbury, and Cranmer volunteered his office for deciding the king's great matter. Next, the Convocation of Clergy declared that Henry's first marriage was void on 5 April 1533. During the same month, the Act in Restraint of Appeals declared that all causes of "matrimony and divorces" would be "definitely adjudged and determined" not by Rome but "within the King's jurisdiction and authority and not elsewhere."[22] On 23 May, Cranmer also found Henry's first marriage to be null and void. Anne's coronation, which More refused to attend, was held on 1 June 1533. Authority from Parliament, the clergy in England, and the archbishop in Canterbury licensed Henry to marry again, and he had already done so. Henry had a legal, if not a political, fait accompli.[23]

The resolution of Henry's great matter by law, however, proved to be a different matter than public acclaim for a new queen. Henry had offered money to anyone who would inform against those who spoke out against his second marriage as late as May and just before Anne's coronation in June. He felt he had to do so because "notwithstanding the orders against it, people will speak of this marriage."[24] Indeed, at the coronation "no one in London or the suburbs, not even women and children," knelt and cried out, "God save the King, God save the Queen." After the people were commanded to do so, someone responded that "the

King could not make them do so."²⁵ The Spanish ambassador to England at the time, Eustace Chapuys (ca. 1490–1556), called the event "a great dissatisfaction" to the "common people." To his mind, "it seems that the indignation of everybody about this affair has increased by a half since the coronation."²⁶ Such testimony, though biased and not entirely accurate, resonates with other accounts and suggests a public backlash. Cromwell's clerks, for instance, kept track of those "in this realm that be not in their minds full pleased and contented that our Sovereign hath married as he hath done." Even if these objectors "forbear to speak at large for fear of punishment, yet they mutter together secretly." The same report warned "if the Pope be excluded out of this realm, the Archbishop must be chief of the clergy here, which will be lightly accepted in the people's hearts"; the commoners, after all, complained of Cranmer precisely because of his decision against Katherine. In response, the hand of another of Cromwell's own clerks noted on the same report that its contents were "reasons" for "abolishing the Pope's supremacy."²⁷ Naturally, More's absence from the coronation and reputation as a Catholic apologist aroused suspicions that he was one of those that "mutter together secretly."

Under these circumstances and no sooner than the coronation concluded, in July 1533, Henry pulled Barton from her convent.²⁸ Barton was questioned, released without charge, questioned again by Cromwell, and sent to the Tower in November. Her support dwindled afterward.²⁹ In March 1534 came her indictment. Barton and her adherents led the people into "murmur" and in "evil opinion" against their king.³⁰

On 20 April 1534—three days after More's arrest—Barton was executed by hanging and beheading along with her associates, including two who had reached out to More about Barton's revelations.³¹ At More's first interrogation also in April, Cromwell told More that his refusal to take the oath would cause Henry to "conceive a great suspicion" against him. The king would now suppose that the "matter of the nun of Canterbury" was contrived by More, an accusation that More denied.³²

The risks involved in More's plans to defend Church unity in the *Treatise* may be appreciated further by noting that Barton's execution was timed to enforce loyalty to Henry's cause. On the same day of her death, Londoners were called to take an oath in support of their king and new queen, affirming the Act of Succession. Charles Wriothesley (1508–62) records in his *Chronicle* that "all the crafts in London were called to their halls, and there were sworn on a book to be true to Queen Anne and to believe and take her for lawful wife of the King and rightful Queen of England."[33] Many took the oath that day. Even More's fool, Master Henry Patenson (d. 1543), did so.[34] "The execution of the Nun of Kent, Henry Gold, and her other adherents on the very day that the oath was demanded," writes Susan Brigden, "had shown Londoners compellingly enough what would happen to those who denied the King, or even spoke disparagingly of his purposes."[35] Although the execution of Barton took place before the Treasons Act forbade Londoners from speaking against their king, her death in combination with the demand to take the oath amounted to the same if not a very similar policy: the king's subjects would pledge themselves in support of his marriage and to the realm's independence from Rome.[36]

More did not join Barton that day in April because his name was removed from the bill, in large part because of his own self-defense. In March 1534, More sent Cromwell his record of his last meeting with Barton. With astonishing foresight, More had retained a copy of the letter he sent to Barton after his 1533 meeting with her in a chapel at Syon. He enclosed a copy of it in his letter to Cromwell, and there the master secretary could read More's words to Barton: "Good Madam, I [doubt] not but that you remember that in the beginning of my communication with you, I showed you that I neither was nor would be curious of any knowledge of other men's matters, and least of all of any matter of princes or of the realm, in case it so were that God had, as to many good folks before time he hath any things revealed unto you such things, I said unto your ladyship, that I was not desirous to hear of, but also would not hear of."[37] More goes on to remind her how he explicitly warned her "from talking with any persons" and especially with "lay persons" about anything pertaining to the "prince's affairs, or the state of the realm."[38] The letter that More shared with Cromwell—written to Barton after More had talked with her but before the Act of Attainder was passed—exonerated him completely.[39] Placed beside the words of the bill itself cited above, More's words sound like a legal rebuttal prepared in 1533 against a charge that would not be made against him until 1534.

Be that as it may, More ended his own letter with a statement of qualified loyalty. Even without Cromwell's investigation and independent of an indictment, More bears himself "in every man's company" such that "neither good man nor bad, neither monk, friar nor nun, nor other man or woman in this world shall make me digress from my troth and faith, *either toward God, or toward my natural prince*, by the grace of Almighty God; and as you therein find me true, so I heartily therein pray you to continue toward me your favor and good will, as you shall be sure of my poor daily prayer; for other pleasure can I none do you."[40] The use of the adjective "natural," as in "natural prince," means "thoroughly legitimate," making Henry into a "natural liege lord" whose rule More accepts and recognizes as lawful.[41] Nothing can make More digress from his "troth" or loyalty to him. Instead of the "one God and one king" formulation from the *Articles*, though, More employed an either/or parallel structure, which can be read alongside his contemporaneous arguments against schism. To paraphrase, no one can persuade More from his duties either to God—and, by implication, and as the *Treatise* argued, to the Catholic Church under the pope—or to his "natural prince" and king. Seen in this light, More held out hope that his loyalties need not be divided.

In correspondence with that same wish, More later contrasted his case with that of Barton. He wrote to his king on 5 March 1534: "For in this matter of the wicked woman of Canterbury, I have unto your trusty Councilor Mr. Thomas Cromwell, by my writing, as plainly declared the truth, as I possibly can, which my declaration of his duty toward your Grace, and his goodness toward me, he hath, I understand, declared unto your grace."[42] The Act of Attainder alleged that Barton pretended to be holy so that she could attack and undermine the king. She was a false prophet and a fraud, a political assassin masquerading under the guise of holiness.[43] By calling Barton "wicked" and Henry "natural" More expresses his agreement with the charges against her.[44]

Here again, the different settings of 1534 and 1557 should be observed. As one might expect, Rastell altered More's letters. He suppressed the first one to Cromwell altogether and deleted More's subsequent characterizations of Barton as "wicked" in the others that made their way to print.[45] In 1557, it would be ill-advised for Rastell to print More's actual words.[46] For the Maid of Kent, so the indictment against her in 1534 reads, claimed "revelation of God that the said Lady Katherine should prosper and do well, and that her issue—the Lady Mary, the King's daughter—should prosper and reign in this Realm."[47] Almost twenty years later, with the ascent of Mary to the throne, this accusation read like a prediction come true, a prophecy spoken by a holy maid and martyr for the Catholic faith.

But before Barton's indictment and on her day of execution in 1534, her defense of Queen Katherine and "Lady Mary" was targeted for suppression. The previous fall, Henry had Mary barred from court and "title, legitimacy, and primogeniture" were deprived her, despite the Spanish ambassador's complaint and appeals on her behalf.[48] On the very same day of Barton's execution, when the oath to the Act of Succession was administered, Wriothesley's *Chronicle* reports that Londoners were also made "utterly to think the Lady Mary, daughter to the King by Queen Katherine, but as a bastard."[49]

Of course, Barton was viewed favorably during Mary's reign. So Rastell changed More's reference to the "wicked woman of Canterbury" to "nun of Canterbury" from More's 5 March 1534 letter to Henry. When More wrote again to Cromwell on the matter, he asked Cromwell to share with the king his "faithful mind," and "that in the matter of that wicked woman there never was on my part any other mind than good."[50] Once again, Rastell altered the text, changing "wicked woman" to "the nun." More's comments and position on the controversy were minimalized for Marian audiences, but these changes also fit with Rastell's overall picture of an author who charitably withdrew from public or worldly affairs in 1534.

More's own response to the political crisis surrounding the nun at Kent is valuable for the insight it provides into his attitude toward his king in the early months of 1534. To More's mind, he shouldn't have to divide his loyalties between pope and king because the latter should acknowledge papal primacy in matters that belonged to the Catholic Church. By the same logic, his *Treatise* warned against schism. Because More had written in the context of the Greek Church, he couldn't be accused of criticizing Henry directly, as Barton did, but his support of Rome remained.

He was treading a finer line, however, with his allegories. In the *Treatise*, More turned the council convened by Caiaphas and the chief priests, for example, into a censure of all "kings" who usurped Church privileges (*CW* 13:73/3). After a statement about how chief priests were ordained in law, More comments upon unlawful selection processes instigated by monarchs: "But afterward, by ambition of the priests, usurpation and covetise [covetousness] of the kings, *the right order of the making or choosing of the bishop was changed*, and they were put in and put out by the kings, sometimes for pleasure, sometimes for displeasure, and sometimes for money too, so that instead of one, now they become many" (73/2–7).[51] Here More conflates the offices of Catholic bishops and Jewish chief priests. The "right order of making bishops," though, is an anachronism for a reason. In writing so, More obliquely criticized Henry for disputing with the archbishop of Canterbury, William Warham (1450–1532), over the appointment of bishops. Like More's criticism of the Greek Church, his comments on kings corresponded with Henry's actions but did not explicitly name them.

More's point would have been recognizable in 1534. We have seen how Cranmer, in effect, was Henry's appointment, but the previous archbishop of Canterbury, who had crowned Henry, made a dramatic stand for Rome on 24 February 1532. On that day and from an upper room in Lambeth Palace, Warham swore to a public instrument that repudiated any statutes since November 1529, including any statutes to be passed henceforth, which were made, or would be made, "in derogation of the Roman pontiff or the Apostolic See," or otherwise threatened the liberties of the Church.[52] Henry responded with a charge of *praemunire* offense against Warham. Fourteen years earlier, one Henry Standish, bishop of St. Asaph, had been consecrated before he had sworn his loyalty to the king, and for this Warham was accused. The stage was set for a battle between king and pope over the appointment of bishops.

Warham died before formal proceedings could take place, but his speech in self-defense remains, which he probably intended for delivery in the House of Lords, and there we read about "the right order" for choosing bishops. "He is made no bishop by his consecration," asserts Warham, "but he is made and provided a bishop at Rome in the Pope's Consistory, and hath before his consecration all things appertaining to spiritual jurisdiction as a bishop." In consecrating Standish, Warham acted in obedience to Rome, following his own duty as primate, as did "Saint Thomas of Canterbury." To place a prince above the pope in the selection process would violate Rome's rights and spiritual jurisdiction, and "it might follow that the Church should have no bishops and consequently no priests by them, and so all the sacraments of Holy Church might cease at [a] prince's pleasure." In contrast to swearing fealty to the king, a "spiritual man" was bound by his "sworn obedience to the Pope" in the consecration of bishops and not to "any temporal law made to the contrary." Warham also told his adversaries that anyone who "lay violent hands upon a bishop, in taking him and imprisoning him is accursed" and cannot be "assoiled but by the Pope."[53] More's ally and Erasmus's patron might have been preparing himself for martyrdom with these words. Warham left his speech undelivered, but his major point resounded in More's blanket criticism of kings who meddled in the "right order" of the selection of bishops.

Even so, Warham and Barton were two different cases. One argued from tradition and law; the other from special and private revelation. Barton's prophesies also assumed and foretold of irreparable division and fomented insurrection. More's "faithful mind," in contrast, would never support armed rebellion or overthrow of Henry. So, More turned to other means of opposition. He meant to address Londoners on the Eucharist, but his discussion of this sacrament would emphasize the need for Catholic unity, or what this sacrament signified: "The thing of this Blessed Sacrament that is signified thereby and not contained therein is the unity of society of all good holy folk in the mystical body of Christ" (*CW* 13:142/13–15), or "the society of all saints in the mystical body of Christ" (143/15–16), and as many grapes flow into one wine, "so be all holy saints gathered together in one, into the unity of Christ's holy mystical body" (143/20–22); "for like as the natural body of Christ is many members in one natural body, so is that society of Saints, many lively members in the unity of Christ's mystical body" (146/6–8).[54] Christ's mystical body was the Catholic Church, which the Eucharist itself signified. Schism would be a rupture in that mystical body, and an attack upon what the Eucharist represented. With such ideas in mind, More began his *Treatise*. Against "one God and one king" would be placed the "unity of society of all good holy folk." By the time of his arrest and Barton's execution, however, a formal and final break with Rome was underway. The mystical body of Christ was being torn asunder, but the opportunity had passed for publishing the *Treatise* in 1534. When Rastell printed it more than twenty years later, More's polemical work was made into devotional literature, a part of *De tristitia Christi*.

A CONTROVERSIAL OR A DEVOTIONAL WORK?

Against the background of the Barton imbroglio and publication of the *Articles*, More's changes in addressing heresy can be explained. He would need to be careful in his writings lest he appear unlike those "true and obedient subjects" who followed the mantra of "one God and one king." If the government had grown wary of and alert to More's controversial tracts as political threats, then he would write under a devotional guise. For this reason, and as I explore in this section, More wrote his *Treatise* to seem like other devotional texts focused upon the imitation of Christ, but with a crucial difference in mind. His treatment of piety demanded a rejection of the Sacramentarian position circulating in 1534. In this way, More's attempt at cultivating piety in readers became inseparable from another assault upon heresy. More's tactic was to catechize and move readers, but he accomplished these aims through polemical writing.

A convenient way into analysis of More's blend of catechesis and apologetics is to point out how More himself distinguished devotional from polemical literature in 1532. In consideration of how to read his controversial exchanges with Reformers, More had offered "Christian Readers" the following advice: "For surely the very best way were neither to read this book nor theirs, but rather the people unlearned to occupy themselves beside their other business in prayer, good meditation, and the reading of such English books as most may nourish and increase devotion. Of which kind is Bonaventure on the life of Christ, Gerson on the following of Christ, and the devout contemplative book *Scala Perfectionis* with such other like, than in learning what may well be answered unto heretics."[55] Here More contrasts the style of his own *Confutation of Tyndale* with the characteristics of books dedicated to the cultivation of personal sanctity. The former consists of citing a passage by your adversary before refuting it—a method that once was More's own.[56] We also learn from the passage above that, although More opposes Tyndale's translation of the Bible into English, he recognizes how reading devotional literature in English, which included selections from scripture, could benefit "people unlearned."[57] In the *Treatise*, More's concern for how uneducated readers should occupy themselves with questions of religious controversy becomes a major point of emphasis. For these readers, More will paraphrase and translate scripture into a narrative that explains the Eucharist as the summit of Catholic sacramental theology. Thus, his polemical and instructive ends became one and the same.

Before leaving the titles of devotional literature listed by More, it should be noted how they are instructive for understanding the *Treatise*, but here not entirely in terms of models for imitation. More's "life of Christ" refers to the *Meditationes vitae Christi*, formerly and inaccurately attributed to Bonaventure (ca. 1221–74), a text subsequently translated into English and printed in 1488, 1495, 1517, and 1523 as *The Mirror of the Blessed Life of Jesu Christ*.[58] More supposed Jean Charlier de Gerson ("John Gerson") (1363–1429), a French churchman and scholar, to be the author of *De imitatione Christi* (*The Imitation of Christ*), a book first printed in English in 1502 by Wynkyn de Worde (d. 1535), but this text was actually written by Thomas à Kempis (1380–1471).[59] The third, the *Scala perfectionis* (*The Scale of Perfection*) by Walter Hilton (ca. 1340–96) was widely known in manuscript from a first edition in 1486 and through five subsequent editions during More's lifetime, the last of which appeared in 1525.[60] Though all highly recognizable titles, only in the broadest sense were these models for More. They represented a reformation of individuals in the spirit of Christ, or an earlier ideal of spiritual renewal before Luther, one focused on an increase in personal sanctity without defiance of Catholic doctrine.[61] Whereas these earlier works assumed a unity of faith, More's *Treatise* stresses how imitation of Christ corresponds only with orthodox but not Reformation doctrine.

Following the example of Christ extends across devotional literature and represents its educative end, a point that More echoed. In the *Imitation of Christ*, Kempis explains the shared method: "'He that follows me,' says Christ our Saviour, 'walks not in darkness, for he shall have the light of life.' These be the words of our Lord Jesus Christ, whereby we be admonished to follow his teachings and his manner of living, if we will truly be illumined and delivered from all blindness of heart. Let all the study of our heart from henceforth be to have our meditation wholly fixed in the life of Christ."[62] The Pseudo-Bonaventure tradition similarly claims that "the Life of Jesus teaches us what we ought to do." The reason why hearkens back to the teaching of Bernard of Clairvaux (1090–1153); namely, that Christ is the source of all virtues. "Where else," we read in *The Life of Christ*, "will you find such virtues—such exalted poverty, exceeding lowliness, profound wisdom, examples of prayer, meekness, obedience, patience, and all other virtues, and doctrine, as in the Life of the Lord of Hosts?"[63] Unsurprisingly then, *following Christ* is what Hilton calls *turning to him*, both in body and heart. "So let your heart be as if dead to all earthly loves and fears," Hilton writes, because your heart is "turned wholly to our Lord Jesus Christ." In turning toward him, you will "fashion yourself within to his likeness, through humility and charity and other spiritual virtues."[64] More makes the same points in his prayer for readers at the start of his treatment of the Passion: "Good lord give us thy grace, not to read or hear this gospel of thy bitter passion with our eyes and our ears in manner of a pastime, but that it may with compassion so sink into our hearts, that it may stretch to the everlasting profit of our souls."[65] Each author values the virtues of humility and charity based upon Christ and in imitation of him as a means of personal growth. Meditation, reading, and prayer "may stretch" one and provide "everlasting profit" to souls.

Despite the shared purpose of imitating Christ, More differs greatly from the devotional literature in English that he recommended. Of note, both the *Imitation* and the *Scale of Perfection* are traceable back to the Carthusian London Charterhouse in extant manuscript copies that date from 1500–1510, and this decade covers the years during which More is reported to have visited or stayed at the same monastery.[66] There, More would have encountered a Carthusian classic in devotional literature, the *Vita Christi* by Ludolph of Saxony (d. 1377/1378). Though the *Vita* was not translated into English, this book and not the ones More recommended in his *Confutation* provided the organizational structure behind More's *Treatise*.[67]

The *Treatise* most resembles Ludolph of Saxony's *Vita* because of a shared scholarly tone and use of traditional sources, especially early Church Fathers, which More deployed in an assault upon Sacramentarians. Hilton, by way of contrast, mentions "disbelief in the sacrament" as a temptation of the devil but provides no theological account of sacramental things and accidents, as the *Treatise* and the *Vita* do.[68] Even Kempis, whose entire last book of the *Imitation* is dedicated to the Eucharist, titles his final chapter "That a man shall not be a curious searcher of the Holy Sacrament." Rather than investigate the Eucharist, Kempis admonishes readers: "Faith and a good life are asked of thee, and not the highness of understanding nor the depths of the mysteries of God."[69]

Contrary to the devotional literature in English recommended by More, his own *Treatise*, like Ludolph's *Vita*, educates readers in sacramental theology. For this reason, both More and Ludolph tend toward abstract or technical discussions of the Eucharist and follow the arguments of Thomas Aquinas (1225–74) from his *Summa Theologica* (1265–74).[70]

Seen in this light, More also distanced himself from his longtime friend and ally Desiderius Erasmus (d. 1536). "Let this be your first and only goal, this your prayer," Erasmus writes in his *Ratio* (1518/19), "pursue this one thing, that you may be changed, that you may be seized, that you may be inspired, that you may be transformed, to those things which you learn." To be transformed by the study of scripture and the early Church Fathers meant allowing texts to move readers, grounding exegesis in affections as much as in thought.[71] Erasmus's own paraphrases of scripture involved "bridging gaps, smoothing rough passages, bringing order out of confusion and simplicity out of complication, untying knots, throwing light on dark places, and giving Hebrew turns of speech a Roman dress" for such a purpose.[72] More's own readers, however, should grow in affective piety *and* in theological knowledge of the Catholic teaching on the Eucharist, a topic Erasmus eschewed.[73] Within More's distinctive framework—and unlike his English antecedents or Erasmus—More seeks to fortify Londoners against reform with a doctrinally clear and essentially Thomistic account of the Eucharist.[74] What scholars have classified as More's devotional literature, in other words, is also an example of polemical theology.

THIS IS MY BODY

More's deviation from devotional literature on the topic of the Eucharist corresponds with his combination of catechetical and apologetical aims. In the *Treatise*, More formulates the Eucharist in terms of sacramental "things." Properly speaking, the word "sacrament" means a sign, but a sign that denotes an existing "holy thing." Washing the body with water, for example, signifies "the washing of the soul by grace," but because the sacrament is efficacious, the actual cleansing of the soul from sin "is called the 'thing' of the sacrament." In the Holy Sacrament of the altar, there are two sacramental signs, one outward and another inward. The outward is bread and wine; the inward, the very body and blood of Christ. The one may be seen; the other remains "unsensible" (*CW* 13:141/11–34). More draws the following conclusion in terms of "signified" and "contained" things of the sacrament: "The thing of the sacrament that is both signified and contained is the very body and the very blood of our Savior himself, therein actually and really present. The thing of this Blessed Sacrament that is signified thereby and not contained therein is the unity or society of all good holy folk in the mystical body of Christ" (142/10–15).[75] The "very body" and "very blood" of Christ are substantially present under the "accidents" of bread and wine; the appearance of "whiteness, redness, hardness, softness, weight, savor, and taste, and such other like, remain and abide in the Blessed Sacrament" (140/27–29). The mystical body of "all good holy folk" are not substantially present but signified, and this sign refers to the Church in its unity, a point of emphasis made to draw attention to heresy and schism. To attack belief in the Eucharist, in other words, excludes one from the Church and the salvation of Christ's sacrifice.

As a pre-Tower Eucharist work, the context of the *Treatise* reflects More's previous polemical efforts, especially against Tyndale. In *The Obedience of a Christian Man* (1528), Tyndale argued for the importance of scripture's literal meaning but not with regard to the Blessed Sacrament. He writes that "the decay of faith" first arose from "allegories" and that "scripture hath but one sense which is the literal sense." Tyndale dismissed all tropological and analogical senses as useless allegories. Only the literal sense never fails, and if one "cleaves" to it, "thou canst never err or go out of the way."[76] Yet in this same text, Tyndale teaches that the word "sacrament" is a "holy sign" that always represents a particular promise by God. Such an "outward sign" would "put a man in remembrance of some spiritual promise, which cannot be seen but by faith only."[77] For Tyndale, the sacrament existed for awaking or strengthening faith. There were no "holy things" but only sacramental significations.

Accordingly, there could be no sacrifice of the Mass or miracle of converting bread and wine into Christ's body and blood during it. In his *Answer to More* in 1531, Tyndale argued against the Catholic teaching of an everlasting sacrifice, a miraculous event at every Mass for the faithful to participate in like the disciples did at the Last Supper. For "Christ is no more killed," Tyndale writes, and the sacrament is only a "sign and memorial of that sacrifice" according to the line "this do in the remembrance of me." Moreover, "the priest touches not Christ's body by your own doctrine," writes Tyndale of Catholic teaching, which held that Christ's body appeared under the species of bread and wine. The priest, therefore, neither sees Christ's body with his eyes "nor breaks it with his fingers" nor "eats it with his mouth." Finally, after the Resurrection, "Christ is impassible," that is, incapable of suffering pain.[78] He cannot undergo his sacrificial death every time the Mass is celebrated.

Tyndale went still further and argued that the institution of this sacrament calls believers to repentance "at the sight of the sacrament or at the breaking, feeling, eating, chamming or drinking" of bread and wine. As a memorial, the sacrament "calls to remembrance the death of Christ, his body breaking and the blood-shedding for all our sins." To eat Christ's body and drink his blood is a sign of how Christians "through faith only" receive forgiveness of sins. "And all that have not this doctrine of the sacrament," Tyndale concludes of his own teaching, "come thereto in vain" or receive Communion without profit.[79]

By the time *The Supper of the Lord* appeared in 1533, Tyndale's previous arguments were enlarged and advanced anonymously in England and threatened to "set the almighty word of God" against those who held to the "devilish doctrine" of the Mass. Instead of the sacrifice of the Mass, faith alone explains Communion: "Faith it is therefore in Christ that fills our hungry hearts so that we can desire no other if we once thus eat and drink him by faith, that is to say, if we believe his flesh and body to have been broken and his blood shed for our sins. For then are our souls satisfied and we be justified." With explicit reference to the formula used in consecration, *The Supper of the Lord* argued that the word *est* meant *significat*, "as much to say, as 'this' signifies my body."[80] *Hoc est corpus meum* should be read as *hoc significat corpus meum*.[81]

In consequence, the unity of the Church would not be found in "Papists & scholastical sophisters" or in their "unwritten words" and "dead dreams," shorthand for Catholic tradition, but in all those who rightly understand how to receive Communion. Who, then, should eat Christ's flesh and drink his blood? The answer in the *Supper* was the same as the one stated in Tyndale's *Answer*: "They that believe his body crucified and his blood shed for their sins—these cleave unto His gracious favor," and this believing is what occurs rather than consuming "material meat." The original apostles themselves understood Christ's words "in an allegorical sense and perceived well that he meant not of his material body to be eaten with their teeth."[82] From defending the literal sense of scripture to debunking it in the case of the Eucharist, the "almighty word of God" prevails.

More rightly noted the contradiction or change in hermeneutical tactics years before his *Treatise*. "But whereas in all their writings they rail upon allegories, and cry out upon such holy doctors as preach them," More writes in his *Confutation*, "yet the holy sacraments themselves, they would, should serve for allegories only and for nothing else."[83] For the question is not, as More continues in his *Answer to a Poisoned Book*, if Christ's words "this is my body" may be explained allegorically, "but whether it may beside all that, be truly expounded of the very bodily eating of Christ's blessed body indeed."[84] More cites John 6:55 to emphasize the literal sense, "My flesh is verily meat & my blood verily drink." An allegorical reading of "this is my body" must account for Christ's insistence on real food and drink.[85] Rather than oppose allegory altogether, More sought to ground it in the literal sense first.[86] At the same time, instead of a departure from his earlier apologetical works, his *Treatise* is an extension of them.

More furthers his argument in the *Treatise* by responding to Tyndale's objection about impassibility. Again, as a polemical work, More is still responding to his opponents rather than turning away from controversy. In the *Treatise*, More agrees that Christ's body "suffered not" when consumed by his apostles at the Last Supper, but that he did suffer later upon the cross. Even so, Christ remains substantially present in the first Eucharist. "But when they received it again sacramentally after his resurrection," More asserts of the apostles, "then was it in eternal glory so confirmed, and in such wise immortal and impassible, that it should never die nor never suffer pain after" (*CW* 13:134/20–27). If Christ's body cannot suffer after his resurrection, though, how could his glorified body be present in the host *before* he rose? In answer, More distinguishes the Last Supper from all subsequent Masses: "And so, though there were in his blessed body and his blood given them in the sacrament before his Passion such a secret wonderful glory of impassibility for the time (as was in his body for the time a visible, open glory at his marvelous transfiguration) yet in the sacramental receiving after his glorious resurrection it had that point of newness which it had not actually before, that is to wit, without loss, diminishment, or intermission, eternal enduring of impassible and immortal glory."[87]

More follows Aquinas in making this point, but he abstains from a scholastic formulation in favor of plain speech. *The Supper of the Lord* used "Thomist" and "Thomistic" as insults and to conjure allegations of theosophistical speculation, but More cleverly avoids any hint of Aquinas's style and language of teaching. What More refers to as "a secret wonderful glory of impassibility for the time," Aquinas states by way of analogy. "Yet there was present in the sacrament," Aquinas stipulates, "in an impassible manner, that which was passible of itself; just as that was there invisibly which of itself was visible."[88] Hence, the paradoxical teaching of the impassible giving of a body that yet was passible.

Further evidence that More's *Treatise* responds directly to the controversy over the Eucharist is found where he reviews the various names of the Blessed Sacrament but takes special aim at the "supper of our Lord"—the very phrase employed by evangelicals to claim that the sacrament was nothing other than a memorial. "For it is called the supper of our lord," More counters, "to put us in mind and to let us know, that it is not another thing, but the selfsame thing that our lord gave there to his apostles, not another supper, but the selfsame supper" (*CW* 13:155/26–29). The "selfsame supper" remains the Last Supper miraculously represented at every Mass.

In all of this, the *Treatise* collects and transfers apologetical information and arguments to readers for the purposes of refuting what may be heard or read in London or otherwise put forward by English Reformers. "Here have I, good Christian readers, rehearsed you some of those many names," More concludes, "that this Blessed Sacrament is called." He did so, More writes, "to the intent that if it happened to you at any time hereafter to hear or read any of these things that are said or written by them that use of some of these names to take occasion of oppugning [attacking] the truth, you may have ready before, at your hand, the fallacy of their sophism solved" (*CW* 13:156/33–157/5). More's *Treatise* is protreptic but tailored to answer previously made attacks upon the Eucharist.

Though under scrutiny in 1534, More wrote anyway because he thought the Sacramentarians posed a frightening dilemma, a point More had emphasized the year before. In his *Answer to a Poisoned Book*, More compares those who disbelieve in the Eucharist, yet still receive it, to Judas Iscariot. An unbeliever will receive the host "to his harm as Judas did, and eateth and drinketh his own judgment and damnation," More warns, "because he discerneth not our Lord's body." Those who believe in the Blessed Sacrament, however, "verily receive and eat the blessed body of Christ, and that not only sacramentally, but also effectually, not only the figure, but the thing also, not only his blessed flesh into their bodies, but also his Holy Spirit into their souls, by participation whereof He is incorporate in them and they in Him."[89] In stark and clear terms, then, More sets forth the decision for English readers between Tyndale's teaching and that of the Church, the way of Judas or that of Christ. There could be no half measures or indifference. Unlike the "devotional More" claimed by critics, his arguments in 1534 were as polemically charged as the ones he made in 1533. Even More's cultivation of piety centered upon English orthodoxy in contrast to Reformation theology.

MORE'S READERS

The propagandistic aims of the *Treatise* are reflected further in More's concern for and written instructions to his readers. To catechize Londoners and prevent the spread of heresy, More distinguished between "unlearned people" and "learned" Christian readers and, therefore, between texts for those who knew Latin and for those who did not, but he wrote his *Treatise* for both types. How did he do so?

At the start of More's presentation of the Passion, he provides "A warning to the reader" that stipulates the different ways in which his book may and should be read. In the first half, his warning to readers with learning, More writes:

> A warning to the reader. Here I will give the reader warning that I will rehearse the words of the evangelists in this process of the Passion in Latin, word by word after my copy, as I find it in the work of that worshipful father Master John Gerson, which work he entitled *Monotesseron*,[90] that is to wit, one of all four, as I have declared you before in my preface, because I will not in any word willingly mangle or mutilate that honorable man's work: but so rehearse it that

learned which shall read it here may have the selfsame commodity thereby that they may have by the reading of the same among his own other works, as in considering such doubts as he sometimes moveth concerning the context of the story,[91] and in searching (if their pleasure be) every word in his own proper place, where it was gathered and taken out of any of the four evangelists, and for their own learning list confer the place and use their own judgment in the allowing or in the controlling of any part of his context, in the gathering and compiling of his present work. (*CW* 13:50/5–21)[92]

More's warning reveals much about his authorial design. He will "rehearse" or narrate the words of the evangelists to tell the story of Christ's passion. Yet More also uses the term "rehearse" to indicate *how* he will represent or relate his source material to readers. More's concern for his source, in this case, consists of accurately representing *the exact words* of Gerson, who compiled the *Monotesseron* (1420), a collection of all four Gospels in a single narrative.[93]

Problems arise, More observes, because Gerson himself has doubts about his organization of the four Gospels. Rather than settle any lingering questions posed by his source, More simply invites his educated readers to use their own judgment: "For their own learning" readers may choose to compare the various individual Gospels against Gerson's ordering and challenge "any part of his context," or any component of Gerson's narrative reconstruction of events.[94]

More's formulation about the "context of the story" translates Gerson's "narrationis contextum" and parallels what Tyndale calls the "order and process of the text."[95] Christ's life, in other words, should be read in context by weighing all the Gospel accounts against one another regarding any single event, action, or saying, according to both More and Tyndale.

"Learned readers," then, were those who understood both English and Latin, and they would be able to see how Gerson arranged or ordered his harmony of the four Gospels in accord with lines in the Vulgate.[96] For More, such *lectores* could also make their own comparison of Gospel texts that present complementary or different views of an issue or event.

If More's emphasis upon narrative context is paramount for learned readers, his stress upon narrative flow is just as significant for "aural" readers or "unlearned people." Indeed, the second section of More's warning raises the question of how educated readers should use his text when sharing its contents with those unable to read Latin. The latter half functions like instructions for how these readers should use More's text to shape public opinion. The scholarly readers with Latin skills will educate those with less learning in matters of religious controversy. More explains:

> But yet will I not fully follow the same fashion in the rehearsing of the same thing in English. For if I should, there neither could any such fruit grow thereof, and also the context of the story should in the eye of the English reader (and yet much more in the ear of the English hearer) seem very far unsavory, by reason of the often interposition of the initial letters, signifying the names of the four evangelists, and some one sentence with so little change so often repeated, and in some place the context so diversely entricked in his collection, that himself with a note in the margin declareth himself to doubt and stand unsure whether in that place he join and link well in one the sundry words of the evangelists or no.[97] And therefore in the rehearsing of his context in English, nothing will I put in of mine own: but out will I not let to leave any such thing as I shall think to be unto the English reader no furtherance but a hindrance to the clear progress of this holy story, which we shall with help of God in this wise now begin. (*CW* 13:50/21–51/4)[98]

Significantly, More will not "fully follow the same fashion in the rehearsing of the same thing in English" for he does not want to hinder "this holy story," which is just as much for the "English reader (and yet much more in the ear of the English hearer)," a telling distinction about the larger audience More hopes to address. Listeners are dubbed "readers." Annotators and those tracing Gerson's arrangement of Gospel verses were one group, but others were "aural" readers, partially literate, or reliant upon others with more education to read aloud to them. More plans his presentation of the Passion narrative for those who will hear it and for those who will read it. When the text is read aloud to those who could not read or read only print English, then educated readers would function as orators or instructors.

Thus, More speaks to readers of Latin not as an isolated group but as leaders in a communal reading process. He does so because of his interest in reaching "aural" English readers, the broadest group of Londoners. Early modern England was neither fully literate nor an oral society.[99] Literacy existed on a continuum, from those who could read print, but not script or secretary hand, a form of Gothic cursive, and extending to those who read Latin.[100] There were also readers beyond these divisions, including those who read Greek or Hebrew. More's polemic aim, however, required him to reach as broad an audience as possible.

According to More's warning, when the *Treatise* is read aloud to those without language skills, the Latin passages will be skipped. The "nota lector," which explains the Gospel abbreviations in the printed text, would be "unsavory" to "English readers," or rather to their *ears*.[101] For the same reason, the questions about Gerson's arrangement of the Gospels in Latin would prove onerous. Even though the context of Christ's passion, or its overall narrative, includes questions "entricked in collection," or inherent in Gerson's compilation, these matters, if voiced, would hinder the flow of the narrative, not to mention the point of the *Treatise*'s defense of the Eucharist.

In More's concern for the flow of narrative, the authorial design of the *Treatise* reveals a rhetorical goal. More cleverly blends scriptures with rejoinders to the Sacramentarians. For More's aims are not consolation but refutation. The work is not primarily meant to advocate fortitude against troubles, for the *Treatise* is not a *contemptus mundi* reflection but a call to action or to education in the scriptural basis of the Mass, and this catechesis seems especially designed for Londoners confused by or misled by evangelical reformers.[102] To persuade his fellow citizens, More's *Treatise* employs or relies upon communal and scholarly reading practices in England and counts upon an educated group of readers to inform and guide those with less learning.[103] Learning materials from scripture, commentary on its meaning, and instructions for educated users are all included.

With the same goal of shaping public opinion, More also addresses all "good readers." When More writes of the chief priests' and scribes' success in betraying Christ, for example, More once again addresses the "good reader" and wonders why men take pride in their mischief, for "if they bring their purpose properly to pass" then "the devil it is himself that bringeth their matters about much more, a great deal, than they." More elaborates his point in a tone reminiscent of the "merry tales" from his earlier *A Dialogue Concerning Heresies* (1529):

> And therefore, good reader, here we may well consider, that when men are in device about mischief, if they bring their purpose properly to pass, cause have then none to be proud and praise their own wits. For the devil it is himself that bringeth their matters about, much more a great deal than they. There was once a young man fallen in a lewd mind toward a woman, and she was such as he could conceive no hope to get her, and therefore was falling to a good point in his own mind to let that lewd enterprise pass. He mishapped nevertheless to show his mind to another wretch, who encouraged him to go forward and leave it not. "For begin thou once, man, the matter," quoth he, "and never fear it; let the devil alone with the remnant; he shall bring it to pass in such wise as thyself alone canst not devise how." I trow that wretch had learned that counsel of these priests and these ancients, assembled here together against Christ at this council. (*CW* 13:78/1–15)[104]

The "good reader," in this instance, is one of those Londoners who will enjoy and recognize More's signature irony and perhaps only hear the *Treatise* read aloud. For this audience, More creates such character types as the "wretch," an evil yet clever advisor, a virtuous maiden, and a young man with a "lewd mind" in order to add vivacity and local color to scriptural commentary. So, too, those familiar with Barton's prophecies could have heard a reference to Henry and Anne in More's anecdote of a man "in a lewd mind toward a woman."[105]

Attention to the audience that More envisions for his *Treatise* reveals both continuity and change in how More approaches and plans his refutation of English Reformers. A year earlier, in April 1533, *The Apology of Sir Thomas More* made a defense of using merry tales. There, More states the charge made against him by William Tyndale, John Frith, and others is that "among the most earnest matters," More brings in "fancies and sports and merry tales." But More justifies his approach by citing the Roman poet Horace (65–8 BCE) because "a man may sometime say full sooth in game." Of importance, More thinks his humor best suits his state: "And one that is but a layman, as I am, it may be better haply become him merrily to tell his mind than seriously and solemnly to preach."[106] Yet the *Treatise* does preach or provide what More calls "lectures" and "homilies," interchangeable terms for him, along with merry tales such as the one above. His willingness to address a reading public through English translations of the Bible is new, but More's public persona as Church apologist remains.[107]

In sum, the distinctions between sacred scripture and literature, educated readers and English ones, Latin and vernacular texts, eyes and ears are blended in the *Treatise* for the sake of defending what More thinks of as the true doctrine of Christ. The reading of approved theologians and sacred scriptures in Latin was restricted to educated readers. General Christian readers, such as the kind addressed in his *Confutation*, will read in English, or be read to by others with more learning.

Accordingly, when More turns to the controversy of the Holy Sacrament, he writes that "in this holy sacrament is the very body and the very blood of him of whom all other sacraments receive their virtue and strength" (*CW* 13:137/7–9). They labor in vain who would "subvert the very true Christian faith" by teaching others that Christ's plain words—"this is my body"—were "other meant than they were" (137/14–16). More then adds: "Yet it is not my present purpose to dispute the matter with them but to show and set forth the truth before *the eyes of the reader*, that he may rather of the truth read, increase in faith, and conceive devotion, than with much time bestowed in the reading of their erroneous fallacies *misoccupy his ears* and heap up in his heart a dunghill of their devilish vanities" (137/25–31). The connection to or transition from the *Confutation* and other earlier apologetical works with the *Treatise* is both clear and ambiguous. On the one hand, More gestures at writing devotionally; on the other, he easily slides into disputation. No sooner than More finishes this paragraph, he goes on the attack: "Howbeit, somewhat of theirs it is, good readers, in my mind necessary that you know, to the intent you may the better beware of their wiliness" (137/40–138/2). Next, More proceeds to refute the "three special engines" or arguments of assault upon the Blessed Sacrament (138/3–32). Afterward, he calls such engines attempts "to deceive unlearned folk," a further indication of how More's own educational or devotional literature remains tied to unmasking or attacking heretics before the people (139/23–4).

RASTELL'S AND MORE'S PLANS FOR PUBLICATION

If Rastell fashioned the Tower Works after his own purposes in 1557, he honored his uncle's polemical intention in a key instance that sheds light upon More's own original design. This curious link between More's plans and Rastell's later folio is the fact that More's *catena*, or compendium of quotations in the *Treatise*, was printed from a previous commonplace book composed by More for apologetical purposes, a text that has been lost.[108]

More had originally provided his own quotations from "old holy doctors and saints, contrary to these new men's tale," because his selections "affirm that in the Blessed Sacrament is the very body and blood of our savior Christ himself" (*CW* 13:160/16–19). The importance of citing Church Fathers was significant because "new men" such as Tyndale and Joye advised their own "Christian reader" that the symbolic nature of the Blessed Sacrament was put "out of doubt" by the testimony of Tertullian (ca. 155/160 to after 220) and Augustine (354–430), whose "own words" were presented "both in Latin and English."[109] More used the same tactic with Latin quotations and English translations of Church Fathers in the *Treatise*. He advised Rastell: "And the Latin sayings should be given and translated after if it seems necessary to add any sayings from those places which we collected formerly, and which are known but not published in that book we published earlier, *De cena Domini*."[110] The title *De cena Domini* most likely refers to one of More's earlier published books that ultimately emerged under a different name, but the instruction of what and where to add quotations illustrates broad leeway granted to the printer. So, too, More's instructions indicate controversial rather than consolatory or conventionally conceived devotional aims. To supply his educated readers with rhetorical ammunition in support of orthodox doctrine, More created a commonplace book within his *Treatise*.

The printing from this earlier commonplace book in the 1557 edition suggests how Rastell followed More's instructions. More's own approach of citing early Church Fathers in a list mirrored that of Henry VIII's *Assertio septem sacramentorum*, and among the quotations from More are two exact parallels to the king's book.[111] Against the citations of Augustine and Tertullian found in the *Supper of the Lord*, More's *Treatise* supplied twenty.[112] Yet of these, the Latin quotations from numbers 9 through 12—including, in order, Basil (329–79), Hesychius (d. ca. 450), Ambrose

(339–97), and Chrysostom (347–407)—appear in large black-ink italic letters in the folio edition. There was no material or bookmaking reason for laying out the text this way. Rather, Rastell's presentation visually orients the reader to what he found to be the most persuasive quotations upon the Eucharistic controversy. Instead of privileging more prestigious fathers, such as Augustine or Jerome (ca. 347–419/420), Rastell enlarged the Latin formulations he thought best in defense of Church teaching.

Rastell's own decisions about how to use, translate, and print More's previous commonplace book in the *Treatise* were extensions of More's own careful distinctions among readers. The Latin quotations are for the sake of educated readers, who can share them or their translations with less educated or illiterate audiences. In the context of a propaganda war, readers of the *Treatise* were carefully grouped, and in this point Rastell honored More's original device.

THOMAS MORE IN 1534

Though scholars continue to sequester More's polemical phase of writing, beginning around 1520 with the *Responsio ad Lutherum*, from his Tower writings, More didn't suddenly change his opinions in the spring of 1534. Instead, he adjusted them to new circumstances. Like how scholars overstated the difference between More's "humanist" phase (1504–19) and his apologetical one (1520–33) because of a critical failure to see how humanist methodologies and religious ideas were intertwined in the period, the *Treatise* is less devotional literature than is recognized.[113] In this chapter I have restored the *Treatise* to its pre-Tower status and extended More's period of theological polemics into 1534. Though Rastell distorted the original compositional circumstances and objectives of More by making the *Treatise* part of *De tristitia*, his edition nevertheless retained some of the editorial apparatus necessary to capture More's plans for shaping public opinion in 1534.

THREE

The (Auto)Biographical More and *A Dialogue of Comfort against Tribulation*, 1534–1535

Though Thomas More's *A Dialogue of Comfort against Tribulation* is often read as a work of consolation literature with universal themes, its characters—the old but wise Antony and his young but fearful nephew Vincent—are from More's own life and circumstances of composition in 1534.[1] In fact, most studies find that More represents his own point of view in the voice of Antony,[2] yet fewer claim, as I do in this chapter, that More writes in defiance of King Henry VIII.[3]

The case to be made here hinges upon what Antony teaches his nephew and how More believes his readership will receive that teaching. Antony provides counsel that echoes the advice More offers to his daughter Margaret More Roper and to himself when beset by fears, but also and notably to all those who could be persecuted for their Catholic faith.[4] Put otherwise, More writes so that his readers will follow Antony's teachings and apply them to the situation at hand in England.

Seen in this way, the biographical context and rhetorical purpose of the *Dialogue* combine in an overall polemical effort. More wasn't writing to provide comfort for his family as much as he aimed at persuading them and others to his cause. Formally, the *Dialogue* is a work of deliberative rhetoric that advises readers what they should do when under a threat such as the kind posed by Henry. Because of its rhetorical structure and political message, the *Dialogue* should be read as another powerful example of More's controversial literature.

THE (AUTO)BIOGRAPHICAL SETTING

The purpose of More's *Dialogue* has generally been taken for granted, but it may be reevaluated by an examination of the author's own circumstances of composition. As with other Tower Works, so-called facts about More's authorship are recycled from early modern and hagiographical accounts to fashion an image of "devotional More," a prisoner who looked heavenward and turned away from politics. Were we to accept this view, we would say he wrote only under the auspices of sanctity and suffering. But More's letters leading up to and surrounding the time of his arrest tell a different story.

In one such letter to Thomas Cromwell from March 1534, fewer than three weeks before Parliament passed the Act of Succession, More spelled out his positions on the king's latest marriage and on papal primacy. Because More remained unconvinced that Henry's divorce from Katherine was licit, the king had exempted him from divorce proceedings. After Henry's marriage to Anne Boleyn, though, More would "neither murmur at it nor dispute upon it." Rastell printed this letter but excised the parts of it in support of Henry's second marriage, to Anne, which can be identified from More's own corrected and signed copy. I reproduce the passage from the *Works* below, but I have inserted in square brackets what Rastell cut:

> Besides this, diverse other ways have I so used myself, that if I rehearsed them all, it would well appear that I never have had against his grace's marriage any manner demeanure whereby his highness might have any manner cause or occasion of displeasure toward me. For likewise as I am not he which either can, or who it could become to take upon me the determination or decision of such a weighty matter, [nor boldly to affirm this thing or that therein,]

whereof diverse points a great way pass my learning, so am I he, that among other his grace's faithful subjects, his highness being in possession of his marriage, [and this noble woman really anointed Queen, neither murmur at it, nor dispute upon it, nor never did nor will, but without any other manner meddling of the matter among his other faithful subjects faithfully pray to God for his Grace and hers both, long to live and well and their noble issue too, in such wise as may be to the pleasure of God, honor and surety to themselves, rest, peace, wealth and profit unto this noble realm] will most heartily pray for the prosperous estate of his grace, long to continue to the pleasure of god.[5]

Rastell cut the sections I have in brackets because to print them would offend Queen Mary.[6] She was the daughter of Katherine, Henry's first wife, and Elizabeth was the daughter of Anne. To present a folio edition of More's *Works* to Mary with passages that refer to Anne as Henry's "noble lady" would be impolitic. Rastell's doctoring of his sources reminds us of how More's circumstances in 1534 differed from those of his nephew in 1557. By restoring More's words in this passage, too, we can reconstruct the confusion experienced by members of More's family about his refusal to placate his king. For what, exactly, was More willing to die?

More declined to state why he would refuse the oath after his arrest, but his family and those at court would have inferred the reason.[7] The preamble to the Act of Succession rejected papal authority and implied royal headship of the Church in England. In Rastell's printing of the same letter to Cromwell, he left intact More's views on papal primacy, which would have pleased a Marian regime. From the standpoint of More in 1534, however, these same views mean that his opposition to a schismatic rupture from Rome was known before his arrest. Of the political dispute between king and pope, More claims he would "nothing meddle in the matter." But More also asserts "that primacy is at the leastwise instituted by the corps [body] of Christendom and for a great urgent cause in avoiding of schisms," and by "schisms" More understood breaches in Church unity not caused by heresy.[8] Before legislation made More's support of papal primacy illegal and as late as 1534, he openly expressed it, as he told Cromwell, "both by mouth and by writing."[9]

Margaret wrote to her father scarcely a month later after his imprisonment in May 1534 and urged him to take the oath anyway. Given More's opposition to Henrician schism, he was disappointed by her letter. Her "lamentable letter" had "abashed" him. For all the terrible things rumored against him, none were "so grievous" as seeing his own well-beloved daughter make the case against his own heart.[10] If Margaret thought she could change her father's mind, More would declare that his decision was firm. He asked her to leave "such labor" and be "content" with his "former answers."[11] But More also softened the blow. He wrote to Margaret and through her to his extended family:

> A deadly grief unto me, and much more deadly than to hear of mine own death (for the fear thereof, I thank our Lord, the fear of hell, the hope of heaven, and the Passion of Christ daily more and more assuage), is that I perceive my good son your husband, and you my good daughter, and my good wife, and mine other good children and innocent friends, in great displeasure and danger of great harm thereby. The let [i.e., hindrance or stoppage] whereof, while it lieth not in my hand, I can no further but commit all unto God.[12]

The "let whereof" refers to the elimination of a threat against More's family, the "danger of great harm," over which More exercises no control, or so he thinks, for he cannot in conscience take the oath. But this is the very question—whether More should take the oath?—that is under dispute and to be argued by father and daughter in the months ahead. More concludes his letter by advising Margaret to meditate upon the passion of Christ, "and if we diligently do so," he includes himself with her, then both "shall find therein great comfort and consolation."[13] From this letter begins the theme of comfort and consolation that would make up the themes of his *Dialogue*, but not before Margaret iterated her position.[14]

Margaret's response in reply was forceful: "Father, what think you hath been our comfort since your departing from us?" More is her source of comfort because of his "godly conversation, and wholesome counsel, and virtuous example." How can she find comfort when he alone teaches her where to find it? Margaret mentions "this bitter time" of More's absence, and doubts not that God will hold "his holy hand" over him, and preserve More, both body and soul, especially now when he has lost all his goods and sits in prison, "gladly and fully" for God's love and "holy protection." Her family remembers and speaks often of him and "live in hope" that they will receive More again soon.[15] Dated to May 1534, this letter would be the last one in which Margaret expresses such hope.

The intimacy and urgency of these letters must have moved More, but Margaret's question—"What think you hath been our *comfort* since your departing from us?"—gave him an idea. He would write *A Dialogue of Comfort against Tribulation* to direct Margaret, his family, and others like them to think of tribulation and persecution in terms of temptations against the Catholic faith. Since Margaret emphasized More's absence, he would craft a character by the name of Antony after himself, using the figure of *conformatio*, which renders an absent person present through speech. The figure was defined in the influential book, *Rhetorica ad Herennium*, which was attributed to Cicero (106–43 BCE) in More's time: it "consists in representing an absent person as present" and "attributing to it [or him] a definite form and a language or behaviour appropriate to its character."[16] Because Margaret writes of More's absence as if it's an absence of comfort in her life, the counsel provided by the character of Antony would represent both More's person and his "definite language" of counsel. Conversely, the "comfort" Antony provides will personify More—her father's own language and behavior. If More couldn't be with his family, his literary persona and voice might "dialogue" with them.

Margaret, like any reader familiar with More's state at that time, could have recognized the title as "A Dialogue with More against Tribulation."[17] In an opening exchange, Vincent is in "need of some comfortable counsel against tribulation" and turns to Antony, who has lived "so long virtuously" and is "learned in the law of god, as very few be better in this country here."[18] Vincent says:

> But now my good uncle, the world is here waxen such, and so great perils appear here to fall to hand, that methinks the greatest comfort that a man can have, is when he may see that he shall soon be gone. And we that are likely long to live here in wretchedness, have need of some comfortable council against tribulation to be given us by such as you be good uncle, that have so long lived virtuously, and are so learned in the law of god, as very few be better in this country

here . . . here shall you leave of your kindred, a sort of sorry comfortless Orphans, to all whom, your good help, comfort, and counsel, hath long been a great stay, not as an uncle unto some, and to some as one father of kin, but as though that unto us all you had been a natural father.[19]

These words channel Margaret's wretchedness and appeal for counsel from her father. So, too, her references to More's extended family are to be found in Vincent's mention of "kindred" and to Antony as "father of kin." Margaret's pathos soars in phrases such as "a sort of sorry comfortless orphans," and More's status as paterfamilias sounds in the idea of Antony being a "natural father" to them all. "This country here" and "the world" are other words for England, even as "now" refers to the time of More's imprisonment.[20] More in the persona of Antony and under these bleak circumstances might provide Vincent—and, by extension, Margaret and More's entire family—with words of consolation.

The contest between Vincent and Antony captures the argument between father and daughter too. When Vincent complains that Antony, so near death, will leave his kindred as orphans without any comfort, Antony replies in words that rebuke Margaret. Her overreliance upon him parallels Vincent's upon his uncle. Antony tells Vincent in words that echo not only More's letters to Margaret but also the Bible: "But whensoever god take me hence, to reckon yourself then comfortless as though your chief comfort stood in me therein make ye, methinketh, a reckoning very much like as though ye would cast away a strong staff and lean upon a rotten reed. For it is not I but God who is and must be your comfort. And a sure comfort he is."[21] Here More and his persona allude to Pauline teaching. Comfort isn't to be found either in Antony or in More but in God. As Paul teaches, God is a sure comfort: "Blessed be god the father of our lord Jesus Christ, the father of mercy, and the god of all comfort, which comforts us in all our tribulation, insomuch that we are able to comfort them which are troubled, in whatsoever tribulation it be, with the same comfort wherewith we ourselves are comforted of god" (2 Corinthians 1:3–4).[22] Antony and More only can comfort Vincent and Margaret with the comfort that is received from above. To seek solace from men ignores "the god of all comfort," who is the source of all encouragement. Antony should be God's messenger, and More could do no better. Though not overt autobiography, we can already see how More begins his *Dialogue* in direct reply to Margaret's letter. She must find comfort in her faith and not in her father.

As the dialogue unfolds, the character of Antony will share More's point of view and love of witty stories, even as Vincent articulates Margaret's own fears, questions, and concerns about how to respond to religious persecution.[23] Vincent's reply to the above call from Antony to find comfort in God, for example, echoes Margaret, who claimed she could not have comfort without More's counsel. "I cannot but grant it for true," Vincent says, "yet if I now had not heard it of you, I had not remembered it, nor it had not fallen in my mind" (*CW* 12:5/19–20).[24] The rejoinder turns the previous correction on its head. The truth might be forgotten. Just as Vincent needs Antony, so Margaret still needs her father.

If Antony speaks on behalf of More, the *Dialogue*, as a whole, also represents how More addresses his own experience of fear, or his previous and ongoing concern for what the king might do to him.[25] In a letter to a priest known only by the name of "Master Leder," More confessed his fear about "violent forcible ways" that could be used against him. In the case of torture, More added: "God would of his grace and the rather a great deal through good folks' prayers give me the strength to stand."[26] Any Christian could wish that he were put to death yesterday for the sake of Christ, as Antony claims, but the obstacle to be overcome stems from anticipation of evils.[27] Indeed, the *Dialogue* enumerates "violent forcible ways"—especially the dangers of imprisonment, torture, and death—and advises readers how to overcome the fear of these when they are imminent threats or probable outcomes. Thus, More seeks courage to remain steadfast, just as his character Antony discusses how to do so under adverse circumstances that mirror those of the *Dialogue*'s author. More is dialoguing with tribulation within himself and with Margaret and with others in similar straits.[28]

The search for the "strength to stand" emerges as a continual spiritual exercise of More's in the Tower, and his *Dialogue* suggests how he did so. "Every tribulation the devil uses for temptation to bring us to impatience and thereby to murmur and grudge and blasphemy," Antony insists, "and every kind of temptation, to a good man that fights against it and will not follow it, is a very painful tribulation."[29] As a result, "a great comfort" is to be discovered in tribulation. Whenever one is tempted,

God responds with strength against the devil's might. "In the fervent heat I say therefore of every temptation," More's Antony declares, "God gives the faithful man that hopes in Him the shadow of his holy shoulders, which are broad and large, sufficient to refrigerate and refresh the man in that heat."[30] Comfort arises from a supernatural view of tribulations as spiritual combat; one trades impatience for hope, and rebellion for faith in God's providence. Man is *refrigerated* and *refreshed* by God in the "heat" of temptation.

Likewise, tribulation as temptation is what More sees at work in Margaret's complaints and in his own fears. In the *Dialogue*, the ills of life—from suffering to death—will be redescribed and reevaluated by reason, but reason informed by Christian faith, a point More had already developed in a letter to Margaret. There, More elaborates upon his own fears. "Many times more than once" he had pondered the threat of death that might come "by the refusing of the oath."[31] Yet he made his decision to refuse the oath before being arrested and explains why he did so:

> And I thank our Lord, Meg, since I am come hither I set by death every day less than other. For though a man lose of his years in the world, [he] is more than manifold recompensed by coming the sooner to heaven. And though it be a pain to die while a man is in health, yet see I very few that in sickness die with ease. And finally, very sure am I that whensoever the time shall that may hap to come, God's knows how soon, in which I should lie sick in my deathbed by nature, I shall then think that God had done much for me, if he had suffered me to die before by the color a such of law. And therefore my reason shows me, Margaret, that it were great folly for me to be sorry to come to that death, which I would after wish that I had died.[32]

In this passage, More comments upon the experiences of pain and death as if he were conjuring defensive maneuvers against Henry's future tactics if not yet "violent forcible ways": years lost on the earth for defying the king are other ways of describing an advance entrance into heaven. Death is reframed as inescapable rather than a trouble to be eluded. If healthy men suffer pain at death, so do sick men; the pain of death is unavoidable, and death comes for all. God, in fact, might favor More by allowing him to come to death by execution rather than by natural causes, for "the color of such a law" are other words for Henry's tyrannical action, and it would be "folly" to die merely for nothing. The last reformulation of adversity occasioned by "such a law" illustrates how More believed allegiance to a unified Catholic faith would be considered rebellion against Henry's designs.

More made the same point in his *Dialogue*, but not as explicitly. There, the thinly veiled More and Margaret, Antony and Vincent, converse in a semiallegorical setting.[33] The dialogue takes place in Hungary in 1527–28, just before its Turkish invasion, and at a time when death, torture, the loss of goods, and slavery were possible outcomes if the Hungarians lost.[34] More adds forced conversion to the Muslim religion as another potential tribulation to sharpen the parallel with abandoning the Catholic faith in England. Though there were no forced conversions historically in the Hungarian war against the Turks, the implication was that Henry VIII's required oaths forced his own people to practice a different religion or to abandon their old profession of faith.[35]

Harpsfield writes that More "does not expressly meddle with those matters" facing English Catholics because of Henry's turn against them. Instead, "so that the book might the more safely go abroad," More "colors the matter under the name of a Hungarian, and of the persecution of the Turk in Hungary, and of a book translated out of the Hungarian's tongue into Latin and then into the English tongue."[36] Harpsfield's claim is partially verified by the title page, which claimed that the *Dialogue* was first "made by a Hungarian in Latin."[37] As with his *Utopia*, More doesn't acknowledge authorship, but, in this case, he uses the pseudonym, "a Hungarian." More "does not expressly meddle," but he *colors matters*, which is to say, he meddles in politics by means of crafting fictive conversation. "For there is no born Turk so cruel to Christian folk," we read in the *Dialogue*, "as is the false Christian that falleth from the faith" (*CW* 12:7/8–9).

In Antony's fabricated dialogue with Vincent, More will speak to Margaret, others in his family, and Catholics in England.[38] So, too, the *Dialogue*'s overall design orients its readers to the universal order that More found in Christendom and in the Catholic Church, and for this very reason More's book proved useful when Rastell printed it under Mary's reign.[39] More colored the matters and events of 1534 with a brand of political theology that Rastell sought to reinvigorate decades after his uncle's death.

THE NOONDAY DEVIL

For Catholics in opposition to Henry in 1534, the greatest tribulations were temptations to abandon their religious profession of belief, or so More believed. After all, faith is what allows tribulation itself to be reframed as a blessing. Without faith, torment awaits absent of all hope. Tribulations, thus, can be described alternatively as tests of faith or as temptations to abandon faith when and if trials are not accepted as blessings. Once tribulations are described as temptations to leave the faith, they may be recognized as invitations to desert the Catholic Church. Within these parameters, Antony addresses religious persecution with Vincent.

Antony relies upon the technique of rhetorical redescription to nudge Vincent into recognizing persecution as a blessing. He notes how persecution and temptation are "incident" to one another. His use of this term is now obsolete, but he means that persecution and temptation are "naturally pertaining or attached to" one another.[40] To be "incident" suggests how evaluative and descriptive terms can refer to the same action but with different moral senses. Antony, in effect, explains redescription as he employs it:

> If we well consider these two things—temptation and persecution—we may find that *either of them is incident to the other*. For both by temptation the devil persecutes us, and by persecution the devil also tempts us; and as persecution is tribulation to every man, so is temptation tribulation to every good man. Now, though the devil our spiritual enemy fight against man in both, yet this difference hath the common temptation from the persecution: that temptation is as it were the fiend's *train*, and persecution, his plain open fight. (*CW* 12:100/12–20; my emphasis)[41]

"Train" is my modernization of the obsolete "trayne," a word More uses to signify a "trap" or "scheme designed to deceive."[42] Antony turns one class of temptations into the devil's more cunning snares and distinguishes them from persecution, which is an "open fight." As do Augustine and other early Church Fathers, Antony separates out subtle temptations that work through "ignorance, obscurity, and darkness" from those that are "blatant and overt."[43] But the overt sense, of note, allows him to redescribe persecution as a temptation to apostasy or heresy or schism. Persecution for being a member of the Catholic Church concomitantly represents a temptation to leave it.[44]

For Antony, such overt persecution is the work of the "noonday devil" (*daemonium meridianum*).[45] You can identify agents of the noonday devil, he argues, by their hatred of Catholicism. Conversely, those who refuse to denounce the Catholic Church emerge as authentic Christians. Antony explains open persecution as spiritual combat in words that likewise justify More's own decision to refuse the oath: "In this temptation, this plain open persecution for the faith, he comes even in the very midday—that is to wit, even upon them that have a high light of faith shining in their heart—and openly suffers [allows] himself so plainly [to] be perceived by his fierce malicious persecution against the faithful Christians *for hatred of Christ's true Catholic faith* that no man having faith can doubt what he is: for in this temptation he shows himself such as the prophet names him, *Daemonium meridianum*, the midday devil."[46] Such persecution identifies "faithful Christians," separating them from other creeds or sects, by their belief in "Christ's true Catholic faith." The midday devil traffics in the "violent forcible ways" More had mentioned in his letter to Master Leder. But apart from defining the midday devil, More has proposed here a means of acknowledging himself as a valiant defender of the faith. If violent ways are to be used against More by the king, they would mark More as a faithful Christian and, by implication, a true martyr.[47]

Antony's account of this temptation also raises the possibility that More could succumb to it. According to Augustine, the noonday devil attacks when a person is tortured repeatedly until he gives way.[48] The name comes from "the incursion and devil of the midday" (Psalm 91:6) and represents "the most bitter sharp and the most rigorous" of all temptations. Yet no man in possession of true faith, according to Antony, will fail to recognize persecution of the "true Catholic faith" as demonic.

This temptation to abandon or modify the Catholic creed constitutes the real matter or essential question under discussion between Antony and Vincent, or More and Margaret, and More and his king. "The Turk is but a shadow," Antony claims, that represents the midday devil, and "the turks are but his tormentors, for [he] himself does the deed" (*CW* 12:317/14–15).[49] It is this devil that "shall send some of you to prison" through his agents here on earth, be they Turks or whoever threatens Catholics, but "without question" it is the "devil's own deed to bring us by his temptation with and force thereof into eternal damnation" (19–22).[50] Imprisonment and the threats of torture and death are demonic means to tempt Christians into renouncing their faith. "Thus may we see that in such persecutions," Antony summarizes, "it is the midday devil himself that makes such incursion upon us *by the men that are his ministers* to make us fall for fear" (24–27; my emphasis). Again, Antony's words are polyphonic, speaking to the theological question and to More's circumstances as prisoner. Henry is but "a shadow" of the real threat, but he remains the midday devil's minister.[51] The personal implication of More's teaching on the noonday devil is that both Henry and Margaret—the one, who doubts the authority of the true Catholic faith enough to replace it with royal power, and the other, who seeks to redescribe the oath as something other than temptation—lack devotion to "the true Catholic faith." Yet to leave this faith was to desert the truth, and "whosoever shrink away with forsaking his faith" falls into "the peril of everlasting fire."[52] One could be saved or damned, depending on whether one stood by or rejected traditional Catholicism and a unified Church.[53]

For reasons such as these, the noonday devil represents the crux of the *Dialogue* and the climax of a dispute between father and daughter. More spells out the matter as in an exercise of deliberative discourse, that is, as a type of speech either for or against a proposed course of action in the future and what would be best. Antony, thus, addresses the noonday devil under the auspices of the following question: "Whether a man should cast in his mind and appoint in his heart before, that if he were taken with Turks, he would rather die than forsake the faith." This is the central question of the *Dialogue* as a whole and, if Henry is taken for a parallel to the Turk, the dilemma facing More. The concomitant consideration is whether More or Margaret should take the oath. The two matters are "incident" with one another.

At this point, we can imagine the voices and positions of More and Margaret in Antony and Vincent most clearly. As More and Margaret both knew, the noonday devil raises the specter not just of torture but also of succumbing to it. The possibility of relenting to extreme pain means that the question about taking Henry's oath wasn't simply a matter of what More wanted to avoid but of how much pain he could suffer. The horrific prospect of torture threatens to change the terms of their dialectical encounter from faith to fear.

On the sensible if not supernatural grounds of fear, Vincent disputes Antony's formulation that one should resolve in advance to stand by his faith. "For the sharpness and the bitterness of the pain," Vincent urges, can lead one "to forsake our Savior" (*CW* 12:297/15). To resolve in advance to die rather than forsake the faith isn't courageous, ultimately, because that resolution seems heedless; it is like the textbook case of gladiatorial miscalculation, where one is reckless rather than courageous.[54] No one can predict how he will respond to torture. In fact, Vincent "heard" of an answer to Antony's position. If a man decides that under persecution he "should stand still in the confession of his faith," such a one could "thereby fall into painful tormentry" and during his suffering "forsake our Savior, and die there with his sin, and be damned forever," despite his earlier good intentions (10–17).

Vincent, as Margaret would have done in conversation with her father, redescribes actions to advance an argument for taking the oath. So, instead of resolving in advance to defy the Turks, Vincent suggests a second scenario. A man could renounce his faith early on and with deception and then return to his faith later and thereby avoid the experience of torture. Vincent goes further still and recommends a course of action that Margaret actually took. A man should forsake his faith when threatened by agents of the noonday devil—not genuinely but verbally, "keeping it still nevertheless in his heart"—to avoid "painful death," and if in error for such verbal renunciation, one may ask for mercy after the threat passes (*CW* 12:297/17–20). In this scenario, one could be spared and "live long and do many good deeds, and be saved as Saint Peter was" (20–21).[55] Peter, after all, resolved to suffer and die with Christ in advance of persecution but later abandoned his master when fear overcame him. "All the pinch is in the pain," Vincent points out, which means the matter is beyond dialectics, for "all the wisdom in this world can never so master pain but that pain will be painful, spite all the wit in this world" (292/15–22). The pinch of pain results in a critical impasse for Vincent and Antony and probably for More and Margaret.[56]

Of note, Margaret suggested to her father the same strategy of verbally taking an oath that one inwardly disavows. She took the oath but with mental reservation, mirroring the advice of Vincent, the character to whom she lent her voice. More's remarks to Margaret concerning the oath and practicing equivocation are recorded in a letter of August 1534, where More is reported to have told Margaret:

> Truly, daughter, I never intend—God being my good lord—to pin my soul to another man's back, not even if he's the best man I know who is alive today; for I do not know where he might happen to carry to it. There is no man living of whom, while he is still living, I can make myself sure. Some might do something for favor, and some might do it for fear.... And some might happen to frame themselves a conscience and think that as long as they did it for fear, God would forgive it. And some may perhaps think that they will repent and be absolved of it, and so God will remit it. And some may perhaps be thinking that if they say one thing while thinking the contrary, God more regards their heart than their tongue, and that therefore their oath goes by what they are thinking and not what they say, as a woman reasoned once. I believe, daughter, you were nearby. But honestly, Margaret, I can use no such ploys in so great a matter.[57]

From this passage we can see how the conversation between Antony and Vincent about mental reservation parallels the debate between More and his daughter. Margaret's and Vincent's positions align, for "God more regards their heart than their tongue." To be "nearby" such a point of view represents More's euphemistic way of identifying his daughter's argument.

In the same letter, Margaret even admits outright to taking the oath, but her words have been excused.[58] Next to Margaret's confession, Rastell's marginal note claimed that Margaret "took the oath with this exception: as far as would stand with the law of God."[59] But his addition isn't in Margaret's quotation from the letter. Rastell's note creates history such that Margaret slipped in the proviso about "the law of God" aloud and it went unrecognized. Far more likely, she took the oath, as she said she did, but in her heart, as in Vincent's recommendation, Margaret silently stipulated the king's right "as far as would stand" with God's law. By taking the oath, she gained admittance to the Tower and the right not just to visit but also to convince her father to swear as she did.

The same 1534 letter will be discussed in chapter 4 in greater detail, but I cannot leave it without noting why More can use "no such ploys in so great a matter." Henry's 1531 Pardon of the Clergy claimed the title of "supreme head" (*supremum caput*) of the Church in England and further asserted that the king had the "care" or "cure" of his subjects' souls (*curae animarum*).[60] Likewise, "the high sovereign over the people," Christopher St. German had announced in royal propaganda, "has not only charge on the bodies, but also on the souls of his subjects."[61] In contrast, More cannot "pin" his soul "at another man's back," not even "the best man" that he knows. More's formulation only seems abstract because no one is named in it. When read in context of Henry's asserted authority over the souls of his subjects, More means not to pin his soul to his sovereign's back.

In the *Dialogue*, Antony's response to Vincent emerges in a series of comments that reveal further More's own state of mind. Antony argues that Christ taught that his disciples should openly profess their faith. Because of this teaching and example, Antony states:

> Finally, when Christ spoke so often and so plain of the matter that every man should, upon pain of damnation, openly confess his faith, if men took him and by dread of death would drive him to the contrary, it seems [to] me in a manner implied therein that we be bounden *conditionally* to have evermore that mind, *actually* some time, and evermore *habitually* that: if the case should so fall, then with God's help so we would. And thus much thinketh me necessary for every man and woman to be always of this mind and … must they call to mind and remember the great pain and torment that Christ suffered for them, and heartily pray for grace, that if the case should so fall, God should give them *strength to stand*. And thus with exercise of such meditation, though *men should never stand full* out of fear of falling, yet must they persevere in good hope and *in full purpose of standing*. And this seems me, Cousin, so far-forth the mind, that every Christian man and woman must needs have. (*CW* 12:198/5–22)[62]

For Antony, everyone should ask the question conditionally or hypothetically of what they would do in the face of open persecution. In answer, each person should resolve to suffer with Christ. "They must call to mind and remember the great pain and torment that Christ suffered for them," Antony insists, "and heartily pray for the grace, that if the case should so fall, *God should give them strength to stand.*" The "strength to stand" here is a formulation that rebuts Vincent's earlier scenario of one who resolved in advance to "stand still in the confession of his faith" but later buckled under the pains of torment. Antony's point is that no one can "stand still" on his or her own without grace. Indeed, Antony's words echo More's letter to Margaret: "God would of His grace and the rather a great deal through good folks' prayers give me the strength to stand."[63] In the longer passage quoted above, Antony repeats iterations of the formulation—"strength to stand"—as More mostly likely did in conversation with Margaret. The position of More and Antony appears identical. By meditating upon Christ's passion, "though men should never stand full out of fear of falling, yet must they persevere in good hope, and in full purpose of standing" (198/19–21). The "full purpose of standing," augmented and strengthened by meditation, will provide "the strength to stand" whether in Antony's theory or in More's decision to refuse the oath.

DELIBERATIVE DISCOURSE IN MORE'S *DIALOGUE*

The (auto)biographical circumstances around the *Dialogue* demonstrate the reason for More's use of deliberative discourse, a formal rhetorical genre, or other words for providing the "counsel" that Margaret desires to hear from her father. More's own plight and training in rhetoric combined in his composition of the *Dialogue*. He responded to his circumstances of imprisonment by writing to convince his family and himself to suffer for Christ and his Catholic Church. Of importance, More's use of deliberative discourse in a fictive setting could extend Antony's teaching to all those so persecuted. We shall see in this section and the next that attention to More's rhetorical strategy will reveal how he wrote his *Dialogue* to persuade others to follow his example and Antony's teaching rather than just writing in a merely consolatory, devotional, or simply dialectical manner. More's *Dialogue* was also controversial literature.

Rhetoric's different genera consist of demonstrative (praise or blame), deliberative (persuade or dissuade about future courses of action), and forensic (accuse or defend), but More's *Dialogue* emphasizes throughout a petition for counsel in the face of impending suffering.⁶⁴ Parallel to Margaret visiting her father in the Tower, the *Dialogue* opens with Vincent coming to Antony. Vincent wants to know how he should react when and if the Turkish invasion succeeds. Thus, More sets up a fictive framework for a deliberative orator, such as Antony, to persuade an audience or interlocutor, such as Vincent, about what one should do in the future.

In the Ciceronian tradition within which More studied, deliberative rhetoric paints a proposed action as *honestus*, a term often translated as "honorable," and here with connotations of rectitude and praiseworthy behavior. To speak of an action as *honestus* means an embodiment of one or more of the four cardinal virtues. The classical example was courage, and its outline reveals Antony's approach against the fears Vincent experiences:

> When we invoke as motive for a course of action steadfastness in Courage, we shall make it clear that men ought to follow and strive after noble and lofty actions, and that, by the same token, actions base and unworthy of the brave ought therefore to be despised by brave men and considered as beneath their dignity. Again, from an honourable act [*re honesta*] no peril or toil, however great, should divert us; death ought to be preferred to disgrace; no pain should force an abandonment of duty; no man's enmity should be feared in defense of truth [*pro rei veritate*]; for country, for parents, guest-friends, intimates, and for the things justice commands us to respect, it behoves us to brave any peril and endure any toil.⁶⁵

In terms of deliberative discourse, Antony will posit that suffering with Christ is a principled decision that constitutes an "honorable" course of action, which in this case will also be courageous in defense of truth, just, and worth doing despite the threats of imprisonment and death. The crucial addition for More and for his Antony will come in redefining the "motive for a course of action." Courage to stand by the faith must first derive from the virtue of faith itself.

Central to deliberative discourse in the *Ad Herennium* and in More's use of it in the *Dialogue* are the techniques of defining terms and redescribing given actions or the situation at hand. Roman theorists distinguished redescription from arguing over the definition of terms, and this difference is essential for understanding how More's Antony argues. For Cicero and Quintilian (35 CE–ca. 100 CE), orators could amplify actions, either to diminish their significance or to elevate them, by merely redescribing them. Redescription differs from definition but remains adjacent to it. To illustrate the shared ethical grounds but difference in technique between definition and redescription, the author of the *Ad Herennium* turns to the example of courage: "That act of yours is not bravery, but recklessness because to be brave is to disdain toil and peril for a useful purpose and after weighing the advantages, while to be reckless is to undertake perils like a gladiator, suffering pain without taking thought."[66] In instances of disagreement over the definition of terms, one party insists upon what the other denies, which in this case is that true courage is deliberative. But there is another kind of disagreement, where both parties agree on the definition of authentic courage but contest whether a particular action was taken with sufficient heed. In such an instance, if an orator wishes to amplify an action as courageous and to arouse admiration for it, he will claim the action was taken with sufficient foresight. If the orator wishes to diminish the action, however, he will call it merely gladiatorial, "suffering pain without taking thought."

So, too, if the orator wishes to persuade his audience that a specific course of action is *honestus*, he will describe the action as virtuous—just, wise, temperate, or courageous. Conversely, if the orator desires to dissuade his audience from taking the same course of action, he will describe the action as unjust, imprudent, immoderate, or without sufficient heed and therefore reckless. "Virtues of this kind are to be enlarged upon if we are recommending them," we read in the *Ad Herennium*, "but depreciated if we are urging that they be disregarded." The latter approach is elaborated upon: "Again, if it is at all possible, we shall show that what our opponent calls justice is cowardice, and sloth, and perverse generosity; what he has called wisdom we shall term impertinent babbling, and offensive cleverness; what he declares to be temperance we shall declare to be inaction and lax indifference; what he has named courage we shall term the reckless temerity of a gladiator."[67] What becomes evident is that moral appraisal and descriptive language are crucial in any deliberative oration and intrinsic to the office of giving counsel. A speaker such as More or his Antony should recommend courses of action with enticing descriptions of them and in accordance with agreed upon definitions of virtues. If a speaker does so eloquently, audiences will admire him and be persuaded by his proposed plans.

Some of these same strategies of deliberative discourse are present in Vincent and Antony's discussion of the "pinch of pain," or whether anyone may rightly decide in advance whether to suffer for religion's sake.[68] If the experience of torment proves to be great and the person under duress reverses himself, then his suffering will have been gladiatorial and reckless rather than martyrological and holy, or so Vincent argues. But how would one know, in advance, his or her ability to resist extreme pain? For Antony, the answer depends on the grace of God; martyrological deaths are not a matter of human strength, but they exemplify courageous witness nevertheless. So Antony argues for trust in God when and if one is persecuted for his religious belief. By implication, More's own "full purpose of standing" by his faith, once understood in light of Antony's descriptions of anyone who would do the same, appears courageous rather than heedless. Seen in this way, Antony's redescriptions are part of More's presentation of himself as a model for any Catholic's faithful resistance to Henrician schism.

DEFINITION AND RHETORICAL REDESCRIPTION

Antony will employ both definition and redescription in his conversation with Vincent, but he first insists on the priority of shared principles or agreed upon definitions of key terms. The *Dialogue* stresses the importance of words such as "counsel" and "comfort" solely in the context of Christian faith. To make the connection between comfort and faith explicit, after suggesting the inadequacy of ancient philosophy to assuage tribulation's blows, Antony states, "Since all our principal comfort must come from God, we must first presuppose in Him to whom we shall with any ghostly counsel give any effectual comfort, one ground to begin withal: whereupon all that we shall build must be supported and stand, that is to wit, the ground of and foundation of faith, without which had ready before, all the spiritual comfort that any man may speak of can never avail a fly."⁶⁹ Here More/Antony distinguishes between comfort (what Margaret/Vincent seek) and spiritual counsel (what More/Antony provide)—that is, a way of deliberating how best to behave when trials come. But "effectual comfort" and "principal comfort" build upon the same spiritual foundation of faith. "For except a man first believe that holy scripture is the word of God and the word of God is true," Antony asks, "how can a man take any comfort of that?" (*CW* 12:12/17–19). To grasp the spiritual grounds of counsel will require not only faith but also belief in scripture. In turn, the effectiveness of scripture in providing counsel will depend on the strength of an individual's faith. Since faith cannot be taken for granted, "we must never cease to call upon God for it" (13/26). Comfort begins in faith, not in reason or philosophy, but reason can help explain the truths of faith, and not all philosophy's medicines are to be shunned.⁷⁰ Thus, the *Dialogue*'s definitions of "comfort" and "counsel" already indicate or dictate the conclusions to which More hopes his daughter will arrive, which are the same points that Antony advances to Vincent.

Like a Ciceronian orator, Antony also begins with a definition to address tribulation. "For tribulation seems generally to signify nothing else," stipulates Antony, "but some kind of grief, either pain of the body or heaviness of the mind" (*CW* 12:1/6–7). He iterates this concept later as "every such thing as troubles and grieves the man, either in body or in mind" (50/19–20) so that Vincent can recognize how there are more kinds of tribulations in the world than he first realized. If tribulation is any interruption in well-being, including "trouble also that grieves the mind," then "many good men have many tribulations that every man marks not" (51/5–7). The expansive nature of tribulation—whether as inward experiences or regarding loss of external goods—multiplies the ways in which tribulation may be described.

By enlarging upon the experience of tribulation this way, the distinction between arguments over definitions and those over descriptions, as we saw in the *Ad Herennium*, operates in More's *Dialogue*. Antony and Vincent will agree upon the definition of tribulation before redescribing its variations. Antony speaks of the distinction between definition and redescription as looking "to the mark": "First must you, Cousin, be sure that you look well to the mark, and that can you not do, but if ye know what thing tribulation is, for since that is one of the things that we principally speak of; but if you consider well what thing that is, you may miss the mark again."[71] To hit the mark, Vincent must not only define his terms ("know what thing tribulation is") but also learn how to describe tribulation ("consider well what thing that is").

So that Vincent will "look well" at tribulation, Antony examines how one may undergo an experience of tribulation with or without faith. First, he provides a taxonomy of replies to suffering from people who will not seek comfort from God. Some fall into despondency and the sin of sloth; others become irritable and impatient and commit the sin of anger; still others seek comfort not in God but in worldly pleasure (*CW* 12:14/15–15/20). But "the other sort" are "those that long and desire to be comforted by god," and such faith guarantees them success. This "mind of theirs may well be cause of great comfort." Because of faith, believers can see for themselves that they search for comfort "where they cannot fail to find it." God "both can give them comfort and will for He is almighty" just as "he that hath faith" cannot doubt God's power or beneficence (15/25–16/5).

Next, Antony compares how tribulations themselves differ between persons of belief and unbelief. Those with faith, for example, find tribulation in being tempted by "the devil, the world, and the flesh" to sin. "To such wretches as care not for their conscience," Antony claims, "many of these temptations be no trouble at all." But the one who stands "in dread of god" will recognize that temptation itself is a trouble that grieves the mind, troubles the heart of the believer, and imparts feelings of grief and anguish to him (*CW* 12:51/8–18).

The *Dialogue* shifts back and forth by way of redescribing tribulation. In an example resonant with Henry's pursuit and longing for Anne, who chastely refused him until he agreed to marry her, Antony seemingly compares Henry's state of mind with that of More's.[72] For one who "cares not for God," Antony stipulates, "let him cast in his mind, if himself hap upon a fervent longing for the thing which get he cannot," and let his frustrated desires torment his mind. Antony specifies that the object of desire in this case is a "certain good woman" who refuses to be unchaste. The anguish of unsatiated lust, Antony claims, will teach the man without conscience what kind of pain faithful men and women are exposed to in resisting temptation while experiencing a "great fear" of falling from grace (*CW* 12:51/19–29).

Antony focuses upon a man without a conscience against the one who does. Formally, what emerges in this comparison is that the same definition of tribulation operates in two very different experiences and correspondingly various descriptions of it: the torment of unfulfilled sexual desire and the suffering of those afraid of offending God. Tribulations remain any trouble that grieves the mind or the body by definition, but by description, tribulations are differently understood human experiences of suffering.

Both believer and unbeliever wrestle with tribulation, but believers have a special aptitude for describing them, ultimately, as blessings. Tribulation may have a multitude of descriptions, but based upon faith, if "we believe to be true all that the scripture says," then we will consider "tribulation as a gracious gift of god," no less than a gift that God gives to his "special friends" (*CW* 12:75/7–12). Thus, the earlier definitions of "comfort" and "counsel" with their emphasis on faith register with how one should think of tribulations.

At the same time, as a Ciceronian orator who aims at inspiring his audience to courageous exploits, Antony recommends tribulations. He lists his reasons why Vincent should agree with him, but these are other words for redescribing tribulation as a good: scripture commends tribulation; uninterrupted prosperity, the contrary state of tribulation, would endanger a soul's salvation; if God doesn't send trials, then believers will need to seek them out through self-imposed penances; tribulation purges people from past sins or preserves them from sins they otherwise would have committed; adversity teaches one detachment from the world and incites people to draw closer to God; trials diminish purgatorial pains or increase heavenly rewards; the way of the cross was the way of Jesus and his disciples, and the cross is the only way to heaven (*CW* 12:75/12–24).

Just as Antony seeks to persuade Vincent, More aims to convince his readers. In redescribing tribulations after this fashion, More makes them sound appealing. The implication of this teaching for how one should understand More's own public and well-known trials in 1534 also becomes clear. Everyone will suffer in body or in mind, but only those with faith like that of More will reap supernatural benefits from the experience.

THERAPEUTIC REDESCRIPTION

We are now able to recognize more fully Antony's strategy for persuading Vincent and More's for inviting others to follow his example. As More knew, the technique of redescription from classical rhetorical theory overlapped with Stoic teaching on therapeutic redescription.[73] Quintilian, as did the author of *Ad Herennium*, taught that any actual behavior may be changed in its nature or character when redescribed.[74] But this oratorical practice of redescription was also part of Stoic meditation. The classic example comes from Epictetus (d. 135 CE), who describes two different ways of thinking about attendance at an event in a large crowd. If you dread crowds, instead of fearing their tumult, imagine that the crowd is a "festival."[75] Like the man who fears crowds, Vincent dreads future tribulations at the hands of the Turkish invaders. To help Vincent, Antony redescribes these tribulations not as "festivals" but as blessings from God.

Both deliberative speech and Stoic meditation employ redescription to determine how best to anticipate and cope with perceived and imminent evils. For this reason, More easily combines Stoic teaching with Antony's attempts at persuading Vincent. The clearest example occurs in Antony's discussion of enslavement. There, we learn that the greatest torment of captivity arises when we are forced to do labor "with our good will" that "we would not." Against forced labor, Seneca (ca. 4 BCE–65 CE) himself "teaches us a good remedy": to do nothing against our will, but to put our good will into whatever we see that we will have to do (*CW* 12:254/4–9). The Stoic precept isn't a paradox, but advice about how to behave in the future. To see *what we will have to do* becomes identical with *what we should do*, and the wise man always does what he should. Seneca's "remedy" is prospective (part of deliberative rhetoric) and prescriptive (part of Stoic therapy) at the same time.

Just as Seneca's adage is deliberative speech, it is also material for meditation aimed at cognitive restructuring or, to be more pointed, a Christian reframing of the evils of enslavement.[76] When Antony cites Seneca's "good remedy" to Vincent, his nephew demurs, telling Antony that the "remedy" is easier said than done. Antony replies by explaining the classic Stoic teaching that passions are forms of false judgment or beliefs: "Our froward mind makes every good thing hard and that to our own more hurt and harm" (*CW* 12:254/12–13). Next, Antony redescribes enslavement from the perspective of faith: "But in this case, if we will be good Christian men, we shall have great cause gladly to be content, for the great comfort that we may take thereby while we remember that in the patient and glad doing of our service unto that man for God's sake, according to his high commandment by the mouth of saint Paul, *servi obedite dominis*, we shall have our thanks and our reward of god."[77] To accept Antony's reframing of enslavement entails cognitive restructuring on Vincent's part. Analytic thinking, based in faith, and Christian well-being correspond. A "froward" or perverse mind "makes every good thing hard." A mind infused with faith, however, makes every hard thing good. So, those enslaved but with faith will recall Saint Paul's words: "Slaves, obey your masters" (Ephesians 6:5). A supernatural perspective such as this means that those condemned to servitude will be able to follow Seneca's charge and never act against their own wishes even while or if they are enslaved by Turkish invaders.

In cases such as these, the *Dialogue* emerges as a combination of ancient rhetoric and philosophy with More's own polemical flair. As a work of deliberative rhetoric, Antony's redescription of tribulations as gifts from God aims to change Vincent's appraisal of imprisonment, loss of goods, and death. As a philosophical practice or meditation, conversation with Antony teaches Vincent how to redescribe human and earthly goods until they either lose their seductive power or Vincent no longer fears their loss. The Stoic admonition "to look from above" becomes analogous to More's prayer "to set the world at naught."[78] As the result of Antony's arguments or by meditation upon his redescriptions of tribulations, Vincent may reimagine his life, whether in terms of desires (for wealth, honor, fame, or office) or fears (of imprisonment, slavery, or death), such that he will flee from false impressions or worldly concerns about them.[79] When reappraised as gifts from God, tribulations cease to cause fear and instill gratitude instead. Whoever "thinks on and remembers well" these teachings will neither "murmur nor grudge" at trials but "grow in goodness" and recognize how God gives them precisely for growth in personal sanctity. Hence, Antony recommends giving God thanks for tribulations (*CW* 12:75/25–76/3).

Antony's goal, however, is not merely to convince Vincent but to free him from the false impressions that govern his life.[80] A redescription of tribulation that is grounded in faith is also a cognitive restructuring of experience. Antony wants to persuade Vincent, but this entails altering how his nephew understands the meaning of life. More wished to do the same for his daughter and his readership, especially with regard to the ongoing trial of religious persecution in 1534. In this, his own rhetorical goals in the *Dialogue* were simultaneously in opposition to the regime's mandate for its citizens to recognize Henry as head of the Church.

RASTELL'S DEPICTION OF MARGARET MORE ROPER

My reading returns More's *Dialogue of Comfort* back to its original context: its composition in 1534–35, his correspondence with Margaret, their conversations in the Tower, and More's polemical aims. We have seen how More's personal, spiritual, and rhetorical objectives coalesced. In his *Dialogue*, More did not put aside his opinions but argued for them. More debated against Margaret in the characters of Antony and Vincent, but his authorial aims were wider. His fictive setting and characters were literary devices designed to encourage anyone in his or her opposition to Henry.[81] For this reason, More defined "tribulation" as first and foremost a temptation to abandon the Catholic faith. Both rhetorical and therapeutic redescriptions valorized More's humanist witness to Catholic unity and, in so doing, proposed a model of resistance to others for emulation. To understand the polemical points of More's *Dialogue*, as in the last chapter, we needed to read without the misleading biographical contexts created by Rastell.

Let us conclude, though, with Rastell's presentation of Margaret. In examining the (auto)biographical setting of the *Dialogue*, I addressed the letter from More to Margaret in May 1534. There, More lamented his daughter's position that he should take the oath and come home. That letter of More's was written in reply to an earlier one from Margaret. We must infer the contents of the latter because Rastell didn't print it. I have fleshed out Margaret's position by reading the *Dialogue* as an extended commentary upon her debate with her father and suggested where and for what reasons Vincent's position aligned with her own. We are in position now to speculate why Margaret's letter isn't extant.

Instead of printing Margaret's letter, Rastell crafted an editorial note, much like his headnotes to More's books. This one fashioned a biographical narrative not just about More but also Margaret. This note posited a motivation behind Margaret's position that More should take the oath, a position that Rastell claimed was Margaret's ruse: "Within a while after Sir Thomas More was in prison in the Tower, his daughter Mistress Margaret Roper wrote and sent unto him a letter, wherein *she seemed somewhat to labor to persuade him to take the oath (though she nothing so thought)* to win thereby credence with Master Thomas Cromwell, that she might the rather get liberty to have free resort unto her father (which she only had for the most time of his imprisonment) unto which letter her father wrote an answer. The copy whereof here follows."[82]

Thus, Margaret's letter is replaced with Rastell's characterization of her position. Rastell's formulation that Margaret "seemed somewhat to labor to persuade" her father suggests that she never meant for More to believe, nor thought herself, that he should take oath. Instead, Rastell advances the story that Margaret duped Cromwell into allowing her to visit her father. By implication, More was content to abide by Margaret's contrivance.[83]

What, precisely, was the purpose of Rastell's note? We have seen how More took Margaret's arguments at face value, both in his letters and in the *Dialogue of Comfort*, and there is no record of his complicity in a deception perpetrated by Margaret. There is evidence, though, of Rastell deleting texts—such as the section of More's letter that states his approval of his new queen—that tailor More or his family's image to Marian tastes. Rather than accept Rastell's note as factual, a better explanation would be that his knowledge of Margaret's position indicates that he had possession of her letter at one time, and that in it she argued too well a case for taking the oath. Like the passages about Queen Anne from More's letter, Margaret's points would be an embarrassment. For these reasons, Rastell suppressed her letter. It's not extant because of him. In 1557, Margaret's position required adjustment. To examine her authentic opposition to her father, we turn to a letter to Lady Alice Alington (1501–63), More's stepdaughter.

FOUR

A Letter from Prison to Alice Alington, 1534

Why would Thomas More, a captive of the Tower, coauthor a letter with Margaret Roper in August 1534? To answer that question, this chapter examines the political and familial circumstances of the letter's composition, its artfully concealed design of forensic oratory, and use of indirect argument, or dissimulation. A careful analysis of the letter's rhetorical strategy will reveal further that More crafted his own defense of conscience with allusion to the question of counsel from *Utopia*: whether or not a philosopher should enter into a king's service. In the *Letter to Alington*, from More's position as an imprisoned, former chancellor of England, he revised civic humanism's call for political engagement into a powerful statement of defiance against Henry VIII.

Against that background, the intensely personal impression of More given in Margaret Roper's *Letter to Alington* (August 1534) turns out to be a masterpiece of rhetorical self-fashioning that marks More's return to *Utopia*, a text first published in December 1516.[1] There, More had portrayed himself as Morus, a character who argues in favor of philosophers serving kings and in opposition to the fictive Raphael Hythlodaeus, a follower of Plato (429–347 BCE).[2] *Utopia*'s debate over service has come to be known as "the dialogue of counsel," a metapolitical issue for humanists, but the question of whether one may serve a king in good conscience is also at the center of the *Letter to Alington*.[3]

Indeed, a comparison of these two texts will show how More fictionalizes himself best when he most cunningly denies doing so. In writing *Utopia*, More imagines a conversation and takes a speaking role within it, all the while eschewing authorship of such a fiction.[4] In More's first dialogue, he pretends as if the substance of the book is a record of Hythlodaeus's words, but Hythlodaeus doesn't exist; in effect, More credits authorship to a character of his own creation. Meanwhile, More plays Morus, a character based upon, if not his own beliefs, his person and office as an ambassador of England to Prince Charles of Castile (1500–1558). The prefatory letters to *Utopia*, including More's own with its "real life" descriptions of his daily occupations, and the subsequent give-and-take of conversation grant the dialogue a sense of verisimilitude, which the *Letter to Alington* matches.[5]

The *Letter to Alington* portrays an equally riveting dialogue and proposes a similar game of authorial attribution. This time, More does not converse with a fictive character but appears in what masquerades as a record of an actual conversation with his daughter.[6] Thus, the speaker or character of "More" materializes within the correspondence between Alice and Margaret and seems to be Margaret's representation of her father. As the primary author of the letter's dialogue, however, More composes his own self-defense against the charge of "scrupulosity" and transforms "Margaret" into the character of a temptress, "mistress Eve."[7] Once again, the subterfuge of an occluded authorship allows for a heightened impression of authenticity in the presentation of More. The letter's readership will assume that Margaret is the author and that her witness is reportorial rather than More's own forensic stratagem.

If *Utopia* and the *Letter to Alington* are More's dialogues of self-dramatization, they are also elegant, complex designs for confounding questions of authorship. After *Utopia*'s publication, More was accused of plagiarizing Hythlodaeus, but when Margaret's letter was first published in 1557, William Rastell, her editor, suggested that More wrote her epistle.[8] *Utopia* is now universally acknowledged as More's work, but controversy over authorship of the *Letter to Alington* persists.[9]

If my previous chapters showed where Rastell's editorial comments misled readers, this one will demonstrate Rastell's grounds for suggesting More's involvement in the *Letter to Alington*. The precedent of More's other dialogues, the prudence of an epistolary hoax in 1534, and the parallel rhetorical strategies of the letter with *Utopia* all suggest More's contribution.[10] Though some believe More abandoned the concerns of his *Utopia* after he became a Catholic Church apologist, More in the Tower not only addresses his particular circumstances as a prisoner but also returns to his earlier denunciation of kings from *Utopia*. Both dialogues should be understood as More's artful means of condemning the corruption at court without explicitly doing so. In *Utopia*, Hythlodaeus voices the allegations against kings, which the character of Morus if not the authorial More rejects, and in the *Letter to Alington*, More's critiques are camouflaged with careful words in the context of an ostensibly harmless letter among sisters.

THE LETTER AND MORE'S DIALOGUES

Let us return to the authorship question of the *Letter to Alington* and examine how plausible it may be that More would have anonymously contributed to a correspondence between his daughters. Though the letter purports to be Margaret's own record of an actual conversation with her father, Rastell prints it with this comment: "But whether this answer were written by Sir Thomas More in his daughter Roper's name or by herself, it is not certainly known."[11] Louis Martz points out on stylistic grounds that Rastell is right to question the authorship of Margaret: "The arguments in this letter are so subtly and ironically given and the language has such a resonance of More's style" that "one ends up with very little doubt" about the letter's true authorship; the letter's "art seems to be all the father's."[12] Yet More had employed such an art before.

In addition to *Utopia*, More wrote two other major dialogues that provide instructive clues for understanding how he planned the composition of the *Letter to Alington*. In *A Dialogue Concerning Heresies* and *A Dialogue of Comfort*, More created thinly veiled portraits of himself and various members of his family. These portraits were not just biographical or historical allegories but dramatic characters in conversation with one another. Such fictive enhancements of family members became characters that could address questions of religion and practices of spiritual counsel during a time of Reformation controversy and political turmoil.

We have seen how the character of Antony voiced More's opinions in *A Dialogue of Comfort*, but before it and after *Utopia*, in *A Dialogue Concerning Heresies*, More most transparently played himself. There, he testifies to heretical proceeding of which his office granted him personal knowledge and defends his faith with reference to the importance of liberal learning and theology.[13] So, too, More's interlocutor, "the Messenger," resembles and is based upon William Roper,[14] Margaret's own husband, a one-time Lutheran, and More's later biographer. As a whole, the content of the dialogue functions like an instruction manual of arguments in defense of Catholicism. Yet the form of dramatic dialogue between invested, intelligent, and sincere interlocutors provides the book its vivacity.[15]

The *Letter to Alington* presents a more compact version of *A Dialogue of Comfort*.[16] To do so, as with Antony and Vincent, More and Margaret must play a "part."[17] Margaret will convey the objections against More for his refusal to take an oath in affirmation of the Act of Succession, leave prison, and come home. In turn, More will perform as advocate of his own cause, providing answers to the objections against him for his opposition to Henry.[18] Neither Margaret's nor More's role is coterminous with her or his actual person. In the letter, they are characters that More and Margaret fashion to "color matters," but, in this case, the dialogue appears in an epistolary correspondence.

There were expedient reasons for doing so. Any transparent manifesto of More's position would be confiscated, examined in detail, and used against him.[19] The oath required subjects to "truly firmly and constantly without fraud or guile observe, fulfill, maintain, defend, and keep to their cunning, wit, and uttermost of their powers the whole effects and contents" of the new law.[20] These "contents" included a preamble that implied royal headship of the Church in England and a rejection of papal jurisdiction. The "whole effects and contents" also referred to the king's "spiritual and temporal" subjects and characterized the papacy as a foreign power.[21] So, too, if any person would "obstinately refuse" the oath "in contempt of this act," such a one should be "taken and accepted for offender in misprision of high treason."[22] More was the only layman called to take the oath with members of the clergy at Lambeth and before royal commissioners on 13 April 1534, and his refusal of the oath and subsequent self-defense relied upon his "silence," the fact that he did not speak or write against the act and its contents.[23]

Under these circumstances, any outright communication about the Act of Succession would be a risk, and so More required a covert outlet for his explanation of why he refused the oath. If not the sole author of the *Letter to Alington*, Margaret proved to be a reliable smuggler of documents on More's behalf.[24] Thanks to her, *A Dialogue of Comfort* emerged from the Tower in 1535; authorities didn't discover its existence until Queen Mary came to power in 1553. Similarly, Rastell did not print the *Letter to Alington* until 1557, but it circulated in manuscript beforehand.[25] Because of Margaret, we have both texts. Her commitment to saving them suggests not only their value in building More's legacy after his death but also, at the time of their composition, that they allowed More to respond to his circumstances and rebut charges against him. Rather than a work of devotional literature, the letter is More's polemical statement of self-defense.

More's penchant for the dialogue's form, the opportunity to spread his own point of view, and his status as prisoner under scrutiny are the most salient conditions of the *Letter to Alington*'s composition, a letter that testified to an ongoing disagreement between father and daughter. In chapter 3, I presented a record of their debate, beginning in the spring of 1534, when Margaret wrote a letter that detailed her objections to her father's position. In reply, More spoke in a general way about his conscience: "I can make none answer, for I doubt not but you well remember, that the matters which move my conscience (without declaration whereof I can nothing touch the points) I have sundry times showed you that I will disclose to no man."[26] More's own letter to Margaret is from May 1534, and Margaret responded during the same month with a question: "Father, what think you hath been our comfort since your departing from us?"[27] We have seen how this exchange could well have given rise to More's *Dialogue of Comfort*, but here I want to emphasize that the correspondence of May suggests authentic filial dissent, a clash of opinions that prefaces and contributes material to the later depiction of More and Margaret in the *Letter to Alington*.

Against that background, the question of Margaret's sincerity must be raised. As with other disputes from More's life that we have examined, this one begins with Rastell and More's earlier biographer, Thomas Stapleton. According to Stapleton, Margaret employed a "ruse" to gain permission for visiting More by writing "a letter in which she seemed to urge him to give up his own determination and conform himself to the King's will," but "these were far from being her real sentiments."[28] Here Stapleton echoed Rastell, who had claimed that Margaret "seemed somewhat to labor to persuade" her father "to take the oath (though she nothing so thought)."[29] Rastell produced no direct evidence, and Stapleton's reason for Margaret's artifice was that "no one understood and sympathized with her father's mind more fully than she."[30] Rastell and Stapleton, thus, unveiled a Margaret unable to think differently from More on this matter.

This version of Margaret represents how many have come to understand her. "Being Thomas More's daughter enabled Roper to be a scholar," writes Elaine V. Beilin, "yet strictly defined the limits of her endeavors." She is resigned "to an uncompetitive, supportive role within the family," a model of private, modest, intelligent devotion.[31] Others retain the same point of unswerving alliance because of "the patriarchal construction of power" within the More family.[32]

Likewise, Rastell's and Stapleton's versions of events lend credence to John Guy's picture of Margaret and More laughing at the charges found in Alice's original epistle. Guy accepts the idea of Margaret's "ruse" and complete union of minds between father and daughter. In a moment of "inspiration," More and Margaret put together "a long 'letter'" in reply, which amounted to a "semi-fictional dramatic realization of what Margaret's exchanges with her father might have sounded like *had she really gone ahead and tried to coax him into taking the oath.*" The *Letter to Alington*, thus, becomes *their* means "to reach out to generations that are yet to be born" to make the case for More's innocence.[33]

Such depictions of Margaret, both early modern and recent, detract from my presentation of her as More's most challenging interlocutor—the very person whose objections led to More's composition of *A Dialogue of Comfort*. Even so, I want to suggest that More and Margaret's exchange of letters from May 1534 indicates that debate between them would have continued into the summer months. After Alice wrote to Margaret in August a letter that accused More on behalf of his old friend, Lord Chancellor Thomas Audley (1488–1544), the most likely scenario is that Margaret used her stepsister's letter to press the case that More should relent. Instead of holding Alice's August letter in derision, Margaret would have expressed genuine alarm that one of More's remaining friends had abandoned him.[34] In this context, Margaret emerges as a proponent of Audley charges in the *Letter to Alington*.

So, too, there is no need to weigh coauthorship claims against an adversarial depiction of More and Margaret. Ordinarily, we might expect more sympathy of mind or agreement between coauthors. In this case, though, the shared aim was to present a lively debate between father and daughter, which, in the words of E. E. Reynolds, shows "their complete confidence in one another" despite their disagreement.[35]

Such "complete confidence" and difference of opinion set the stage for writing another polemic against Margaret's position and, therefore, against all those who took the oath. The very act of committing their dispute to paper and secretly dispatching it out of the Tower suggests both More's and Margaret's desire for a wider readership than just that of Alington. The dialogue was More's apologia, but it testified to Margaret's tenacity. What More would or did not disclose to her in May, he sheds light upon by August for others to read, and it was his daughter's opposition to him that caused him to do so.

Margaret's intelligence and scholarly acumen need not be rehearsed here, but her loyalty to More should not be equated with agreement between them about taking the oath.[36] "How now daughter Margaret?" More asks her in the letter. "What how Mother Eve? Where is your mind now?" More finds her "musing with some serpent" to concoct some "new line of persuasion by which to offer Father Adam the apple once again" (*TMSB*, 333/1–4). The "apple" refers to taking the oath, which Margaret had already done.

In fact, she continued to press for her father to take the oath even after the delivery of and debate over Alice's letter to More's cell. From the official record of More's final interrogation in June 1535, he testified that Margaret "had written to him before divers letters, to exhort him and advertise him to accommodate himself to the King's pleasure, and specially, in the last letter, she used great vehemence and obsecration."[37] What the August *Letter to Alington* captures, then, is an argument that would continue in the months to come.

FORENSIC DISCOURSE AND THE FAMILIAR LETTER

Unnoticed by most readers, the contest between father and daughter employs judicial oratory, a rhetorical genre that resolves an issue through speeches of defense and accusation. Formally, the *Letter to Alington* provides a *controversia* on More's refusal to swear the oath.[38] At the same time, such contest occurs within the parameters of a familiar letter, an epistolary genre that represents conversation between absent friends in a simple style.[39] The easiest answer to the conundrum of the letter's blending of genre would be to read it as a mere report about More from Margaret's intimate correspondence with her sister. A closer examination, however, shows how this familiar letter hides a forensic design of classical oratory, the structure of a single oration of self-defense. To recognize this forensic design, we must consider first the familiar letter and how More used it.

Though the genre of the familiar letter affords wide latitude, the Erasmian aim in writing letters is to write intimately, what Cicero first describes as *scribere familiariter*.[40] Erasmus, as did Petrarch (1304–74) before him, emphasizes the connection between letter writing and *familiaritas* when he teaches that "letters which are deficient in true feeling and do not reflect a man's actual life do not deserve to be called letters"; instead, true epistolary writing reveals "the writer's character and fortunes and sentiments, and the state of affairs both public and private."[41] The emphasis upon artistry, however, remains: "If there is something that can be said to be characteristic of this genre, I cannot define it more concisely than by saying that *the wording of a letter should resemble a conversation between friends*."[42] Conceived so, the letter, as a rhetorical genre, would replace the oral, immediate forms of conversation, dialogue, or debate.

Yet the connection between classical oratory and the familiar letter is also clearly drawn. Erasmus summarizes his list of epistolary forms in *De ratione studii*, what he calls "the argument of the persuasive, dissuasive, exhortatory, dehortatory, narrative, congratulatory, expostulatory, commendatory, and consolatory letter."[43] With the possible exceptions of narrative, congratulatory, and consolatory letters, each kind falls into one of the three categories of classical oratory: the deliberative, which persuades an addressee to take or refrain from particular courses of future action; judicial or forensic, which argues opposite cases of prosecution and defense; demonstrative or epideictic, the speeches of praise or blame.[44] As a result of these oratorical genres, letters incorporate formal divisions of speech that correspond to Cicero's original, six-part rhetorical scheme: (1) *exordium* or *salutatio* (introduction or greeting); (2) *narratio* (statement of facts); (3) *divisio* (an outline of what will be discussed); (4) *confirmatio* (proofs); (5) *refutatio* (refutation of counter arguments); and (6) *peroratio* (conclusion with an appeal from pathos).[45] Erasmus recommends that letters "conceal rather than reveal their order," even though "they are in fact carefully constructed," and permits freedom in the alteration or reorganization of its parts.[46] The end of letter writing, however, remains the same for each kind of letter and its arrangement: to write in a style that displays "simplicity, frankness, humor and wit" and resembles a "conversation" among friends.[47]

By Erasmian standards, the *Letter to Alington* marks a fascinating rhetorical choice, in part, because of what it refuses to attempt. Long before More's imprisonment, his correspondence illustrated a rhetorical mastery of epistolary forms. More wrote in formal or friendly styles to Wolsey, Erasmus, or to his own wife, Lady Alice More (ca. 1474–ca. 1551).[48] More's humanist letters, especially his *Letter to Dorp*, are paragons of Erasmus's theory, a combination of Roman oratory with the etiquette or decorum of the personal letter.[49] Though More was expert in composing such Erasmian letters, he put aside the opportunity for an outright oratorical defense of his actions in the form of a personal letter. The very kind of letter Thomas Cromwell might have expected from More never materializes.

To recognize More's contribution to the *Letter to Alington*, we should note where epistolary rules of arrangement are wed to forensic discourse. One of the most popular and widely printed rhetorical handbooks among humanists was the *Rhetorica ad Herennium*, a text whose authorship remains unknown, but one that accurately represents the Ciceronian tradition from which Erasmus drew and More followed. For example, the opening to the *Letter to Alington* eschews a *salutatio* in favor of an *exordium*, what the *Ad Herennium* dubs "the Direct Opening" or the *principium*.[50] In forensic speech, if your cause is of "the honourable kind"—what the Latin refers to as *honestum genus*—then an orator may employ the *principium*, a straightforward introduction.[51] So the *exordium* begins with Margaret's statement that she will show Alice's letter with its accusations against their father to More himself. The case against More seems "honorable" because Alice's news details how More's "scruple of conscience" will force his friends into forsaking him. Within the fiction of a correspondence, Margaret allies herself with Alice from the start; both daughters hope to save More from himself. But the letter's beginning (*exordium*) also neatly introduces the subject of the dialogue—is More guilty of scrupulosity?—as a *quaestio iudicii* (some "question for decision") that the rest of the letter must resolve in a judicial contest.[52]

Next, the question about how to judge More's "scruple" is developed. To do so, More deployed a special kind of *narratio* that reviews an issue in light of the persons involved. Such a "narrative," we read in the *Ad Herennium*, "should present a lively style and diverse traits of character," such as "austerity and gentleness, hope and fear, distrust and desire, hypocrisy and compassion, and the vicissitudes of life," including a "reversal of fortune."[53] True to form, Margaret and More represent the austerity of their disagreement alongside "gentleness" toward one another. Where Margaret fears for her father, he hopes she will be merry. Both speak in the context of "the vicissitudes of life," More's political free fall and its consequences, and to the family's punishing "reversal of fortune." The author of the *Ad Herennium* cautions that not all of the prescribed character traits need inclusion in a rhetorical exercise, but More's actual case and his position vis-à-vis his daughter provide a real-life paradigm of the *genus narrationis quod in personis*.[54]

From a narrative that involves persons, the transition to dialogue occurs. Formally, a *narratio* will review a case, and, according to Erasmus, such review "can be greatly enhanced by the figure some call *sermocinatio*, a dialogue in which we assign suitable utterances to one or more persons."[55] Accordingly, Margaret and More, in short speeches and in conversation, flesh out the nature of the case against him, dramatizing the *narratio* both as characters and within the context of judicial oratory. Margaret begins with the accusation that More may "stubbornly refuse to do" what the king wants, though her father could "do it without displeasing God"; alternatively, he may refuse the oath and leave "a great blot" on his honor and perhaps put his "soul in danger too" (*TMSB*, 319/24–29). More replies by calling her "mistress Eve" and claims the opposite disjunctive: "If in this matter it were possible for me to do the thing that might content the King's Grace without God thereby being offended, there is no man who has taken the oath already who has done so more gladly than I would," yet "I have no way out of the bind that God has me in" (320/13–16, 24). The roles for the ensuing debate are cast as the dialogue emerges from the partitioning of forensic speech.

That same oratorical framework remains throughout the rest of the letter, but its components abide within the form of dramatic dialogue that is shared between two speakers. Margaret voices the *divisio* (points to be contested) in terms of Audley's objections to More's conscience. The *refutatio* of Audley follows before More's *confirmatio* (arguments of self-defense), a defense that emerges in further dialogue between father and daughter. These latter exchanges allow More to elaborate upon his central position, namely, that conscience must align with the general councils of the Church and its consensus, or traditional teaching. The letter, finally, forgoes any farewell from Margaret to Alice and, instead, emphasizes More's trust in God and call "to be merry and rejoice" in what God wills, a peroration.[56] The hidden yet operative parts of a forensic speech reveal the design of a single oration in defense of More and once again hint at his contribution.

As the *Letter to Alington* becomes More's vehicle for self-defense, a forensic display, the dialogue achieves the letter's overall goal of writing *familiariter* by providing a seemingly private and close proximity to *his* thoughts. Rather than a report or mere summary of More's words, More appropriated his daughters' correspondence as a clandestine outlet for his own defense. The letter invites Alice (and all subsequent readers) to imagine dynamic, improvisational, intimate conversation with More, but readers also are exposed to a formal forensic defense disguised to appear as such.[57]

Once the letter's oratorical design is recognized, the compelling depictions of the dialogue's interlocutors may be viewed as artistic touches, a function of rhetorical craft and historical fact.[58] For Erasmus, *sermocinatio* is the technical term for all dramatic dialogues of debate, including scenes of disputation from epic poems or those found in ancient histories. In the latter case, historians "put speeches into the mouths" of actual people whom Erasmus nevertheless designates as "characters."[59] In the context of Erasmus's teaching, More provides a mimetic and historical account of a face-to-face encounter between him and Margaret. As a result, the description of their conversation is vivid enough to convey the impression of lifelike speakers and exchanges, just as in poetry or histories.

When More turned to self-dramatization and defense in 1534, he didn't simply stumble upon the most convenient means to speak during a time of surveillance. The correspondence between Margaret and Alice provided him cover to provide an apologia, a statement piece that would move readers because of the dramatic conflict between father and daughter. Though the forensic arrangement was hidden, his self-defense was a robust polemical piece of literature that responded to his incarceration.

DIALOGUES OF COUNSEL AND CONSCIENCE

Attention to the underlying genres of rhetorical discourse in the *Letter to Alington* and *Utopia* reveal their philosophical symmetry and, as we shall in the next section, a shared strategy of indirect argument. In *Utopia*, a debate over "counsel" employs deliberative speech, the arguments over whether it is noble to a serve a king. Deliberative rhetoric addresses the future—in this case, should Hythlodaeus or the authorial More join a king's council?—according to the categories *honestas* and *utilitas*, the moral and expedient points of view.[60] Hythlodaeus is adamant that no philosopher may do so, but Morus or More argues in favor of service. The second and later dialogue features forensic discourse, what happened in the past, and whether More is guilty of obstinacy, failure to serve his king.[61] As the subject of "counsel" turns into that of "conscience," More faces the charge of forsaking Henry to cultivate a reputation for wisdom. In other words, More could be painted in terms of the character he created, Hythlodaeus, because both author and character voice opposition to kings.

In fact, the first attack More responds to in the *Letter to Alington* comes from Audley's discussion of so-called wise men from Aesop's fables. The very selection from Aesop cleverly juxtaposes the simplicity of Audley against the learning of More. "I am very glad that I have no learning outside of a few of Aesop's fables," Audley says, "of which I shall tell you now one":

There was a country in the which there were almost none but fools, saving a few which were wise. And they by their wisdom knew that there should fall a great rain, the which should make them all fools that should so be fouled or wet therewith. They, seeing that, made them caves under the ground till all the rain was past. Then they came forth thinking to make the fools to do what they list, and to rule them as they would. But the fools would none of that, but would have the rule themselves for all their craft. And when the wise men saw they could not obtain their purpose, they wished that they had been in the rain, and had defiled their clothes, with them.[62]

To illustrate the fable's relevance, Audley explains how he "would not" have More "so scrupulous of conscience" (TMSB, 318/1). Instead of More's opposition to Henry, Audley wishes his old friend would leave his cave (prison cell) and get wet (risk corruption) with the rest of the realm.

The point and position of the fable thus frames the subsequent dialogue between Margaret and More, but the fable also significantly alludes to *Utopia*. Instead of the accommodating diplomat played by Morus, the imprisoned More is turned into a Hythlodaeus-like figure, a wise man who prizes his distance from fools. Hythlodaeus explains: "Plato by a very fine comparison shows why philosophers are right in abstaining from administration of the commonwealth. They observe the people rushing out into the streets and being soaked by constant showers and cannot induce them to go indoors and escape the rain. They know that, if they go out, they can do no good but will only get wet with the rest. Therefore, being content if they themselves at least are safe, they keep at home, since they cannot remedy the folly of others."[63] Thus, when More foregrounds Audley's use of the fable in the *Letter to Alington*, he also revisits his own, earlier reference to Plato from *Utopia*. He both sharpens and ironizes Audley's charge in the process. For Plato's point, like that of Hythlodaeus, is that the wise should rule. Morus says as much to Hythlodaeus: "Your favorite author, Plato, is of the opinion that commonwealths will finally be happy only if either philosophers become kings or kings turn to philosophy." What Morus proposes as an argument in favor of service, though, Hythlodaeus turns into gloomy prognostication. "Plato was right in foreseeing that if kings themselves did not turn to philosophy, they would never approve of the advice of real philosophers," rejoins Hythlodaeus, but the outstanding problem remains that kings "have been from their youth saturated and infected with wrong ideas."[64] Plato is correct about philosopher counselors only if there are educable, potentially if not yet actual philosopher kings. The fable, therefore, not only equates scrupulosity with preening wise men but also associates More with Hythlodaeus's position, a coincidence that ironically casts Audley, More's accuser, into the role of Morus.

Seen in this light, Audley reasons as Morus did. As in the case of corrupted kings, politics prioritizes the passions and pride of real human beings—"fools"—who will stick to their own "craft" instead of utopian ideals or philosophy.[65] Such realism approximates Morus's point in rejoinder to Hythlodaeus: "What you cannot turn to good you must at least make as little bad as you can. For it is impossible that all should be well unless all men were good, a situation which I do not expect for a great many years to come."[66] To make things less bad means working with imperfect men. In terms of More's refusal to take the oath, his "conscience" may appear like a self-indulgent excuse for abandoning the ship of state, howsoever foolish are its helmsmen.[67]

In the *Letter to Alington*, More replied by identifying Audley's fable as a favorite of Cardinal Wolsey. When dissension arose in Europe because of the French king's taste for war, Wolsey advocated taking sides. Though it might seem wise for England to remain neutral, the "fools" at war in Europe would eventually ally together against the English. "And so," Wolsey concluded, "if we were to be so wise as to sit in peace while the fools fought, they would not fail afterwards to make peace and agree among themselves and eventually all fall upon us" (*TMSB*, 322/24–26). For Wolsey, to be rained upon entails military conflict, but cave-dwelling neutrality signals myopic strategy.

Once again, More's recollection of Wolsey's "counsel" in the *Letter to Alington* comments upon and harkens back to *Utopia*'s dialogue (*TMSB*, 322/28). Hythlodaeus relates that when advisors to the French king argue for the seizure of Italy, a host of practical if morally questionable ploys emerge. A treaty may be made with Venice and later broken when "convenient," France might bribe Swiss mercenaries, the king of Aragon could be duped with a settlement, and the prince of Castile ensnared by a marriage alliance. In the rush of such suggestions, "the most perplexing question of all comes up: what is to be done with England?" The "most perplexing question" appears like an irrelevant concern to the capture of Italy until justified by the French belief that "the English should be called friends but suspected as enemies" at all times. The Scots, as a result, should be poised to attack England before the invasion of Italy commences.[68]

The example of the French king from *Utopia* would seem to illustrate the prescience of Wolsey's use of the fable, a conclusion that More undermined both in Hythlodaeus's rejoinder and in the epigrams on kingship that prefaced the 1518 editions of *Utopia*. For Wolsey, war's inevitability circumscribes the deliberations of England's own privy council such that peace falls outside the range of possibilities. The impossibility of peace, however, Hythlodaeus pounces upon as a central reason why philosophers cannot serve at court. He tells Morus:

> Suppose I proved that all this warmongering, by which so many nations were kept in a turmoil on the French king's account, would, after draining his resources and destroying his people, at length by some mischance end in naught and that therefore he had better look after his ancestral kingdom and make it as prosperous and flourishing as possible, love his subjects and be loved by them, live with them and rule them gently, and have no designs upon other kingdoms since what he already possessed was more than enough for him. What reception from my listeners, my dear More, do you think this speech of mine would find?[69]

That last question could have been asked by More himself about the publication of his epigrams with *Utopia*. Hythlodaeus above, at least, paraphrases the poems on how kings should rule.[70] As More puts it in one epigram, "a devoted king will never lack children [*liberis*]; he is father to the whole kingdom. And so it is that a true king is abundantly blessed in having as many children [*liberis*] as he has subjects."[71] *Liberis* may translate "children" or "free men," a pun that iterates Hythlodaeus's call for gentle rule. In a related poem, "On the Good King and His People," More emphasizes how "a kingdom in all its parts is like a man" because "love" holds the body politic together.[72] Just as More's poems echo Hythlodaeus's ideal, they also mirror his fears. More writes: "Among many kings there will be scarcely one, if there is really one, who is satisfied to have one kingdom. And yet among many kings there will be scarcely one, if there is really one, who rules a single kingdom well." The title of this poem is "On the Lust for Power," a distillation of Hythlodaeus's overall point.[73]

The argument from Hythlodaeus and the epigrams illustrates More's irony behind his reply to Wolsey's use of Aesop's fable in the *Letter to Alington*: "I will not dispute his Grace's counsel, and I trust we never made war but as reason would dictate" (*TMSB*, 322/28–29). Yet More means precisely the opposite; he did distrust England's own pugnacity because it defied reason. Henry VIII went to war with France, forgoing England's neutral position between France and Spain. According to one recent estimate of the years between 1509 and 1520, Henry spent 1 million pounds of a total of 1.7 million in overall expenditures on his military.[74] "But yet his telling of this fable," More adds of Wolsey, "did in his day help the King and the realm to spend many a fair penny" (322/29–33/1). Hythlodaeus's call for a prosperous realm contrasts with "warmongering" because the latter drains resources and destroys a people. Seen in this way, More's comment upon Wolsey in the *Letter to Alington* recalls Hythlodaeus's earlier critique from *Utopia*.

As for those wise men who wished to rule, More claimed that they "were stark fools before the rain" because it was impossible to govern fools in any case (*TMSB*, 323/21). In context, More here rebuffs the charge that he covets office with the suggestion that the king and his courtiers are unworthy or unable to be ruled by wisdom, an audacious retort. So More put that critique of court conversely, or with respect to what the wise ought to have done. "For if they'd had any sense," More says of them, "they might well have seen that if they had been fools too, that would not have sufficed to make them rulers over the other fools, no more than the other fools over them, and that of so many fools, not all could be rulers" (323/10–13). To venture forth into the rain and join the foolish would simply displace and condemn the wise, not elevate them. By implication, the courts of kings are replete with corruption, a repetition of Hythlodaeus's critique. Because the rejoinder is so sharp, More qualifies his answer with more irony. "Anyway," he sums up, "whom my Lord [Audley] takes here for the wise men, and whom he means by the fools I cannot very well guess" (323/22–24). Yet More knows very well who calls whom a fool and for what reason. Because More's presentation associates Audley with the fallen chancellor, Wolsey, and hearkens back to his most celebrated and well-known work, *Utopia*, More's readers would recognize his ironic voice.

AN INDIRECT APPROACH

More's use of irony also points to a shared rhetorical strategy at work in both dialogues, a device More espoused as *ductus obliquus*. In the first place, More meant an indirect approach to a controversial matter, a special form of polemical writing. To mask a high-minded moral or political point of view within a hostile environment calls for more than just avoiding inflammatory speech. In *Utopia*, Morus put the matter this way: "You must not force upon people new and strange ideas which you realize will carry no weight with persons of opposite conviction. On the contrary, by the indirect approach [*oblique ductus*] you must seek and strive to the best of your power to handle matters tactfully. What you cannot turn to good you must at least make as little bad as you can."[75] In the context of polemical strategy, *ductus* represents structure. An argument could be *simplex*, a straightforward presentation; *subtilis*, as with More's irony, when an author implies something different from what he states; or *figuratus*, when a speaker conceals his meaning because of fear or shame.[76] A *ductus obliquus*, however, best illustrates the potential for crafting arguments of dissimulation, whether oral or written.[77]

Virginia Cox has argued that the concept of *ductus obliquus* not only represents a decorous tactic for giving counsel but also More's approach to writing *Utopia*. Specifically, More's dialogue employs what the humanist George of Trebizond (1395–1486) defined as a *ductus obliquus*, or an argument that combines *ductus simulatus*, when a speaker disguises his reasons for supporting his case, with *ductus contrarius*, "where he subtly seeks to persuade his audience of precisely the opposite of what he is saying." Cox proposes a "hermeneutic hypothesis" for the whole of *Utopia* that considers Hythlodaeus's "speeches" and More's "written text" as "parallel and specular, both advancing the same theses, but one using a simple and one an oblique *ductus*." In the dialogue of counsel, the character of Hythlodaeus allows authorial More to state critiques of kings while Morus makes those points tactful by his opposition; in the process, *Utopia* shows "how radical thinking might be brought in from the wilderness and insinuated into political discourse in an urbane and 'deniable guise.'"[78] The "indirect method," then, emerges as a strategy well suited not just for a courtier's speech but also for authors.

The *Letter to Alington* also calls for an indirect approach.[79] Although a familiar letter between sisters camouflages More's forensic design and points, the letter could nevertheless be captured and used as evidence against him.[80] So More must defend himself in a contest without breeching his public stance of "silence," a seemingly impossible task. In *Utopia*, Morus had recommended "a part without words" to those who would speak inappropriately and ruin the political drama at hand, that is, the plays of the powerful.[81] In More's own case, to speak against the oath in public would make for "strange and out-of-the-way speeches," which would have no effect on those who are "firmly persuaded the other way."[82] Yet the *Letter to Alington* produces More's most substantial statement of self-defense during the same time that he had pledged silence in answer to his accusers. How did he do so?

More needed to make a case of self-defense with plausible deniability about doing so, and so he returned to the practice of *ductus obliquus*. In *Utopia*, Hythlodaeus argued simply and Morus obliquely, but these speaking roles parallel Margaret's *simplex* approach and her father's dissimulation. Similar to how an apparently innocuous conversation between father and daughter masked forensic rhetoric, More would conceal and reveal his specific arguments against the king's new law by replicating the *ductus* typology from *Utopia*.

Like Hythlodaeus, Margaret illustrates the effect and drawback of a *ductus simplex* within her consideration of the political and moral questions at hand. First, she recounts Audley's observation of how "all the nobles of this realm, and almost all other men too, are boldly going forth with the contrary" of More's position (*TMSB*, 321/8–10). Second, she elaborates upon the charge: "But, Father, those who think you should not refuse to swear this thing that you see so many—such good men, and so learned—swear before you, do not mean that you should swear in order to bear them fellowship, or go along with them for companionship's sake. They mean, rather, that the credence that you may reasonably give to their persons on account of those aforesaid qualities should well move you to think the oath such of itself that everyone may well swear it without endangering their soul" (328/19–26).[83] Finally, she makes the first and second points personal, for she has taken the oath. So Margaret quotes Master Harry Patenson, More's own fool, with respect to herself: "Why should you refuse to take the oath, Father? For I myself have taken it" (333/12–13). The association with the family fool hearkens back to the fable of wise and foolish men, but, even so, each of her arguments varies the first one. Throughout, Margaret offers a straightforward question or position that does not admit accommodation.

In contrast, More argues accommodations and adjustments to the question of whether or not he is bound to take the oath. He employs the *ductus simulatus* in disguising his reasons to refuse the oath. Just because "the law of the land" should be obeyed, it does not follow that he is "bound to swear that every law is well made, or bound upon pain of God's displeasure to perform any point of the law that is actually unlawful" (*TMSB*, 328/35–329/2). To show why this is so, More posits an abstract case of a local law or from "some particular part of Christendom" that does not have the approval of a "General Council of the Church or by a general faith grown by a universal working of God through out all Christian nations." Such a law lacks the authority to "command and compel" any man to change his own opinion and transfer his own "conscience from the one side to the other" (329/13–31). More elaborates upon the question of jurisdiction with the case of a Marian feast in celebration of her sinless birth, a doctrinal issue unresolved at the time, and an example that elides More's central and most pertinent point: Unless a general council grants Henry his title as head of the Church, England cannot attribute it to him. "But Margaret," More concludes, "for what reasons I refuse the oath, that—as I have often said to you—is something I will never tell you, neither you nor anybody else, except if the King's Highness should choose to command me" (330/34–36). With such a presentation, More makes his point but covers his reasons for doing so.

In response to Margaret's emphasis upon "such good, learned men," More employs the *ductus contrarius*. He does so by crafting an exoneration of those who have taken the oath, which simultaneously functions as a condemnation of them. The assumed "good, learned men" now in accord with the king's caesaropapistic designs are the same men who "clearly said and affirmed the contrary of some things that they have now sworn to in the oath, and did so then upon their honor and their learning, and not in haste or suddenly, but often and after very diligently exerting themselves to see and find out the truth." More "never heard the reason for their change being any new, further thing found in the words of some authority." Of note, More defends these same "good, learned men" by wondering aloud if some old text or argument suddenly took on a new light. "Of the very same things that they saw before, if some seem otherwise to them now than they did before," More explains, "I am for their sake a great deal gladder" (*TMSB*, 331/12–17). So More perhaps insincerely rejoices in the fortuitous lability of these "good, learned men" because they may swear the oath in conscience.

Thus, the exoteric, public position of More becomes evident: "I do not take it upon myself either to define or to dispute in these matters, nor do I rebuke or impugn any other man's deed." The denial is sweeping. "Nor have I ever written, nor so much as spoken to anyone, any word of criticism about anything that parliament has passed." He finishes by making the point with regard to conscience: "Nor have I meddled with the conscience of any man who either thinks or says he thinks contrary to mine" (*TMSB*, 332/23–28). From public disputes and private criticisms, More abstains. His silence seems absolute.

Against that silence, however, More undermines his earlier defense of those whom Margaret prizes by considering what others might say of them. He is careful to distinguish his opinion above from what "some would perhaps say" (*TMSB*, 332/23–28). By putting objections in the mouths of others, More can speak through them without legally reneging upon his promise of silence. In a long winding sentence, More includes a crucial parenthetical remark:

> Now, as for things that some would perhaps say—*such as, that I might with good reason take into less account those people's change, and be less inclined to change my conscience on account of any example of theirs, because their desire to keep the King happy and avoid his indignation, their fear of losing their worldly possessions, in consideration of the discomfort this would cause their relatives and friends, might have made them swear otherwise than they think or else frame their conscience afresh to thinking otherwise than they thought*—any such opinion as this, I will not conceive of them. (331/20–28; my emphasis)[84]

Here More provides an alternative explanation for why people reversed their thinking in a sentence that denies he holds such an opinion himself. His argument in favor of Margaret's "good, learned men" cunningly suggests an argument against them. Theirs could be a decision made in fear and against Christian belief.[85]

More also begs and answers the question of how to define or judge who is good and learned: "But, indeed, if, on the other hand, a person were on some issue to take a way all by himself, going by his mind alone, or with some few, or with however many, against an evident truth appearing by the common faith of Christendom, this conscience is very damnable, yes" (*TMSB*, 330/21–24). Even if the "issue" is "not fully plain and evident, yet if he sees but himself with the smaller side thinking the one way, against the far larger side," such a one should "conform his mind and conscience" to the larger group (330/25–33). Here the arguments of Margaret turn against her because "the rest of Christendom" sides with her father (332/6). Indeed, More is "plenty sure" that "of all those holy doctors and saints, who no Christian doubts are long since with God in heaven, whose books we still to this day can get our hands on, many thought in some of these things as I think now" (332/14–18). As a result, the conscience of those who swore contradicts the rest of Christendom and the thought of "holy doctors and saints." The refutation of Margaret's position, thus, includes More's *ductus contrarius*, a refutation of *his* own arguments in defense of those who took the oath.

By implication of and inference from the above, More revealed his thoughts about the king's latest prerogative in law. As More wrote to Cromwell and iterated in his *Treatise upon the Passion*, schismatics should align themselves with Rome. In effect, the oath required More to affirm a transfer of moral and spiritual authority from the Catholic Church to the king via Parliament's legislation.[86] Yet More believed neither the king nor Parliament could make such a claim. Many "good, learned men" in England, including Henry, once thought so too.

FIVE

The True Martyr in *De tristitia Christi*, ca. 1535

Imagine Thomas More imprisoned in what he calls his "shop" with books that he refers to as his "implements." There, he composes his *De tristitia Christi*.[1] On 12 June 1535, More's books and writing materials are confiscated. According to More's early biographer, Thomas Stapleton, More keeps his blinds drawn down day and night afterward. When his jailer asks why, More replies: "Now that the goods and the implements are taken away, the shop must be closed."[2] Less than a month later, More's trial and execution occur.

What are these "implements" that More values so much? We know he uses both the *Catena aurea* (ca. 1262–64) of Thomas Aquinas and Jean Gerson's *Monotesseron* as his "basic tools" for composing *De tristitia Christi*. The *Catena* is a compendium of exegetical comments by Church Fathers, which Aquinas compiles and condenses. His *Catena* thereby becomes a "golden chain" of linked biblical commentary on specific sections of the four Gospels. The subtitle of *Monotesseron* is *Unum ex quattuor* ("one from four"), which indicates how Gerson integrates the four Gospels into one "harmony" by combining corresponding verses. Gerson's book aided More in his writing of the *Treatise upon the Passion* in the spring of 1534. Gary Haupt, More's modern editor, rightly surmises that "nothing could more appropriately express More's intense concern for the unity of Christendom" than his selection of Gerson's harmony and Aquinas's collection of excerpts from the Church Fathers.[3] Clarence Miller's commentary on *De tristitia* acknowledges especially Aquinas's *Catena* as a source upon which More "relies heavily" because it provides "the groundwork" of More's biblical exegesis.[4] Unity among evangelists and within the tradition is symbolized in More's selection of texts and suggests the cause for which he was jailed.

Church unity also represents More's polemical agenda. Contrary to previous studies that have emphasized the devotional aspects of *De tristitia* or how this text revealed More's "inner" life, I will examine it as his final contribution to apologetics.[5] More's own circumstances as a prisoner in the Tower, as in the *Dialogue of Comfort*, remain inseparable from how he understands the theological and political landscape in England. In *De tristitia*, however, More goes a step further. He portrays the bishops in England as "sleepy apostles," who abandoned Christ and his Catholic Church, and he rewrites martyr literature to reflect his own refusal to submit to Henrician schism.

Indeed, *De tristitia*'s teachings cannot be separated from More's reaction to his king's claim to be supreme head of the Church in England.[6] As early as 1532, Henry VIII had commissioned French and Latin translations of *A Glass of the Truth*, a tract in defense of his claims for divorce and case against the papacy. The polemic was designed to attract English and Continental support.[7] Similar printed works were dispersed to foreign diplomats who were in England. Meanwhile, Henry's diplomats used such texts in presenting the theoretical basis of supremacy abroad.[8] What began in 1532 culminated by the end of 1534 when Parliament passed the Act of Supremacy and severed ecclesiastical connection with Rome.

Of course, there was no equivalent print campaign in England to respond to that of the government, but More's writings did make a reply. From the Tower, he composed his *Dialogue* and *De tristitia*, the one for consumption at home, the other as a trumpet blast to Latin readers and, therefore, for those beyond England's boundaries; both served to rebut royal propaganda. For More, the theory of supremacy entailed schism and plunged Christendom into crisis.[9] To counter such disaster, More presented to English and European audiences accounts of the importance of suffering for Christ's Catholic Church.[10] Rather than retirement, More's public persona as champion of Church unity continued in *De tristitia* but through an explicitly Christological lens that invited others to ponder the significance of his own witness.

DATE AND CIRCUMSTANCES OF COMPOSITION

Against that background, More might have begun *De tristitia* from the day of his arrival to the Tower but, we shall see in this section, I think it most likely that he composed it sometime after the bill of attainder was passed against him, and that his final major work was written predominately in the spring of 1535. Once the legislative case for supremacy grew in November 1534, so did More's awareness that—no matter how unlawful the charges against him were in the spring—he could be convicted of treason. Seen in this light, the regime's pursuit of him influenced his cast of mind and defense of fearful martyrs in *De tristitia*. As More's interrogations grew more combative and Parliament's laws more stringent, More suspected his execution was imminent and reacted against its prospect with fear. The case or type of a fearful martyr became one and the same with that of his own state. As the legal noose tightened, so did More's focus upon the passion of Christ as "a mysterious image of future times," as a "paradigm," and a "clear and sharp mirror image" of his own day.[11]

More hadn't arrived at this position when his incarceration began. To the contrary, he thought himself to be safe in silence, or in his refusal to discharge his conscience. Master Cromwell had used the Act of Succession, passed by Parliament in March 1534, to demand an oath from More on 13 April. Upon More's first refusal of the oath, he told Cromwell:

> Surely as to swear to the succession I see no peril, but I thought and think it reason, that to mine own oath I look well myself, and be of counsel also in the fashion, and never intended to swear for a piece, and set my hand to the whole oath. Howbeit as touching the whole oath, I never withdrew any man from it, nor never advised

any to refuse it, nor never put, nor will, any scruple in any man's head, but leave every man to his own conscience. And methinketh in good faith, that so were it good reason that every man should leave me to mine."[12]

The "whole oath" required More to accept the act's preamble, which implied Henry's supreme headship of the Church in England and rejected papal jurisdiction. More would swear to the succession, but not to royal supremacy. Even so, More never "advised" anyone to refuse the "whole oath." Everyone should leave More to his own conscience, just as he ostensibly left others to theirs. More was imprisoned anyway on 17 April.[13]

More's response suggests why he didn't directly tell Margaret, or anyone else, the reasons he refused "the whole oath." The Act of Succession clarified that anything written maliciously against it was high treason and thus punishable by hanging, drawing, and quartering; anything spoken against the act meant misprision of treason, punishable by loss of all goods and imprisonment. So, too, any adult male subject could be called to take an oath. If anyone should "obstinately refuse" to do so, "then every such person" would be found guilty of misprision of treason.[14] To give an answer why he refused the "whole oath" risked the statute's penalties. More's own partial answer was already a dangerous if truthful evasion: "that in my conscience this was one of the cases in which I was bounden that I should not obey my prince."[15] Refusal of the prince in this case, More claimed, was his right of conscience.

Conversely, silence would avoid violation of the statute, according to More, for his silence wasn't obstinate. "Before the world," More writes to Margaret of his interrogation, "my refusing of this oath is accounted a heinous offense, and my religious fear toward God is called obstinacy toward my Prince." More calls his own interrogators as his witnesses. The lords of the council saw More's "heaviness of heart" in refusing the oath. Instead of obstinance, More explained that his silence was charity because he would rather not speak and "endure all the pain and peril of the statute" than declare his reasons and "give any occasion of exasperation" to his sovereign. Rather than simply a strategy to avoid implicating himself, More formulates his refusal in terms of loyalty and his firm reluctance to give offense: "And now you see, Margaret, that it is no obstinacy to leave the causes undeclared, while I could not declare them without peril."[16]

We should note in passing that More's personal explanation of silence appears different from the ones often attributed to him.[17] The Guildhall Report of his trial first painted More's defense as based in silence because by common law silence indicated consent.[18] Archbishop William Warham invoked the same principle when the convocation of clergy approved Henry's title as "Supreme Head, insofar as the law of Christ allows."[19] Roper's version of More's trial, however, makes no mention of the assumption that silence means consent.[20]

In contrast to feigned agreement, More forthrightly claims under questioning that swearing to the contents of the oath would place his soul in danger: "I could not swear without the jeopardizing of my soul to perpetual damnation."[21] Under investigation, More speaks with lawyerly precision but without reference to any subterfuge of consent; he will abide by the law but not speak to its merits or deficiencies. Quite the contrary, he clarifies that his reasons for silence or "causes undisclosed" would anger his prince.[22] If silence in law means consent, More clarifies that his silence safeguards his conscience.

Such a defense obviously implies that the "causes undeclared" would give offense or fall under the statute's penalties if they were declared. But More also refused to say what he thought because the king and his councilors already knew his mind.[23] The preamble condemned the "bishop of Rome" for interferring in the "jurisdiction" of England, contrary to the "great and involiable" grant of dominion "given by God immediately to emperors, kings, and princes."[24] We have seen how More's *Letter to Alington* and *Dialogue of Comfort* opposed Henry's title as supreme head of the Church in England. In the *Dialogue*, Antony suggested how kings such as Henry were ministers of the midday devil, agents of an open persecution of English orthodoxy, and how More found such orthodoxy to be inseparable from obedience to the Holy and Roman See. In the *Letter to Alington*, More's "silence" was paradoxical. He never explicitly iterated his support of papal primacy because his previous statements spoke for themselves and for him.[25] Instead, he pointed out the discrepancy between belief and behavior in those who agreed with him but took the king's oath anyway.

Only in settings that permitted private and familial talk would More speak freely. On the same point of the first oath offered More, Roper's biography reports More's words to Margaret: "I may tell thee, Meg, they that have committed me hither for refusing of this oath not agreeable with the statute, are not by their own law able to justify my imprisonment. And, surely, daughter, it is a great pity that any Christian prince should by a flexible council ready to follow his affections, and by a weak clergy lacking grace constantly to stand to their learning, with flattery be so shamefully abused."[26] This proves that More could be critical of the king's council outside of its interrogation chambers, but it suggests something else besides. Without an oath whose text was specified in the Act of Succession to be sworn, there were no grounds for claiming More obstinately refused the oath offered to him. Accusations of "obstinacy" ignore how the "oath" is not "agreeable" to the statute. More could always argue that the oath provided him did not agree with the statute since the oath's absence from the bill created a legal lacuna.

Rastell, who was an attorney and a printer, believed that More was unlawfully imprisoned "because the oath contained more things than were warranted by the act of succession."[27] Here Rastell may have had in mind the following clause: "the bishop of Rome had no greater authority conferred upon him by God in this kingdom of England than any other foreign bishop."[28] Authorities tendered this clause, which spelled out the point of the act's preamble, with the oath offered to the clergy and probably to the one and only layman called to swear with them, More himself, on 13 April.[29] After More offered to swear to the succession without affirming the "whole oath," the king rejected any such compromises. Instead, Rastell reports, Henry kept More and Fisher in the Tower "until the next session of Parliament, and then made an act to make sure their wrongful imprisonment as rightful from the beginning."[30] The act Rastell refers to here was supplementary legislation about the oath and, in particular, to the following: "An Act ratifying the oath that every of the King's Subjects hath taken hereafter be bound to take for due observation of the act made for the surety of the succession of the King's Highness in the Crown of the Realm."[31] This law fixed the original Act of Succession by specifying the form of the oath to be taken.

An Act Ratifying the Oath to Succession emerges as a direct reply to More's previous legal maneuvering and laid out the path he must take if he wanted to live. Every adult male subject should have taken the oath and demonstrated his support for Henry's dynastic succession. There could be no vacillation or lawyerly cavillation, which is to say, there were no legal grounds for thinking or speaking differently from Henry on the topic of Church authority in England. The last part of the act clarified that any refusal to take the oath would result in an indictment—such persons "shall be compelled to answer thereunto as if they were indicted."[32]

The oath's significance becomes clearer in context of the parliamentary session and its laws in the fall of 1534. By that time, More's support of papal primacy and the Roman or Latin Church couldn't be upheld alongside Henry's own claims to rule the Church of England.[33] The Act Ratifying the Oath mandated loyalty to the king alone and in contrast to any "foreign authority," such as that of the pope: "Ye shall swear to bear Faith, Truth, and Obedience alonely to the King's Majesty and to his heirs of his body of his most dear and entirely beloved lawful wife Queen Anne begotten & to be [begotten] and further to the heirs of our said Sovereign Lord according to the limitation in the Statute made for surety of his succession in the crown of this Realm mentioned and contained, and not to any other within this Realm nor foreign authority or Potentate."[34] We have seen how More consented to the succession of Henry and Anne's offspring and even acknowledged her as rightfully anointed queen. Though More did not attend Anne's coronation, he knew that the service entailed recognition of her office, an oath taken by her, and anointing of her with holy oil; the last was a sign or seal of divine approval. Even so, Henry's caesaropapism went beyond his "great matter."

Henry had made the pope merely "bishop of Rome" by way of his previously published *Articles*, but now Parliament arrived with other new laws.[35] In the single month of November, Parliament passed "An Act concerning the King's Highness to be supreme head of the Church of England & to have authority to reform & redress all errors, heresies, & abuses in the same."[36] The Supremacy Act solidified the king's absolute authority, even though Henry had already claimed to be God's "vicar" in the Act in Restraint of Appeals from 1532. Next, the Act of Treasons elevated malicious speaking from misprision of treason to high treason.[37] In effect, a citizen could be put to death for merely speaking against the king's new title because such speech was a prima facie case of malice against the sovereign.[38] Already in November 1534, the Supremacy Act and Treasons Act clarified the king's jurisdiction as sole vicar in England.

Before Parliament convened, More's arguments of defense displayed expert knowledge of existing laws, so Cromwell needed new ones. The onslaught of legislation must have turned More's mind toward his final (and increasingly probable) punishment. In concert with the Supremacy and Treasons Acts, Parliament passed a bill of attainder against More for his previous refusal of the oath, which now could be shown as unlawful. "I refused to swear," More wrote to Margaret of his first time before Cromwell and legal representatives of the Privy Council, but "I would not declare any special part of that oath that grudged my conscience, and open the cause wherefore." More offered to disclose his conscience upon the safeguard of "gracious licence" by royal letters patent. More was told that such a license would not save him. "But yet it thinketh me," More iterated in another letter to Margaret, "that if I may not declare the causes without peril than to leave them undeclared is no obstinacy."[39] The point was brilliant when first used. What was ambiguous obstinacy or difficult to prove in the spring of 1534 became an easier charge to make in the fall.

The bill of attainder left little doubt that More could or would be convicted for treason. Spoken malice could be determined by any rejection of or refusal to admit to the king's title in the Treasons Act, and this same language of sedition was part of More's attainder:

> Sir Thomas More contrary to the trust and confidence aforesaid being lawfully and duly required, since the first day of May last past unnaturally and contrary to his duty of allegiance, intending to sow and make sedition murmur and grudge within this the king's realm amongst the true obedient and faithful subjects of the same, that obstinately, frowardly, and contemptuously refused to make and receive such corporal oath as was ordained to be accepted of every Subject of this Realm for the surety and establishment of the succession of our said Sovereign Lord in the imperial Crowne of this Realm.[40]

More's intentions are declared for him in the bill. Sedition need not be proved when legislation proclaims More's attempts "to sow and make sedition."

Similar sentiments were expressed, just before More's trial, in Henry's "Order to Publicize the Guilt of Fisher and More" on 25 June 1535. There, Fisher and More "by divers secret practices of their malicious minds against us intended to seminate, engender, and breed amongst our people and subjects a most mischievous and seditious opinion."[41] This declaration of guilt, though, might just as easily have been written from the bill of attainder.

From Cromwell's point of view in late 1534, the problem posed by More's silence and the wrangling over what constituted "obstinance" was solved. Refusal to take the oath alone caused murmur and seditious grudge within the realm. More had not spoken out against the oath or disclosed his reasons for refusing it, but that no longer mattered. His silence would sow rebellion rather than consent.

With the "Act concerning the Attainder of Sir Thomas More," Cromwell's men raided and confiscated his estate and isolated him from others.[42] "Father, what moved them to shut you up again," Margaret wrote to her father of his solitary confinement, "we can nothing hear." But she speculates. Because her father was content to remain in prison with the liberties afforded him in the Tower, the king decided to "restrain" More from the Church and the "company" of his wife and children.[43] More was denied access to a priest—and, as a result, the possibility of receiving the sacrament of confession—even while Margaret was prohibited from seeing her father.[44] From this time forward, More's thoughts turned toward the composition of *De tristitia*.

Events from the spring of 1535 might have further inspired him. Margaret was allowed to visit her father again on Tuesday, 4 May. On that same day, More and Margaret watched as a Bridgettine monk, Richard Reynolds (ca. 1492–1535), accompanied Carthusians to Tyburn to be executed for denying an oath in affirmation of the king's new title. Reynolds, who was charged and tried at the same time as the others, had spoken out at his trial on 28 April 1535 that "all good men of the kingdom" stood with "the rest of Christendom" and against the king, including "dead witnesses" like "all the General Councils" and "holy doctors of the Church for the last fifteen hundred years." When the king learns of these truths, he will become "indignant against certain bishops" who have misadvised him.[45] By coincidence or by way of influence upon More, these same points previewed similar ones that More would make at his own trial.[46]

The deaths and final words of these men most likely prepared More for death rather than deterred him from it, albeit their brutal demise would have terrified him. The same four monks and one secular priest were "hanged with great ropes," and, while still alive, they had their hearts and bowels removed. Then "they were beheaded and quartered." There was "no change" in their "tone of speech" while their execution occurred, and they *preached* "obedience to the king in everything that was not against the honor of God and the Church."[47] Such preaching again anticipated and perhaps inspired More's last words, "I die the king's good servant *and* God's first."[48] Obedience to God and Church, in other words, should not make one in law a disobedient subject to the king, even if such arguments would not keep men from the scaffold.

Cromwell had arranged Margaret's visit so that the fate of the Carthusians would make a king's threat frighteningly immediate to More. We can infer something about Cromwell's plans for intimidation because, days before Margaret's visit, Cromwell had asked More if he had read the statute proclaiming the king as head of the Church. When More admitted that he had, Cromwell said the king demanded to know More's opinion on the king's title and prerogatives. More's response, at first glance, is stunning: "Whereunto I answered that in good faith I had well trusted that the King's Highness would never have commanded any such question to be demanded of me, considering that I ever from the beginning well and truly from time to time declared my mind unto his Highness."[49] Why did More think Cromwell was lying about the king's command? More surmises it because, as we have seen and Henry well knew, More had given his opinion on papal primacy many times "from the beginning well and truly from time to time." From More's first response to Luther in 1523 all the way to his defense of the Council of Florence as late as 1534, More privileged Rome and condemned schisms. He had expressed substantially the same opinion against schism to Cromwell in his letter from March 1534.

In hopes of persuading More to change his mind, in a second interrogation from 3 June 1535, Cromwell returned to the question of the king's title and papal primacy. Again, the matter of Henry's second marriage or Anne's rights as queen were not addressed. The king demanded acceptance of his title. Cromwell tells More to "make a plain and terminate answer." Either "confess it lawful that his Highness should be Supreme Head of the Church of England" or "utterly plainly" his malignity.[50] When More refuses to do so, Cromwell replies that the king may compel More to answer.

At this juncture of the interrogation, More had arrived at the very situation Antony and Vincent discussed in *A Dialogue of Comfort against Tribulation*. There, the question to be answered was when and if the "pinch of pain" would cause a man to falter.[51] Cromwell's use of the word "compel" raises the same dilemma. Less expansive than Antony, More replies that Cromwell's solution of brute force seems "somewhat hard." For it is "a very hard thing" to compel him to lose his soul, or to violate his conscience, by supporting the king's title, or to destroy his body for denying the same. Once again, More is blatantly transparent in his opposition to the Supremacy Act without saying so.[52]

Cromwell, next, wonders what the difference would be between coercing More to speak and those bishops who forced suspected heretics to answer whether the pope was head of the Catholic Church. Before Henry's reversal on the topic, after all, this question was a litmus test for Lutheranism, and those who denied the pope's authority were swiftly condemned.[53] Since there is a law that now stipulates the king as supreme head, More should answer. Those who previously denied papal authority, Cromwell reasons, were as "well burned" as those who now would defy the king's governance of the Church.[54]

In reply, More again alludes to schism without making mention of the term. "I said there was a difference between those two cases," he reported to Margaret, "because that at that time, as well here as elsewhere through the corps of Christendom, the Pope's power was recognized for an undoubted thing." That time when the pope's power was acknowledged occurred when More was chancellor of the realm. In contrast, after the legislation from the fall of 1534, what had been an "undoubted thing" now seemed "not like a thing agreed in this realm," even though the contrary is "taken for truth in other realms."[55] The authority of the papacy, in other words, should be a thing agreed upon.[56] In More's play between "this realm" and others, he previewed his trial defense, which iterated how one realm, that of England, cannot make a law "disagreeable with the general law of Christ's universal Church."[57] These arguments under interrogation paralleled those to be made later because, in effect, More was on trial already.

In Cromwell's interview of More in early May 1535, the master secretary had informed More that the king is merciful to those who are "confirmable" and will "submit," but the June interview revealed how Margaret's visit and the deaths of the Carthusians made no difference. In May, More "might be abroad in the world again" if he were "confirmable." In reply, More answered in words that suggested his composition of *De tristitia* was his entire focus. "My whole study should be upon the passion of Christ," More declared after declining Cromwell's offer, "and mine own passage out of this world."[58] A month later, More asserted that he would never swear any oath again while he lived.[59] Again, Cromwell questioned why More shouldn't speak out plainly against statute, especially if he wanted to die: "I have not been a man of such holy living, as I might be bold to offer myself to death." There was a proviso. "Howbeit if God draw me to it Himself, then trust I in his great mercy that he shall not fail to give me the strength to stand."[60] More's words here about the "strength to stand," as we have seen in chapter 3, reflect Antony's position in a *Dialogue of Comfort*, but they also suggest that More might have written sections of the *Dialogue* and *De tristitia* at the same time.

When, then, did More begin his *De tristitia*? During More's months of isolation, after November and up to the confiscation of his books, he composed *De tristitia* and finished his *A Dialogue of Comfort against Tribulation*.[61] After the Treasons Act went into effect in February 1535, More could be demanded to speak, and if he did so, as his captors knew, he would be found guilty. From February on, the subject matter of Christ's passion and what More increasingly recognized as his own coming martyrdom combined in his consideration of Christ's last days.[62]

OF CHRIST'S FEAR

More's confession that God might "draw" him to death parallels his treatment of how Christ experienced fear in *De tristitia*. "For in good faith," More confessed to Margaret, he knew "few so faint hearted" as himself.⁶³ Except, that is, for Christ. In fact, More believed that "faint hearted" martyrs best identified with Christ because they shared with him an intense dread of pain, suffering, and death.

A convenient way into discussion of how More came to understand Christ's own experience of human passions is to review what Erasmus had already taught him. The Christological topic, after all, was not unfamiliar to More nor were its theological implications. More knew of Erasmus's own "short debate" on the "distress, alarm, and sorrow of Jesus," or *De taedio Iesu*, which testified to a dispute between Erasmus and John Colet (1467–1519) at Oxford in October 1499.⁶⁴ More's friends debated whether Christ experienced a truly human fear of death. Colet found it "inappropriate and inconsistent to suppose that he, who loved the human race with such passion, could have approached death not merely with reluctance but with great trepidation." Christ, as "the very pattern of charity," died for humanity out of love; love of oneself is not love at all. Rather, Christ experiences passions because he wills to suffer out of love for humankind.⁶⁵ If Christ experiences fear or grief, Colet argued along with Saint Jerome before him, it is not in anticipation of his own physical suffering on the cross but for the fate of the Jews or the grief and terror about to befall upon the apostles.

In reply, Erasmus argued the same position More did thirty years later by explaining how Christ's perfect humanity meant that he truly experienced passion, distress, sorrow, even an intense fear of death:⁶⁶ "I do not consider it wicked at all to give Christ these emotions, which certainly do lead to sin—but in us, not in him." Because Christ "put on a human nature that was subject to many of the ills arising from original sin but free from any taint of sin itself, he could not in fact be lured towards evil by the passions natural to us."⁶⁷ Though Erasmus considered the many ways in which Christ might have assuaged his anguish in the garden, he argued the contrary position: "Jesus allowed himself none of these to help alleviate the miseries that he took on with our nature." Instead, Christ "assumed a soul that was endowed with the most acute sensitivity in every one of its faculties." As a result, "he felt every kind of mental anguish." Christ's death, in fact, "should be more painful than any other, since it alone was to atone for so many other deaths and to wash away the sins of the world."⁶⁸

Unlike More's later treatment, however, Erasmus prosecutes a general Christological point that More will simply assume to be true. Erasmus had reminded Colet of Christ's two natures and correspondingly two wills, divine and human, and how "the Church has stamped its authority so firmly on this theory of the two wills that anyone who thinks differently is branded a heretic." By referring to the theory of two wills, Erasmus alluded to the divide between early Church Fathers and later scholastic theologians, which stemmed, in part, from the fact that the doctrine that Christ possessed only a single will, or *monothelitism*, was not formally condemned until the Sixth Council of Constantinople in 685. The earlier problem before the Sixth Council was that Christ's perfect humanity would be sullied by passionate excess if he were allowed to suffer like human beings do. Yet this dilemma, Erasmus believed, could be resolved with the distinction between human and divine natures and wills. Christ, in other words, could experience a human fear of death and pray to his Father to "let this cup pass from me" even as he reaffirms to do what the Father, not he, wills.[69]

Thus, Erasmus's position placed him with scholastic theologians and in opposition to Colet's return to the early Church Fathers.[70] John W. O'Malley rightly observes that Erasmus's *De taedio Iesu* "serves to qualify most generalizations that have been made about Erasmus's relationship to the scholastics."[71] Scholastic thought, of course, isn't monolithic, yet Aquinas also teaches that Christ did not allow his higher faculties to affect his experience of even physical suffering, and this position appears essentially like that of Erasmus.[72] Because of such connections, Erasmus advertised his alliance with scholasticism and invited Colet to join them: "I must ask, along with the modern theologians, why do you refuse to allow that death filled Christ with dread, even if it were only an emotion Jesus assumed temporarily and not an essential part of the nature he assumed? I know that you are generally quite happy to disagree with the new breed of theologians, but let us carry out the test recommended by Plato in the *Parmenides* and see whether the view I hold with them is in any way unreasonable."[73] The "modern theologians"—the new breed, as it were, which opposes the earlier Church Fathers—refers to scholasticism. By invoking Plato, Erasmus suggests that Colet's possesses an unreasonable prejudice against it.[74] Yet in following Jerome and other Fathers like him, "Colet's position on this issue was consistent with his overall aim of purifying theology by pruning it back to its roots in the holier and wiser age of the Fathers," according to James D. Tracy.[75] Erasmus attacked this "consistency," which he believed prevented Colet from recognizing an important Christological truth. So, Erasmus concludes his letter by praising the opinion—which he shares with "modern theologians," who appear better at keeping with "the words of the evangelists"—of those in favor of Christ's truly human experience of suffering. Since More agreed with this point, he followed the *recentiorum theologorum*.[76]

THE FEARFUL MARTYR FOR CATHOLICISM

Within this framework of More's inherited and Erasmian assumptions, we can see how he constructed his case for fearful martyrs from the *Catena aurea* of Aquinas. In *De tristitia*, More elaborates upon and extends Erasmus's position in consideration of the words "My soul is sad unto death" from Matthew 26:38 and Mark 14:34 (*CW* 14.1:43/5–45). Miller observes that the *Monotesseron* presents More with three points of discussion on this verse—the selection of Peter, John, and James; the sadness and fear of Christ; and Christ's command to pray with him—but More is "primarily interested in the second point, to which he devotes more than fifteen times as much space as to the other two points combined."[77] In the Valencia manuscript of *De tristitia*, More's own autograph of this text, the canceled passages show how More revises, striking his treatment of first and third points so he may elaborate upon Christ's sadness and fear. Of note, More also repeats Christ's complaint in Latin—*tristis est anima mea usque ad mortem*—in his own collection of scripture verses found in the same manuscript.[78] But why such an intense focus upon this single verse?

Though Christ's complaint appears only in Matthew and Mark, the *Catena* repeats it verbatim and often. From that compendium, More discovered how the iteration of a single verse articulates a Christological controversy in miniature. First, from Matthew, by John Damascene (ca. 676–ca. 749), who cites it as proof that "in Christ nothing befell of compulsion, but all was voluntary; with His will He hungered, with His will He feared, or was sorrowful. Here His sorrow is declared." And second, by Origen (ca. 185–ca. 254), who after citing the same verse, paraphrases it: "Sorrow is begun in me, but not to endure forever, but only till the hour of death; that when I shall die to sin, I shall die also to all sorrow, whose beginnings only are in me." The last comes from Theophylactus (ca. 1050–ca. 1109): "For since He had taken on Himself the whole of human nature, He took also those natural things which belong to man, amazement, heaviness, and sorrow; for men are naturally unwilling to die. Wherefore it goes on: And he saith unto them, *tristis est anima mea usque ad mortem.*"[79] In Theophylactus and Damascene, More finds the position that he himself believes: Christ wills to suffer torments in the garden, allowing his human nature to fully experience sadness and fear. In Origen, however, there is only the "beginning of sadness" rather than an utterly complete experience of it. From this same section of the *Catena*, the partial or initial sense of fear and sadness are explained in Jerome's voice, which maintains that Christ is sorrowful not because of death but *unto* death, that is, until the completion of his salvific sacrifice.[80]

More synthesizes these various and contrary opinions with his own by imagining the scene. Unlike Erasmus, who announces the points to be disputed, More describes how the threat of impending death would affect a nature such as Christ's, which could more keenly experience physical and mental sufferings.[81] Though More's doctrinal position agrees with many theologians, he focuses upon Christ's subjective and emotional state:

> A huge mass of troubles took possession of the tender and gentle body of our most holy Savior. He knew that His ordeal was now imminent and just about to overtake Him: the treacherous betrayer, the bitter enemies, binding ropes, false accusations, slanders, blows, thorns, nails, the cross, and horrible tortures. Over and above these, He was tormented by the thought of His disciples' terror, the loss of the Jews, even the destruction of the very man who so disloyally betrayed him, and finally the ineffable grief of His mother. (*CW* 14.1:47/1–48/3)[82]

In these lines, More incorporates Colet's and Jerome's argument that Christ is sad unto death—sad until he could save those he loves—with their emphasis upon Christ's sorrow for the loss of Judah, the terrified disciples, and Judas himself.

Yet More blends these accounts with the overall positions of Erasmus, Bede (673/4–735), Theophylactus, Aquinas, and Bonaventure, all of whom advocate that Christ fully experiences the passions of sadness and fear.[83] "Since He was no less really a man than he was God," More summarizes, "He had the ordinary feelings of mankind" (*CW* 14.1:51/6–7). In More's hands, the *Catena*, with its rich variation, spurs More's poetic re-creation of the agony.

Indeed, this same collection of scripture commentary also allows us to see where or from whom More developed his own position on fearful martyrs. More turns to the objection that Aquinas reproduces from Hilary (ca. 310–ca. 367) in the glosses upon Matthew 26. Aquinas's citation of Hilary reads: "I suppose that there are some who offer here no other cause of His fear than His passion and death. I ask those who think thus, whether it stands with reason that He should have feared to die, who banished from the Apostles all fear of death, and exhorted them to the glory of martyrdom?"[84] Miller observes that "this is a strong argument not considered by Erasmus (or Colet),"[85] yet it is the very one More elaborates upon: "But here, perhaps, you may object, 'I am no longer surprised at His capacity for these emotions, but I cannot help being surprised at His desire to experience them. For He taught His disciples not to be afraid of those who can kill the body only and can do nothing beyond that; and how can it be fitting that He Himself should now be very much afraid of those same persons, especially since even His body could suffer nothing from them except what He Himself allowed?'" (*CW* 14.1:53/3–10).[86] Even the last lines of this passage paraphrase the same quotation from the *Catena* because Hilary also asks, "And what pangs of death could He fear, who came to death of the free choice of his own power?"[87] More raises objections Erasmus's *De taedio Iesu* never considers, in part, because he finds and borrows them directly from Aquinas's quotations of Hilary.

More goes still further and amplifies Hilary's case when he explores the potential harms created by Christ's alleged bad example. More asks, "Shouldn't He rather have been especially careful to set a good example in this matter . . . so that others might learn from His own example to undergo death eagerly for truth's sake, and so that those who suffer death for the faith with fear and hesitation might not indulge their slackness by imagining that they are following Christ's precedent?" Those who refuse martyrdom, after all, might cite Christ's own fear when "their reluctance would both detract a great deal from the glory of their cause and discourage others who observe their sadness and fear." Again, this objection does not appear in *De taedio Iesu* but, writes Miller in an important observation, "it has a special force for More, who was actually facing martyrdom."[88] Seen in this light, More's own intense fear of martyrdom drew him to Hilary's objections, which, in turn, provoked a sustained treatment of Christ's fear.

The crucial consideration here is how More's treatment of Hilary makes the case for fearful martyrdom. Against Hilary's unqualified support of Christ's admonition that his disciples should not fear death, More rebelled. The prohibition against fear of death was not made against feeling a natural aversion to it but given as a warning so that one will not "flee from a death which will not last, only to run, by denying the faith, into one which will be everlasting." Christ wishes his followers to be brave yet prudent: the brave bear up under blows; the senseless don't feel them. The prudent do "not allow any fear of suffering" to divert them from a "holy way of life," but a "foolish man does not fear wounds" (*CW* 14.1:55/6–59/10).[89] Fear will remain because of human nature, but faith and reason, working together and against this passion, may overcome it.

The significance of Christ's example, which Hilary develops, More continues to explore, crafting a defense of fearful martyrs in the process but with an autobiographical impulse. Contrary to "requiring us to do violence to our nature," Christ "even leaves us free to flee from punishment," which is the very "cautious advice of a prudent master" that almost all the apostles follow at one time or another (*CW* 14.1:63/1–7). For God's mercy is such that he "does not command us to climb this step and lofty peak of bravery, and hence it is not safe for just anyone to go rushing on heedlessly to the point where he cannot retrace his steps" (67/2–5). Thus, the fearful martyr should take solace in God's providence. "If anyone is brought to the point where he must either suffer torment or deny God," More writes, "he need not doubt that it was God's will for him to be brought to this crisis. Therefore, he has very good reason to hope for the best" (69/2–4). Writing from the Tower under threat of execution for failure to acknowledge the king as head of the Church, More discovers reason for hope because, like the fearful martyr in *De tristitia*, "he must either suffer torment or deny God." Or, as More put it while under interrogation, "I could not swear without the jeopardizing of my soul to perpetual damnation."[90] Or again, in terms of the fearful martyr, to swear would deny God and to refuse the oath would mean suffering torment.

Under these circumstances, though there was no doctrinal imperative to do so, More elevates the fearful martyr over the brave one. Those in danger of death because of their faith will find confidence on the day of engagement because God does not allow "you to be tempted beyond what you can stand." Just as the Turk was minister of the midday devil in More's *Dialogue*, persecution for faith in *De tristitia* promises heavenly reward: "Therefore, when things have come to the point of hand-to-hand combat with the prince of this world, the devil, and his cruel underlings, and there is no way left to withdraw without disgracing the cause, then I would think that a man ought to cast away fear and I would direct him to be completely calm, confident, and hopeful" (*CW* 14.1:71/3–8). Before such engagement, fear is natural, an invitation for struggle and therefore an "immense opportunity for merit" (73/1–4). Take the case of a fearful soldier, who nevertheless fights and achieves victory: "he ought to receive even more praise" because "he had to overcome not only the enemy but also his own fear, which is often harder to conquer than the enemy himself" (85/5–7). Like a fearful yet dutiful soldier, "our Savior Christ" did not allow his intense feelings to "prevent him from obeying His Father's command" (85/7–10).[91] More elevates the fearful martyr above the brave because the former merits greater praise. Finally, the fearful martyr most closely imitates Christ's own agony in the garden.[92]

THE CONTROVERSIAL MARTYR

More's entry into the above debate meant that he could identify with a suffering Christ in the form of a fearful martyr but, as we shall see in this section, such self-fashioning amounted to a theological and political message.[93] "Blessed are they which are persecuted for righteousness' sake: for theirs is the kingdom of heaven" (Matthew 5:11) was a rallying cry for members of minority religious groups throughout the period, and More was no exception.[94] In *De tristitia*, the true martyr experiences anxiety and sadness, just as Christ did in Gethsemane and More does in the Tower. Put differently, the Christological and biographical aspects of More's composition complement one another and create a work of distinctive prison literature. More's account of the Passion reinforces the idea that following Christ entails loyalty, even martyrdom, in obedience to his Church, an obligation that includes unity under the papacy.[95] By the same logic, true martyrs are to be distinguished from pseudomartyrs; the former alone witness to the "true Catholic faith."[96] As the author of *De tristitia* and a prisoner of the regime, More's account of himself as a reluctant or fearful martyr offers an example to Catholics and a rebuke to Henrician schism.

Developed in this way, the Christological questions become a consideration of the merits of fearful martyrs such as More himself. "And yet for everyone who reads with the knowledge of this writer's situations," states Louis L. Martz, "the defense of the faint-hearted, fearful kind of martyr takes on a poignant personal application that cannot and should not be avoided."[97] In fact, More did confess to Margaret: "I found myself (I cry God mercy) very sensual and my flesh much more *shrinking from pain and from death* than it seems to me the part of a faithful Christian."[98] So, too, More's words to Master Leder, a priest to whom More writes from the Tower, amounts to a paraphrase of the above point from *De tristitia* about how the fearful martyr becomes brave: "And I trust both that they will use no violent forcible ways, and also that if they would, God would of his grace and ... a great deal through good folks' prayers give me strength to stand." In his letters, More appears fearful but reliant upon grace.

In another sense, More's famous "silence" against his accusers is no longer just a legal or prudential strategy. His reason for silence also comes from *De tristitia*. When More tells Master Cromwell that, unless God "draw" him to death, he cannot be "bold" in offering himself to that possibility, More advertises himself as a reluctant martyr.[99] More's strategy of silence parallels the prudent yet ultimately brave martyr, who nevertheless lives in fear before the moment of crisis arrives. Like the fearful martyr, More believes, if God brings him to the brink, he will provide the "strength to stand." From this standpoint, More's careful legal self-defense emerges as a test to see if God is drawing him to death.

Be that as it may, More identifies Christ's own fear as a source of strength for others such as himself in *De tristitia*. Christ foresaw how many "would be convulsed with terror at any danger of being tortured," and "He chose to enhearten them by the example of His own sorrow, His own sadness, His own weariness and unequalled fear, lest they should be so disheartened as they compare their own fearful state of mind with the boldness of the bravest martyrs" (*CW* 14.1:101/2–7). More, then, envisions Christ speaking to such a fearful one:

> O faint of heart, take courage and do not despair. You are afraid, you are sad, you are stricken with weariness and dread of the torment with which you have been cruelly threatened. Trust me. I conquered the world, and yet I suffered immeasurably more from fear, I was sadder, more afflicted with weariness, more horrified at the prospect of such cruel suffering drawing eagerly nearer and nearer. Let the brave man have his high-spirited martyrs, let him rejoice in imitating a thousand of them. But you, my timorous and feeble little sheep, be content to have me alone as your shepherd, follow my leadership; if you do not trust yourself, place your trust in me. See, I am walking ahead of you along this fearful road. (101/1–10 to 105/2)[100]

More, thereby, reverses Hilary's position and provides a counterintuitive conclusion by showing how the temporarily yet overwhelmingly fearful are closer to Christ than the constantly brave.[101] Christ does not set a poor example because he experiences human passion. Rather, he acts as a paragon. More triumphs in this dispute by creating a speaking Christ to counter an objecting Hilary, but he also drafts words of consolation for his own plight, for others, and for all those who will oppose heresy and schism in 1535.

In passages such as the one above, More develops his analysis of the Passion not only from the *Catena* but also in light of his own unique circumstances: "Indeed, the *De tristitia* gives us the fullest and deepest explanation of why More strove so intently to save himself from death by hiding behind the law, and it tells us better than anything else why More died, the motive of his martyrdom," writes Miller.[102] On that premise, More discloses his "motive" in developing materials from the *Catena* and by using them in his defense of fearful martyrs.

Like Martz's insistence upon the "personal application" of More's treatment of the Passion, Miller's "fullest and deepest explanation" pays tribute to the "devotional More" without reference to the political connotations of the pseudomartyr debate so important to More himself.[103] In other words, the "personal application" of More's writings on martyrdom also provides a political message that cannot and should not be avoided.

Before his arrest, More painted a catastrophic vision of rebellion, heresy, schism, and social chaos. These forces could "frame this realm" of England like "some other parts of Germany," where Lutheran sects had "pulled down the churches, polluted the temples, put out and spoiled all good religious folk, joined friars and nuns together in lechery, despited all saints, blasphemed our blessed lady, cast down Christ's cross, thrown out the Blessed Sacrament, refused all good laws, abhorred all good governance," and so on.[104] Though the gates of hell would not prevail over Christ's Church because of scripture's promise, Christ's words didn't protect countries beset by religious errors that had "swallowed whole countries up." "In other realms," thousands were "killed by schisms" already.[105]

Under these terms, defiance of the Catholic Church could never make for saints or martyrs. According to More, those who had died for the cause of evangelical reforms were the devil's martyrs.[106] When William Tyndale claimed that executed heretics were holy martyrs, More replied that "the great feast and glory of Tyndale's devilish proud heart dispiteous heart" was to take delight and even rejoice "in the effusion of such people's blood." Tyndale was proud of these deaths as a monument to himself. For his own "poisoned books had miserably bewitched" such people, "and from true Christian folk turned into false wicked wretches."[107] Even repentant heretics, More insisted, were not martyrs, but their executions could cleanse them of sin. Thomas Bilney, burned in Norwich on 19 August 1531, was More's case in point.[108] God accepted Bilney's "pain" as "that poor man's purgatory" and "hath forthwith from the fire taken his blessed soul to heaven," where Bilney prays for those he misled while on earth.[109]

For More and for most of the medieval theological tradition that he inherited, heresy was the result of pride, a deliberate choice and grave sin, an erroneous position to which one held with obstinacy, and for which one was damned to hell.[110] Pride was the mother of heresy and anarchy and so required urgent redress for the sake of peace in the realm and for a united Christendom.[111]

In contrast, More established the doctrinal grounds for valid martyrdom by his definition of the Church, which he called the commonly acknowledged "Catholic people, clergy, lay folk, and all which whatsoever their living be." These stand together "and agree in the confession of one true Catholic faith, with all old holy doctors and saints, and good christen people, beside that are already passed this fifteen hundred years before."[112] Such a Church began with Christ and "Peter his vicar after him," and "always since" the successors of Peter upheld Christ's "holy faith, and his blessed sacraments, and his holy scriptures delivered."[113] In More's view, true martyrs suffer for the sake of Catholicism, but pseudomartyrs do so for schismatic breaks or heresies.

With More's death, he became a martyr according to his definition of the Church, a witness to the "one true Catholic faith." Like the Carthusians who went before him, More's death amounted to what Anne Dillon calls "a new form of martyrdom," which was exclusively Catholic and witnessed to the authority of the pope.[114] To put it another way, More was a "new martyr" because he died in rejection of Henry VIII's denial of papal authority.[115] *De tristitia*'s originality, ultimately, owes less to its theological teaching and more to what that teaching imparts to its author and to his subsequent witness upon the scaffold in 1535.

Rastell recognized and appropriated this new kind of martyrdom.[116] He placed "a devout prayer, made by Sir Thomas More, knight, after he was condemned to die, and before he was put to death" in a collection of prayers that follows More's treatment of the Passion. There, More writes, "Good Lord, give me the grace in all my fear and agony to have recourse to that great fear and wonderful agony, that thou my sweet savior had at the mount of Olives before thy most bitter passion, and in the meditation thereof, to conceive spiritual comfort and consolation profitable for my soul."[117] Here "my fear and agony" parallel "my soul" and both formulations indicate the personal and political position of the petitioner in Rastell's presentation. More seeks comfort for himself, but he is also a type of the new kind of martyr, who is a fearful martyr besides. "Whoever is utterly crushed by feelings of anxiety and fear and is tortured by the fear that he may yield to despair," More writes in lines that applied to those persecuted like himself, "let him consider this agony of Christ, let him meditate on it constantly and turn it over in his mind." As such a new martyr, Rastell could see More suffering, like

Christ, for his friends, for the sake of English Roman Catholicism, and for a united Christendom.

More himself, though, had already imagined that others would follow his example as he followed Christ's own: "And in our agony remembering His, let us beg Him with all our strength that He may deign to comfort us in our anguish by an insight into His" (*CW* 14.1, 253/3–255/3). Others like More may humbly expect and faithfully hope for profitable "spiritual comfort and consolation" and the "strength to stand" against Henry. What More might have told his jailer after his books were removed takes on a new meaning. More closed his shop because his "implements" already produced the goods he needed.

OF SLEEPING APOSTLES

The propagandistic rather than devotional aims of More, finally, become most clear in analysis of his allegories. Just as More identified himself with a suffering Christ, so he associated the apostles, who abandoned their master in the garden of Gethsemane, with the bishops in England. In these sections of *De tristitia*, More's treatment of the Passion is no mere academic dispute or personal means of meditation.

More's concern over the sleeping apostles, after all, was personally involved and polemically motivated. He contrasts the alert Judas, who is wide-awake and intent upon betraying Christ, with the apostles who are buried in sleep, even after the third time that their lord returns to them, inciting them to stay awake and pray. More, in turn, expands the Gospel episode into an image of his times: "Does not this contrast between the traitor and the apostles present to us a clear and sharp mirror image (as it were), a sad and terrible view of what has happened through the ages from those times even to our own? Why do not bishops contemplate in this scene their own somnolence? Since they have succeeded in the place of the apostles, would that they would reproduce their virtues just as eagerly as they embrace their authority and as faithfully as they display their sloth and sleepiness!" (CW 14.1:259/7–261/1).[118]

To heighten the above, More called upon "the story of that time when the apostles were sleeping as the Son of Man was being betrayed" as a "mysterious image of future times" (*CW* 14.1:341/3–6): "I think we would not be far wrong if we were to fear that the time approaches when the son of man, Christ, will be betrayed into the hands of sinners." For such betrayal occurs "as often as we see an imminent danger that the mystical body of Christ, the church of Christ, namely the Christian people, will be brought to ruin at the hands of wicked men" (345/7–347/3). When the Church is destroyed or attacked, Christ's mystical body is crucified, an overtly polemical claim in 1535 against both heresy and schism.

Indeed, sleep becomes More's metaphor for placing the faith in jeopardy in general and for the dissolution of the Church in England. For the bishops "are sleepy and apathetic in sowing virtues among the people and maintaining the truth, while the enemies of Christ, in order to sow vices and uproot the faith (that is, insofar as they can, to seize Christ and cruelly crucify him once again), are wide awake" (*CW* 14.1:261/1–5). Judas-like, the enemies of the Church are energetic and cunning in their assaults. Meanwhile, Christ's representatives through apostolic successions are fearful or numbed by ambition or worldly pleasures. Because negligent bishops represented the apostles, while Cromwell and Henry played "other governors and other caesars" who sought the destruction of the Catholic Church, More claimed his age was the mirror image of this very scene of the Gospel.[119]

Such a final statement on the bishops of England represents not simply denunciation but also change in More. Though More had criticized clergy in the past, before the Submission of the Clergy to the royal supremacy on 15 May 1532, More had held many of England's bishops in high regard.[120] He wrote his *A Dialogue Concerning Heresies* to assist the ordinaries by defending their courts and techniques of investigation into heresy, a position he maintained in subsequent works, from his *The Debellation of Salem and Bizance* through to *The Apology of Sir Thomas More*, both of which were published in 1533 and after More resigned the chancellorship.[121] To give a sense of the sheer volume of ink poured in defense of clerical magistrates and courts, the *Debellation* and *Apology* alone run from pages 845 to 1034 in Rastell's edition, a total of 189 pages.[122]

In the *Dialogue*, More's admiration extended to the learning and leadership of bishops.[123] There, Tyndale's translation of and call for the scriptures in English meets with condemnation, but not because the

New Testament shouldn't appear in English. "It might be with diligence well and truly translated" either by some "good Catholic and well learned man" or a committee of them. "And after that might the work be allowed and approved by the ordinaries, and by their authorities so put unto print, as all the copies should come whole unto the bishops' hand."[124] In this way only could the "holy bible . . . be spread abroad in English." More was optimistic about this possibility in 1529, in part, because of England's prelates. The king himself may "move this matter unto the prelates of the clergy." Of these, More boasts: "I have perceived some of the greatest and of the best of their own minds well inclinable thereto already."[125] England's bishops are like good fathers, More concludes, and their discretion protects and guides their children in matters of faith.[126] As a result, the translation of scripture into English should be left in their hands.

These same great minds and good fathers, however, later caved to the king and left More without important allies. "It is well known," More lamented to Margaret, "that of them that have sworn it, some of the best learned before the oath [was] given them said and plain affirmed the contrary of some such things as they have now sworn in the oath."[127] In fact, the bishops "said and plain affirmed the contrary" in their oath to Rome. At their consecration, as Henry himself said, they made "an oath to the pope, clean contrary to the oath that they make to us." The bishops, Henry continued, had been the pope's "subjects" and "not ours."[128] By 1536, the bishops belonged to the king.

All the orthodox or conservative bishops—John Fisher (1469–1535), Henry Standish (d. 1535), Richard Nix (ca. 1447–1535), Cuthbert Tunstall (1474–1559), Stephen Gardiner (1483–1555), and John Longland (1473–1547)—were threatened or intimidated by Henry.[129] With the exceptions of Fisher and such bishops as Robert Sherborne (ca. 1440–1536), who resigned in 1536 in opposition to the royal supremacy, the rest capitulated.[130] Standish was forced to make his renunciation of papal authority on 1 June 1535, just a little more than a month before he died on 9 July.[131]

In *De tristitia*, More compares all bishops who relented to cowards who neglected their duties. They have abandoned their call as pastors out of fear and sadness. In commenting upon the sleepy apostles from the Passion, More writes:

> If a bishop is so overcome by heavy-hearted sleep that he neglects to do what the duty of his office requires for the salvation of his flock—like a cowardly ship's captain who is so disheartened by the furious din of a storm that he deserts the helm, hides away cowering in some cranny, and abandons the ship to the waves—if a bishop does this, I would certainly not hesitate to juxtapose and compare his sadness with the sadness that leads as [Paul] says, to hell; indeed, I would consider it far worse, since such sadness in religious matters seems to spring from a mind which despairs of God's help. (*CW* 14.1:265/1–10)[132]

The sadness of a fearful martyr, therefore, juxtaposes the sadness that leads to hell. A fearful martyr may be transformed by meditation upon the example of Christ, but fear and sadness can also become a person's undoing. If a bishop despairs of God's help, he will neglect to do "what the duty of his office requires for the salvation of his flock" and, returning to a comparison More makes often, he becomes "like a cowardly ship's captain."

The solution is to remain awake, a point More iterates frequently, but especially in regard to Christ's admonition that the apostles "stay awake and pray." We learn in these words, claims More, how prayer is "not only useful but also extremely necessary," for without it "the weakness of the flesh" holds back our mind and will, despite our best desires. Prayer sharpens reason and checks passion, allowing our better selves an opportunity to act or "reason to rule" (*CW* 14.1:167/7–171/5).

In More's association of constant prayer with alert captains, he expands upon the piloting metaphor for governance that he employs most famously in his *Utopia*, which urges political engagement and service because "you must not abandon the ship in a storm because you cannot control the winds."[133] In *De tristitia*, the Latin term for Miller's "ship's captain" is *gubernator* (helmsman/pilot). In *Utopia*, More refers to an effective helmsman who must guide the ship of state through tempests of difficulties.[134] But in *De tristitia*, More specifies energetic attention to duties of one's own state, which for bishops consist of unflagging attention to the common good of the flock brought about by the practice of incessant prayer. The polemical development from *Utopia* that More makes in *De tristitia* connects abdication of duty with sadness, a sadness that leads "to hell" because of the sin of despair.[135]

According to Roper, More complained to his daughter about England's "weak clergy," but in *De tristitia* we discover the standards by which More judges.[136] Bishops may experience sadness because they grieve for Christ's Church or, like others who supported the king, because they are "numbed and buried in destructive desires." Whether the causes are laudable or not, sadness must be "checked by the rule and guidance of reason." Otherwise, "sorrow so grips the mind that its strength is sapped and reason gives up" (*CW* 14.1:263/1–15). More's contrast between sleeping and wakeful states, finally, reveals his ideal: a bishop who should be a vigilant pilot or steersman of his own soul and of Christ's Church. Vigilant, awake, and alert pilots of the Church may experience fear, but the vocation and glory of a fearful martyrdom will be the surest sign of their discipleship.

RASTELL'S READERS AND MORE'S TIMES

By the time Rastell published More's *De tristitia*, some of the bishops More had criticized would have been alive to read it. Like others who served during the reigns of Henry VIII and Edward VI, a handful drifted along into the regime of Mary, returning to the Catholic positions where they first stood in opposition to the claims of royal supremacy.[137] Even so, I have argued how Rastell's audience in 1557 constituted a different readership and that More's original objectives were far more polemical than scholars have recognized.

More proposed a figurative reading of the Gospels that focused upon historical events and persons of his times and last days. These were the years of 1534–35 and especially the spring of 1535, the very same period when More witnessed the dismantling of Roman Catholic unity in England. He took these events to signify a second crucifixion, a sharp mirror image of the passion of Christ, because the mystical body of Christ, or his Church, was divided by schism. Rather than a retired or politically disengaged author, More painted a dramatic if not quite apocalyptic picture of the passion of Christ and loss of England's soul.[138] The bishops of his day were sleeping apostles, who despaired of help from God, or they were "drunk with the new wine of the devil, the flesh, and the world"; these slept "like pigs sprawling the mire" (*CW* 14.1:263/1–3). More wrote in Latin so that what happened in England would be a warning for the rest of Christendom. He made his Christ speak prophetically and perennially about "other governors and caesars," who could come for Christ's disciples in any age or regime.

Thus, attention to More's "inner man" or to his affinity with Erasmus's thought does not capture fully More's defiance of Henrician reforms. More's polemical design contrasts fearful martyrs with despairing minds. The former follow Christ unto the death, but others "cower away in a cranny" and leave the ship of state or the Church to tempests. In 1535, More's picture of fearful martyrs and despairing minds would have presented a stark disjunctive for Catholics under Henry: to "deny God" or "suffer torment" for true religion's sake.[139] Instead of quietism or apolitical contemplation of scripture, More's *De tristitia* boldly articulates a new kind of martyrdom, a call to give witness to Rome. More's treatment of the Passion, his selection and exegesis of commentary from the *Catena*, and his figurative readings all reveal how he understood his political situation as a person of Catholic faith caught between Henry VIII's agenda and the papacy in 1535. My reevaluation of *De tristitia* not only draws attention to a neglected area of source study but also suggests how More countered royal propaganda from his "shop" in the Tower of London.

Conclusion

The Case of Malicious or Merry More

In the popular imagination, More's stand against his king is best defined by either Fred Zinnemann's film *A Man for All Seasons* (1966) or Hilary Mantel's novel *Wolf Hall* (2009). Both focus on More's trial but diverge on the role played by Richard Rich (ca. 1496–1567). In the film version, which won six Academy Awards and was based upon Robert Bolt's play of the same title, Rich commits perjury. He receives the post of attorney general of Wales in exchange for it: "Why Richard, it profits a man nothing to give his soul for the whole world.... But for Wales!"[1] In the novel, which won the National Book Critics Circle Award and the Booker Prize, More is the one who denies his jury the truth, which Rich provides in his testimony. More's attack upon Rich's character is a subterfuge, an unfair assault, which conceals More's rebellious thoughts. Despite the stark contrast in these two depictions of the same trial, what More believed about the Church in England and his king's claim over it remains a subject of intense scrutiny and deep fascination.

May the same be said for More's last writings? We have seen how scholars gloss over the controversial aspects of More's Tower Works because they don't fit within Rastell's original canonical breakdown from 1557. According to Rastell's folio and early modern biographers, More stopped writing polemical literature in 1533. Hence scholars theorize multiple Mores. There is an early humanist, the subsequent hunter of heretics, and finally a heavenly minded saint.[2] The last is referred to as "devotional More," an author and person described as "charitable" by 1534 and in contrast to the figure immediately preceding him in 1533, the public author and controversialist More, or "the real Thomas More," a psychologically deranged man and crude propagandist.[3] Against the background of Rastell's pervasive and ongoing influence, scholars have been reluctant to reassess More's prison writings as works written in reply to his adversaries and in opposition to the Henrician Reformation.

What should we say about multiple Mores? Herein I have hoped to demonstrate how such divisions in More's canon and biography are serious distortions and failures to recognize, if not More's continuity in thought, then his complexity as an author. The hiatus between More's arrest in late April 1534 and the day his books were removed, 12 June 1535, provided him with productive months of writing. Immediately after his arrest, More began composing letters to this daughter that gave lawyerly and detailed accounts of his various interrogations, leaving a record of what was said and done, a record that exonerated him. Over the summer, he began work on his *Dialogue of Comfort* and finished the *Letter to Alington* by the end of August. Both were powerful rejoinders to Henry VIII's political maneuvering against him in 1534. More's *Letter to Alington* returned to rhetorical devices found in *Utopia*, and *De tristitia* revisited humanist roots, in particular, the debate between Erasmus and Colet over Christ's human nature from 1499. *De tristitia* was not just a humanist work of scholarship, but also a rebuke to the emergent Church of England. "Humanist More" and "controversial More" and "devotional More" were one and the same man. Of course, More adjusted his thought and language to the changing and evolving circumstances of 1534–35, yet his principles remained constant. For this reason, as I have argued, the last "phase" of More's canon may be read as polemical literature.

Let us return to More's exchange with Rich and examine how plausible it may be for More to have remained disputatious until the end. In the record of that conversation, we find More advancing his position according to his circumstances by the putting of cases, a ubiquitous practice among lawyers at the time. In Tudor law, "putting cases" was a form of "mooting" that referred to legal debate through forensic argument, pleading, and litigation.[4] Law students trained by discussion of a hypothetical case, otherwise known as a "moot."[5] A moot should be uncertain or doubtful, unable or difficult to be firmly resolved.[6] These hypothetical cases would help students learn how to apply "the sayings and order of the Bench"—or the legal precedents of common law—to a fabricated but difficult case.[7] "Putting the case" was a rhetorical exercise and a means of analysis, even an imaginative exercise. Moots might be absurd or without consequence because training in "the putting of cases" was "designed to stretch the mind."[8] Moots, finally and of note, were also a form of silence under the law. If one put cases, you speculated or hypothesized but didn't necessarily disclose what you thought.[9]

As Bolt and Mantel knew, More's most famous experience of "putting the case" occurred in his conversation with Rich on 12 June 1535. In the Tower of London, where More was imprisoned for his refusal to swear the "whole oath" to the Act of Succession, Rich put forward a "case" about the powers of Parliament. Suppose it were enacted by Parliament that he, Rich himself, should be king, would it be a treasonable offense to deny him the office? More consented Parliament could make Rich king. Then, More put a higher case. He asked if an act of Parliament could declare that God were not God. Rich conceded that Parliament could not and replied with a "middle-level case." If More agreed that Parliament could make Rich king, why wouldn't he consent to Parliament making King Henry VIII supreme head of the Church in England? "To this," so reads the indictment, "the said Thomas More falsely, treasonously, and *maliciously* persevering in his said treachery and *malice*, and desiring to put forth and defend his aforesaide treasonous and *malicious* proposal and appetite, responded to the aforesaide Rich that the cases were not a like because a king can be made by Parliament ... but to the case of a primacy, the subject cannot be bound."[10] Of the four indictments against More at his trial, this was the only one he lost and, on its count alone, was sentenced to execution. Putting cases about the king's new title, contrary to conventional practice, was not without criminal consequence. In the regime's pursuit of More, even speaking hypothetically could be enlarged unlawfully into a charge of malice and used against him.[11]

Or so More argued in his own defense. He denied Rich's testimony at trial, but he did propose or put a case in his defense: "And yet if I had done so indeed, my lords, as Master Rich hath sworn, seeing it was spoken in familiar secret talk, nothing affirming, and only in putting of cases without other displeasant circumstances, it cannot justly be taken to be spoken 'maliciously.' And where there is no malice, there is no offence."[12] More's characterization of his exchange with Rich indicates a collegial conversation according to the norms of the legal profession. "If I had so done indeed," More told his jury by way of proposing still another hypothetical case, then what he said "in familiar secret talk" was nothing other than the exercise of putting cases. More's points, if he said what Rich alleged, would be moot. The putting of cases was a technical form of legal discourse for exploring questions that differed from the discharge of conscience. More affirms nothing about what he believes in arguing this way. If he affirms nothing, he cannot be found guilty of malice.

More's defense on this point cleverly called attention to the extreme scope of the Treasons Act, which redefined "high treason" for the first time since 1352. Previously, "to compass or imagine" the death of the king, his queen, or his eldest son and heir was declared treason, but the new act expanded that crime to any "wish, will, desire, by words or writing," that the king should be denied his titles.[13] To argue against the laws of 1534, More claimed, would result in the destruction of his body. But support of them would mean the loss of his soul.[14] At his trial, even the putting of cases about these laws emerged as grounds of high treason, which at the same time was an assault upon how law could be discussed and analyzed. Legal argument itself could be grounds for execution. Such were the consequences when "malice" became the vehicle or excuse for conviction of high treason by words or verbal offense alone.

Even so, Rich's testimony and accusation seamlessly fit with years of legislation aimed at, in part, prosecution of More. The first instance of "malice" used against him came from the Act of Succession, where misprision of treason was applied against those who by "any words without writing, or any exterior deed or act, *maliciously* and obstinately publish, divulge, or utter anything or things to the peril of your Highness, or to the slander or prejudice of the said matrimony solemnized between your Highness and the Queen Anne, or to the slander or disherison of the issue and heirs which shall be inheritable to the crown of this realm."[15]

What was "maliciously" done took prominent place in the Treasons Act also, the same bill used in More's indictment, which declared it was treason to "*maliciously* publish and pronounce, by express writing or words that the king our sovereign lord should be heretic, schismatic, tyrant, infidel, or usurper of the Crown."[16] Variants of "malice," too, resound in the records of More's trial. At the start, we learn that More pleaded not guilty "and so reserved unto himself advantage to be taken of the body of the matter, after verdict, to avoid that indictment." But More also added that "if those only odious terms—'*maliciously*, traitorously, and diabolically'—were put out of the indictment, he saw therein nothing justly to charge him."[17] More's words here accurately pointed to the grounds of his conviction.[18] Malice or maliciousness were the key terms to be used against him, and they carried wide latitude and application. The laws quoted above illustrate the king's extension of malicious behavior from those who would deny his second marriage to anyone who found him to be a tyrant or schismatic.

Such a caveat, "if I had done so indeed," may also raise a question about what More did say or write about his king and the theological and political controversies of 1534–35. In other words, the debate between More and Rich suggests another hypothetical case to be made against More, whether he was malicious against his king in composing the Tower Works. Were his writings other instances of "secret, familiar talk" otherwise known as private and prayerful meditation? Or else were they fictive dialogues about suffering, "nothing affirming" about the events surrounding his imprisonment? Put differently, the charge of malice should be brought against "devotional More," who critics find to be charitably and serenely disengaged from theological and religious controversy.

In the preceding chapters, we have seen how More might have been accused on grounds more solid than Rich's testimony if only his last writings could have been submitted in evidence against him. More's *Treatise upon the Passion* invoked the Council of Florence and rebuked the Greek Church for schism, but the same point could be made against all breaks with Rome, including Henry's own. In *A Dialogue of Comfort*, Henry emerged no different from the Turk, a tyrant who worked on behalf of the midday devil, persecuting Christ's true disciples, or forcing them to declare, or convert to, a new religion. The *Letter to Alington* went further by juxtaposing all of Christendom against one part of it, a not so oblique way of contrasting England with the rest of the European Church still under the See of Rome. More's last major work, *De tristitia Christi*, compared ruptures in Christ's mystical body or in his Church to the Crucifixion itself. To be a true martyr meant being orthodox and obedient to the pope.[19] Throughout, More never referred to the king's new title explicitly. "If I had done so indeed" are words More used to adjust what he might have said against the claims of royal supremacy in "familiar talk" with Rich, but in his late writings we discover not what More hypothesized but what he believed.

So then, was More malicious or charitable, a polemical voice to be silenced or a devout mind better left to heaven? More protested that his beliefs, even before his trial and during the same period when he composed his Tower Works, coexisted with good will toward his king. "I am," More told Cromwell in May 1535, "the King's true, faithful subject." More famously adds: "I do nobody harm, I say none harm, I think none harm, but wish everybody good. And if this be not enough to keep a man alive in good faith I long not to live." Cromwell follows up by asking More to "confess it lawful that his Highness should be Supreme Head of the Church of England or else to utter plainly," of note, More's "malignity." More informs Margaret of this exchange that "I had no malignity and therefore I could utter none." So, he tells Cromwell, "I know very well that the time shall come, when God shall declare my truth toward his Grace and before him and all the world."[20] Instead of malice, More relies upon God to declare his truth to Henry.

What did More mean by invoking God as witness to his "truth"? What becomes evident in More's interrogations and in his prison writings is that good will carries two sets of connotations, where one sense of the term corroborates the charge of malice and the other implies heavenly charity, what More will refer to as "merriness." From the standpoint of the regime, any claim of good will means unflinching loyalty to the Crown.[21] To be a good subject entails acceptance of all the king's titles. Such an understanding represents not only the stance of Cromwell but also the king himself. Under these terms, More's defiance in his last writings is criminal. In contrast, More believed that his loyalties should not be divided between pope and king because Henry should give primacy to Rome in all matters that concern Church teaching. When there could be no way out from this impasse, Greg Walker argues, More's "assertion of good will took on an almost mystical association with the long durée of Catholic history viewed from the vantage point of eternity." Good will, thus, emerges in terms of heroic charity because "to wish all well in the face of the manifest malice of others was to be, like the first martyrs, part of a convivial communion of Christian fellowship."[22] For Walker, instead of showing malice, More rises above the malice shown by his adversaries against him. Seen in this light, More's prison writings would express his desire for "convivial communion" within Christendom and in obedience to the pope.

With these two senses of good will in mind, both More's defiance and his charity may be recognized at his trial. Or, if you prefer, both the "controversial More" and "devotional More" appear in the same person. As to the first, after receiving the verdict against him, More exposed the contradictions of Henry's case by calling attention to the Magna Carta, which secured the Church's freedoms in England against claims of empire. More referenced the king's coronation oath—Henry's own pledge to protect the Church, whose representatives he now labeled foreign and hostile powers. Henry had perjured himself, but More was jailed for his refusal to do the same. "No more might this realm of England," More said in an echo of the same thought we have seen in his polemical writings, "refuse obedience to the See of Rome than might the child refuse obedience to his own natural father." The bishops who agreed with royal supremacy made no difference. Outside of England, "well-learned bishops and virtuous men" agreed with More, as did the general councils of Christendom.[23] In sum, More spoke all that he avoided saying under interrogation in sentiments that expressed messages similar to those found in his last works.

With regard to charity, however, More's trial provided something equally important for understanding his *Dialogue*, *Letter to Alington*, and *De tristitia*, especially. In his final address to jurors, More made allusion to "Saint Stephen" and, instead of malice, invoked merriment. When asked if he had anything else say, More replied,

> More have I not to say, my lords, but like as the blessed apostle Saint Paul, as we read in the Acts of the Apostles, was present and consented to the death of Saint Stephen, and kept their clothes that stoned him to death, and yet be they now both twain holy saints in

heaven, and shall continue there friends forever, so I verily trust, and shall therefore right heartily pray, that though your lordships have now here on earth been judges to my condemnation, we may yet hereafter in heaven merrily all meet together, to our everlasting salvation.[24]

Under sentence of death, More's final words to his jurors were a customary mixture of humility and humor, irony and honesty—devotional and polemical considerations. His words both excuse and accuse. More's prayer to be merry with his jurors in heaven rebuts the charge of "malice" made against him, a word specially privileged in the charges against him. In terms of courtroom drama, "merry More" refutes the "malicious More" of the indictment.[25] There is also reprimand or sting. In drawing a parallel to Paul's approval of Stephen's death, More redescribes his guilty verdict in terms of religious persecution. More will accept the role of true martyr, sketched out already in *De tristitia*, but he will do so as he looks forward to the time when all shall be merry together in heaven. More wrote his Tower Works with the same hope.

APPENDIX
Key Dates

1532

24 February: William Warham, archbishop of Canterbury, publishes a formal protest, repudiating anything done in violation of Rome's ecclesiastical rights and authority.

March: Publishes *The Confutation of Tyndale's Answer I–III*. Act in Conditional Restraint of Annates passed.

13 May: House of Lords, under Thomas More's leadership, refuses to approve the Submission of the Clergy.

15 May: The Submission of the Clergy.

16 May: Resigns as chancellor of the realm.

Summer: More writes his epitaph, has it engraved on his tomb, and sends the text to Erasmus for publication. Archbishop William Warham is threatened with *praemunire* and prepares his speech in self-defense and on behalf of the liberties of the Church by invoking Thomas Beckett twenty-eight times; there are no formal proceedings, however, because Warham dies in August. His successor, Thomas Cranmer, marries in Nuremburg.

December: Anne Boleyn is pregnant. More writes his *Letter against Frith*.

1533

25 January: Henry VIII marries Anne in secret.

4 February 1533–7 April 1533: Parliament in session. The Act in Restraint of Appeals passed, declaring England an empire.

Spring: Publishes *The Confutation of Tyndale's Answer IV–VIII*.

30 March: Cranmer installed as archbishop of Canterbury and disavows papal authority.
April: *The Apology of Sir Thomas More* is published.
11 April: Cranmer's letter to Henry asking to judge the validity of the king's marriage to Katherine.
12 April: Henry grants permission to Cranmer. That night, Anne is presented at court as Henry's queen for the first time.
23 May: At Dunstable, Katherine of Aragon and Henry's marriage declared null and void by Cranmer.
28 May: At Lambeth, Anne and Henry's marriage declared valid by Cranmer.
1 June: Anne crowned in Westminster, but More doesn't attend her coronation.
11 July: Papal sentence conditionally excommunicating Henry.
11 August: Elizabeth Barton is questioned by Cranmer.
7 September: Anne gives birth to the future Elizabeth I.
November: Publishes *The Debellation of Salem and Bizance*.
16 November: Barton confesses her guilt.
23 November: Barton is forced to do penance at Paul's Cross in London.
December: Publishes *The Answer to a Poisoned Book* and *Letter against Frith*.
End of year: *Articles Devised by the Whole Consent of the King's Most Honourable Council* published.

1534

January: William Rastell, More's printer, is interrogated by Thomas Cromwell to determine whether More had written a reply to the *Articles Devised by the Whole Consent of the King's Most Honourable Council*.
15 January 1534–30 March 1534: Parliament in session. Bishops John Fisher and Cuthbert Tunstall told not to attend. Attainder of Elizabeth Barton and others passed. The Act in Absolute Restraint of Annates [and Election of Bishops] passed: Royal nomination of bishops and domination of the election of bishops becomes law; bishops now make an oath in fealty only to the king and his successors. The Act of Succession passed, which includes misprision of treason for oral attacks on Henry's marriage to Anne or for any

"obstinate" refusal to take an oath affirming the statute; effective 1 May 1534. The text of the oath is not specified.

January–April: More composes his *Treatise upon the Passion of Christ* in defense of the Eucharist and Catholic Church unity.

February: More writes to Cromwell that he did not publish or write against the king's recent *Articles*. Henry asks for More's indictment as an accomplice to Barton, but More's name is eventually removed from the final bill of attainder.

March: More writes to Cromwell and Henry to prove his innocence in the Barton case. Barton and six of her followers are indicted for high treason.

12 April: More summoned to Lambeth.

13 April: More refuses to take "the whole oath" to the Act of Succession.

17 April: More is sent to the Tower.

20 April: Barton is executed with her associates; on the same day, Londoners are summoned to take the oath to the Act of Succession.

May: More starts writing *A Dialogue of Comfort against Tribulation* from the Tower.

August: More writes the *Letter to Alice Alington* with Margaret More Roper, which addresses whether taking the oath is lawful. Cromwell reminds More that Parliament will reconvene.

3 November–18 December: Parliament in session. An Act Ratifying the Oath to Succession: includes the form of the oath considered valid. More is attainted of misprision of treason for not taking the oath: He loses his property, Margaret's visits are prohibited, and Cromwell's men raid More's estate. The Supremacy Act passed: Henry "justly and rightfully is Supreme Head of the Church of England" with no saving clause "as far as the law of God allows." The Treasons Act passed: it is high treason to deny the king or the royal family any of its titles, even by words, or to call the king a schismatic, tyrant, or heretic; takes effect 1 February 1535.

Christmas: Lady Alice writes to Henry, pleading for mercy and pardon for More.

1535

ca. January–June: More works on his *De tristitia Christi* (*On the Sadness of Christ*).

16 January: More writes to Master Leder, "a virtuous priest," that he trusts the king will use "no violent forcible ways." If torture is used, he prays that God will grant him the "strength to stand."

4 May: Margaret is allowed to visit her father again. More and his daughter watch three Carthusian priors and one Bridgettine monk leave for Tyburn, where they will be hanged, drawn, and quartered for their refusal to take Henry's oath and to deny that the pope is the true head of the Catholic Church.

7 May: More interrogated.

20 May: Fisher is made cardinal by Pope Paul III.

3 June: More interrogated.

12 June: More and Richard Rich "put cases" about the relative powers of Parliament and popes. More's books and writing materials are confiscated.

14 June: Final interrogation.

17 June: Trial of Fisher.

22 June: Execution of Fisher.

25 June: Henry orders that Fisher's and More's guilt be publicized.

1 July: More's trial at Westminster Hall.

6 July: Execution of More on Tower Hill.

1547: Edward VI becomes king after Henry VIII dies.

1553: Mary I becomes queen after Edward VI dies.

ca. 1556: William Roper writes his biography of More and commissions Nicholas Harpsfield to write an official biography.

1557: Publication in London of More's *English Works* in folio edition. Both Roper's and Harpsfield's biographies of More circulate in manuscript.

1558: Elizabeth I becomes queen after Mary I dies.

1563: Publication in Basil of *Thomae Mori Lucubrationes*.

1565: Publication in Louvain of More's Latin works, *Opera omnia*.

1588: Thomas Stapleton's *Tres Thomae* is printed at Douai.

1626: Roper's *Life of Sir Thomas More, Knight* is printed at St. Omer.

1886: Fisher and More are beatified by Pope Leo XIII.

1932: Harpsfield's *The Life and Death of Sir Thomas More, Knight* is published by Oxford University Press.

1935: Fisher and More are canonized by Pope Pius XI.

2000: More proclaimed patron saint of statesmen by Pope John Paul II.

NOTES

INTRODUCTION

1. The Convocation of the English Clergy, however, included only a handful of bishops present, and William Warham (ca. 1450–1532), archbishop of Canterbury, later argued that Henry's attack upon the rights of the papacy could not stand. See J. J. Scarisbrick, "Introduction to Archbishop Warham and His 1532 Defense," *Moreana* 58, no. 2 (2021): 206–17; and for Warham's argument, see Scarisbrick, "Archbishop William Warham's 1532 Defense," *Moreana* 58, no. 2 (2021): 218–35.

2. All quotations from Thomas More's writings are cited according to the list of abbreviations in the front matter. I have retained the Yale translations of More's Latin texts and cite the original language in my notes only for block quotations. A solidus (/), is used after the notation of page(s) to indicate cited line numbers for the Yale editions, letters from *Corr.*, and the *Letter to Alington* from *TMSB*.

3. For the *Apology*, see *CW* 9; for the *Debellation*, see *CW* 10; for *Answer*, see *CW* 11. All three were written in 1533.

4. More wrote against Henry's propagandist, Christopher St. German (ca. 1460–1540), whose attacks upon the clergy, John Guy has shown, were part of "royal propaganda justifying and exploring the nature of Henrician schism" (*CW* 10:xxi–xxii). At his resignation, More told Henry that he would not meddle in the king's public affairs, but St. German published anonymously, and this gave More an opportunity to write against the regime's policies without explicitly attacking Henry (see *CW* 10:xxiv–xxv). For discussion of the debate between St. German and More, see Henry Ansgar Kelly, "Thomas More on Inquisitorial Due Process," *English Historical Review* 123, no. 503 (2008): 847–94. On the rivalry between the Rastell family, printers of More's works, and the king's printer, Thomas Berthelet, see J. Christopher Warner, *Henry VIII's Divorce: Literature and the Politics of the Printing Press* (Rochester, NY: The Boydell Press, 1998).

5. On what constitutes the Tower Works, see *CW* 13:clxviii; *CW* 12:lvii–lix.

6. *CW* 12:200/21; 12:75/10. See the entry for "catholic" in the *OED*, I.1.a.iii and at I.1.b. "The term 'Catholic' acquired its modern meaning in the polemics of the sixteenth century"; see Lee Palmer Wandel, *The Eucharist in the Reformation* (New York: Cambridge University Press, 2006), 14. Kristen Deiter points out that More referred to the Catholic Church in "a strikingly modern sense" because, even though the Reformation began in England in 1534, "it had been raging in Europe since 1517," and More was an early, prolific, and public opponent of it; see Deiter, "Building Opposition at the Early Tudor Tower of London: Thomas More's *Dialogue of Comfort*," *Renaissance and Reformation* 38, no. 1 (2015): 40n61.

7. "And therefore sith all Christendom is one corps," More wrote to Cromwell in 1534, "I cannot perceive how any member thereof may without the common assent of the body depart from the common head" (*LL*, 54).

8. *CW* 8.1:478/1. In fact, More styled himself a defender of "any point of the common belief of Christ's Catholic Church" (*CW* 6.1:8/31–32; and see 6.1:116/24–25).

9. Jasper Ridley, *Statesman and Saint: Thomas Wolsey and Thomas More* (New York: The Viking Press, 1982), 276; William A. Clebsch, *England's Early Protestants, 1520–1535* (New Haven, CT: Yale University Press, 1964), 304. Early twentieth-century or "hagiographic" critics of More had emphasized More's early humanism or later "devotional" phases; see R. W. Chambers, *Thomas More* (London: Jonathan Cape, 1935; repr., Ann Arbor: University of Michigan Press, 1958; citations refer to the Michigan edition); and C. S. Lewis, *English Literature in the Sixteenth Century, Excluding Drama* (Oxford: Clarendon, 1954), 164–81, 191–92. Later "Revisionist" critics claimed to discover "the real Thomas More" in his polemics. For the founder of this school of thought, see G. R. Elton, "Thomas More and Thomas Cromwell," in *Studies in Tudor and Stuart Politics and Government*, Vol. 4, *Papers and Reviews, 1982–1990* (Cambridge: Cambridge University Press, 1992), 144–60; Elton, "Thomas More," in *Studies in Tudor and Stuart Politics and Government*, Vol. 3, *Papers and Reviews 1973–1981* (Cambridge: Cambridge University Press, 2002), 344–54. "Hagiographic" and "Revisionist" critics, however, agree that More's polemical phase of writing ended in 1533.

10. Joanne Paul, *Thomas More* (Cambridge: Polity Press, 2017), 87.

11. On the celebratory welcome by Catholics of Queen Mary to London, see Susan Brigden, *London and the Reformation* (Oxford: Clarendon, 1989), 525. On the Marian revival of More, see Roper, 254, which juxtaposes the wisdom of Emperor Charles with the folly of Henry VIII in a biography of More

composed in 1556. On how Roper designed his biography in praise of More, see R. S. Sylvester, "Roper's Life of More," *Moreana* 36 (1972): 47–59. On Thomas More's posthumous and early modern reputation, see Eamon Duffy, *Fires of Faith: Catholic England under Mary Tudor* (New Haven, CT: Yale University Press, 2009), 179–86. See, too, James K. McConica, "The Recusant Reputation of Thomas More," in *Essential Articles for the Study of Thomas More*, ed. Richard S. Sylvester and Germain Marc'hadour (Hamden, CT: Archon Books, 1977), 136–49; and Anne Dillon, *The Construction of Martyrdom in the English Catholic Community* (Burlington, VT: Ashgate, 2002), 36–52. On the legacy of More's thought, see Paul, *Thomas More*, 116–40.

12. More's death gave rise to the idea of "a merrier England," whether in reference to bygone days or to better ones in the future, according to Greg Walker, *John Heywood: Comedy and Survival in Tudor England* (Oxford: Oxford University Press, 2000), 183, and on the "politics of merriment," see 185–206.

13. The consensus view divides More's polemical works, ending in 1533, and his devotional ones, starting in 1534. See Louis A. Schuster, "Thomas More's Polemical Career, 1523–1533," in *CW* 8.3:1135–1268; Rainer Pineas, *Thomas More and Tudor Polemics* (Bloomington: Indiana University Press, 1968); Brendan Bradshaw, "The Controversial Sir Thomas More," *Journal of Ecclesiastical History* 36 (1985): 535–69; William J. Rogers, "Thomas More's Polemical Poetics," *English Literary Renaissance* 38 (2008): 387–407; David Lowenstein, "Religious Demonization, Anti-Heresy Polemic, and Thomas More," in *Treacherous Faith: The Specter of Heresy in Early Modern English Literature and Culture* (Oxford: Oxford University Press, 2013), 23–68; Uwe Baumann, "The Humanistic and Religious Controversies and Rivalries of Thomas More (1477/78–1535): A Typology of Religious Forms and Genres?," in *Forms of Conflict and Rivalries in Renaissance Europe*, ed. David A. Lines, Jull Kraye, and Marc Laureys (Göttingen: V&R unipress BmbH, 2015), 79–108. All these studies assume that More's polemical phase ends in 1533.

14. The "real Thomas More" is from Elton, "Thomas More," 344. For the biography of More approved by Elton, see Richard Marius, *Thomas More: A Biography* (New York: Vintage Books, 1985). For Elton's influence on Marius, see John Guy, *Thomas More* (London: Arnold, 2000), 49.

15. Lowenstein, "Religious Demonization, Anti-Heresy Polemic, and Thomas More," 23–25, and Alistair Fox, *Thomas More: History and Providence* (New Haven, CT: Yale University Press, 1985), 209, see also 1, 199–205, 209–53; Elton, "Thomas More," 344–54; and on More's supposed inner conflicts, see Marius, *Thomas More*, 519–20.

16. Cf. Elton, "Thomas More," 354: "The Thomas More of the 'Tower Works,' and of those last letters to Margaret Roper is, on the face of it, a very

different person from the persecutor of protestants, and the hammer of poor Christopher St German."

17. J. H. Baker, "William Rastell," in *ODNB*, 83.

18. In all, Rastell printed eighteen letters of More's.

19. On Totell's first printing of More's *Dialogue* in 1553 and Rastell's improvement upon it in the subsequent *Works*, see *CW* 12:xlix–lv. Rastell also included "A treatise to receive the blessed body of our lord, sacramentally and virtually" (less than six pages), and a miscellany of prayers and "certain devout and virtuous instructions, meditations."

20. *CW* 13:xxxvi.

21. For discussion of Rastell's distortions, see McConica, "Recusant Reputation," 138–49. Perhaps the most famous mistake, however, belongs to Harpsfield, 134–35, who claimed the *Dialogue of Comfort* and the *Treatise upon the Passion* were written with a piece of coal. We know from the Valencia manuscript of *De tristitia* that More had supplies of ink and pen. See *CW* 14.

22. In addition to the folio of More's *Works* and during the same year, Rastell published *The Collection of All the Statutes*, which contained all the public legislation still in force. A. W. Reed called the latter "an equally important work" to that of the *Works*; see Reed, *Early Tudor Drama: Medwall, the Rastells, Heywood, and the More Circle* (London: Methuen & Co., 1926), 87. Rastell's edition of the *Statutes* "was reprinted at the end of almost every session of parliament until the 1620's" (Baker, "William Rastell," in *ODNB*, 83).

23. K. J. Wilson, "Introduction," in *EW*, vii.

24. *CW* 13:xxxv, and *CW* 8.3:1422.

25. Wilson, "Introduction," vii.

26. *CW* 8:1423.

27. A. W. Reed, "William Rastell and More's English Works," in *The English Works of Sir Thomas More*, ed. W. E. Campbell, intro. and philological notes A. W. Reed (London: Eyre and Spottiswoode, 1931), 1:11, writes of Rastell: "His edition of the *English Works* was the fulfilment of a duty which he felt he owed to More, his religion and his country. Everything that William Rastell undertook to do he carried through."

28. Dale B. Billingsley, "The Editorial Design of the 1557 *English Works*," *Moreana* 23, no. 89 (1986): 43.

29. More was officially canonized at St. Peter's Basilica on Sunday, May 19, 1935, but Rastell already presented him as martyr and saint in 1557. John Guy reports that More's canonization was "hardly welcomed with open arms by the British establishment" when the moment finally arrived; Guy, *Thomas More: A Very Brief History* (London: Society for Promoting Christian Knowledge, 2017), 78. For discussion, see William Sheils, "1535 in 1935: Catholic Saints

and English Identity: The Canonization of Thomas More and John Fisher," in *Reformation Reputations: The Power of the Individual in English Reformation History*, ed. David J. Crankshaw and George W. C. Gross (Cham, Switzerland: Palgrave Macmillan, 2021), 159–88.

30. In More's time, New Year's Day was celebrated on 1 January, but the new year officially began on 25 March. Herein all dates are cited in New Style, marking the beginning of the year to 1 January.

31. The reigning critical consensus includes the *Treatise upon the Passion* as a Tower Work. For examples, see Seymour Baker House, "'The field is won': An Introduction to the Tower Works," in *A Companion to Thomas More*, ed. A. D. Cousins and Damian Grace (Madison, NJ: Fairleigh Dickinson University Press), 226; Peter Marshall, "The Last Years," in *CCTM*, 123; and Paul, *Thomas More*, who writes that More "continued to write in the Tower, producing there his *Treatise on the Passion*, his *Treatise to Receive the Blessed Body* and his *De tristitia Christi* (*On the sadness of Christ*)" (87). House and Marshall acknowledge William Rastell's 1557 edition as the basis for this grouping of texts.

32. On how More's earlier vernacular polemics were shaped by his responses to specific circumstances, events, and other authors, see Eamon Duffy, *Reformation Divided: Catholics, Protestants and the Conversion of England* (New York: Bloomsbury, 2017), 10–11, 50–132. Duffy uses More "to open the discussion of reformation as a field of contestation, between Catholics and Protestants" (11). The Tower Works, as polemical writings, extend that discussion. In contrast to a field of contestation so defined and for an account of reform movements, both Catholic and Protestant, over a two-century span, see Carlos M. N. Eire, *Reformations: The Early Modern World, 1450–1650* (New Haven, CT: Yale University Press, 2016). For studies of the English Reformation but with a focus on religion, see Peter Marshall, *Heretics and Believers: A History of the English Reformation* (New Haven, CT: Yale University Press, 2017); Richard Rex, *Henry VIII and the English Reformation*, 2nd ed. (New York: Palgrave Macmillan, 2006); and Alexandra Walsham, *Charitable Hatred: Tolerance and Intolerance in England, 1500–1700* (Manchester: Manchester University Press, 2006). For a compact overview of and introduction to "reformations" underway in early modern England, Alec Ryrie, *The English Reformation: A Very Brief History* (London: Society for Promoting Christian Knowledge, 2020).

33. The "Blessed Sacrament" receives such attention because it is "the most excellent, and of all holy sacraments the chief" (*CW* 13:152/23–25). For an introduction to Reformation disputes over the Eucharist, see Wandel, *The Eucharist in the Reformation*.

34. More calls his instructions "A warning to the Reader" (*CW* 13:50–51).

35. Clarence H. Miller's balance between political and devotional analyses of More's *De tristitia* should be applied to the *Dialogue*. For Miller, More wrote not only "to find relief from his emotional distress," but also to encourage "the suffering members of Christ's body," which included "his family and friends" and "all those who face martyrdom" during "his own and later times" (*CW* 14.2:748). The depiction of More as a politically disengaged author, in contrast, correlates with readings of the *Dialogue* as devotional or consolation literature alone. These eschew More's personal circumstances in favor of universal concerns and more literary rather than political readings. See Andrew W. Taylor, "'In stede of harme inestimable good': *A Dialogue of Comfort against Tribulation*," in *CCTM*, 216–38; R. J. Schoeck, "Thomas More's 'Dialogue of Comfort' and the Problem of the Real Grand Turk," *English Miscellany* 20 (1969): 23–37; and Manley, ed., *CW* 12:cxxi. Conversely, political readings reveal More's controversial purposes. Brad S. Gregory, for example, calls the Turkish invasion More's "thinly veiled reference to the Henrician religious settlement," in Gregory, *Salvation at Stake: Christian Martyrdom in Early Modern Europe* (Cambridge, MA: Harvard University Press, 1999), 108; and Leland Miles referred to More's book as an "allegorical smoke screen behind which to attack Henry VIII"; see Miles, introduction to *A Dialogue of Comfort against Tribulation* (Bloomington: Indiana University Press, 1965), xliii.

36. For More's *Dialogue* as a polemical reply against Henry, see Gabriela Schmidt, "'This Turk's persecution for the faith': Thomas More's *Dialogue of Comfort* and the Reformation Debate on Martyrdom," *Moreana* 45, no. 175 (2008): 209–38, who argues how the *Dialogue* is "the most enduringly successful" of all More's "polemical works" because of how it justifies his martyrdom. See also Ruth Ahnert, "Writing in the Tower of London during the Reformation, ca. 1530–1558," *Huntington Library Quarterly* 72, no. 2 (2009): 168–92, especially her comment on More's Tower writings: "Most of all, though, by writing, More is asserting that he is not daunted" (192). On the rebellion implicit in More's *Dialogue* and the contrast between More's sense of Catholicism and that of Henry VIII's, see Deiter, "Building Opposition at the Early Tudor Tower of London," 27–55, esp. 43 and 52.

37. For More's letters and his self-presentation, see Alison V. Scott, "More's Letters and 'the Comfort of the Truth,'" in Cousins and Grace, eds., *A Companion to Thomas More*, 53–76. "More's letters construct the icon of saintliness and 'other-worldly' detachment that is his legacy, but their contents are carefully contrived" and "cannot be taken at face value"; John Guy, *Thomas More* (London: Arnold, 2000), 175. On the *Letter to Alington*, see Elizabeth McCutcheon, "Decoding the Alice Alington–Margaret More

Roper Letters," *Moreana* 57, no. 2 (2020): 144–70; McCutcheon finds More to be "the chief writer."

38. Rather than focus on More's attempt to receive personal consolation by writing in the Tower, I follow Seymour Baker House's suggestion that More chose the scene in Gethsemane "to bear witness to those who will face similar persecution in the near future"; see House, "Endgame: The Genesis of More's *The Sadness of Christ*," *Moreana* 45, no. 174 (2008): 34.

39. Often ignored by commentators, More condemns schism with heresy and on equal terms because "never shall that country long abide without debate and ruffle where *schisms and factious heresies* are suffered a while to grow" (*CW* 8.1:29/27–29; my emphasis).

40. Anne Dillon, *Michelangelo and the English Martyrs* (Burlington, VT: Ashgate, 2012), 34–35 for quotations.

41. Peter Marshall, *Heretics and Believers*, 225, also notes that More believed "papal headship was the indispensable cement of orthodoxy and unity." But Marshall adds: Henry VIII's attack upon the papacy "was turning Catholics—some Catholics—into *Roman* Catholics." As a result, Henry "was the creator of English Roman Catholicism just as much as he was the progenitor of 'Anglicanism.'"

CHAPTER ONE

1. For "devotional More," see Lowenstein, "Religious Demonization, Anti-Heresy Polemic, and Thomas More," 23–25.

2. I showed in my introduction that the breakdown of More's canon into separate phases represents scholarly consensus. For another representative statement of More's overlapping life and works, which includes "a humanist phase from 1506 to 1516; a polemical, anti-Lutheran phase from 1520 to 1533; and a devotional phase from 1534 to 1535," see James Simpson, "Rhetoric, Conscience, and the Playful Positions of Sir Thomas More," in *The Oxford Handbook of Tudor Literature*, ed. Mike Pincombe and Cathy Shank (Oxford: Oxford University Press, 2009), 128. Simpson's designations mirror Rastell's own. On how such divisions traffic in overgeneralizations and errors, see Travis Curtright, *The One Thomas More* (Washington, DC: Catholic University of America Press, 2012).

3. *EW*, sig. C$_2$.

4. On King Edward VI's advance of Reformation teachings through print, see Andrew Pettegree, "Printing and the Reformation: The English Exception," in *The Beginnings of English Protestantism*, ed. Peter Marshall and Alec Ryrie (Cambridge: Cambridge University Press, 2002), 157–79, who

concludes that the "Protestant publishing offensive was deliberately fostered by those at the very heart of the Edwardine regime" (173).

5. The title page even references its Marian audience: *The Life and Death of Sir Thomas More, Knight, Sometimes Lord High Chancellor of England, Written in the Time of Queen Mary by Nicholas Harpsfield.*

6. Eamon Duffy, *Fires of Faith: Catholic England under Mary Tudor* (New Haven, CT: Yale University Press, 2009), 179–81. Duffy shows that Roper's and Rastell's development of More's writings and reputation should not be separated from Cardinal Pole's wider plans for the restoration of Catholicism and that Harpsfield composed his *Life of More* at the end of 1556. See also Dillon, *Construction of Martyrdom*, 45, who calls Harpsfield's *Life* "a compendium" because it included "the Vita of a humanist martyr," "an outline of Catholic teaching through a review of More's works, and it was a polemic and justification of the religious persecution of the Marian Church through a reiteration of More's teaching on heresy and through his own martyrdom."

7. Harpsfield, 5.

8. On the date when More's books were removed, see *CW* 14.2:738n4.

9. *EW*, 1035: "by sir Thomas More knight. Anno. 1533. after he had geven over the offyce of Lorde Chauncellour of Englande."

10. More's message to the Christian reader first appeared in 1533, and Rastell subsequently printed it in multiple copies of the *EW* from 1557. There, however, More's note is printed on a leaf tipped in between sigs. CC_5v and CC_6 (pages 1138 and 1139) that divided controversial works from 1533 and Tower Works from 1534: "Nor never purpose while I live, wheresoever I may parceive, either mine adversary to saye well, or my self to have saide otherwise, to let for us both indifferently to declare and saye the truth. An surely if they would use the selfsame honeste plaine truthe towarde me, you shold sone see good reders all our contecions ended."

11. See Hitchcock's editorial notes in the marginalia for Harpsfield's extensive use of Roper in Harpsfield, 171–204. Roper also consulted the prison letters that Rastell planned to print. See Guy, *A Daughter's Love*, 274, 328.

12. Roper, 241 (my emphasis).

13. Roper, 239, with glosses inserted from 239n8–9; and cf. Harpsfield, 171.

14. *EW*, 1349.

15. *EW*, 1350.

16. The running head "A treatice upon the passion" covers the entirety of *De tristitia*. See *EW*, 1319–1404.

17. "Syr Thomas More wrote no more of this woorke: for when he had written this farre, he was in prison kepte so streyght, that all his bokes and

penne and ynke and paper was taken from hym, and sone after was he putte to death" (*EW*, 1404).

18. "and after all the apostles were fledde away, and finallye after the yonge manne whom they were not able to kepe (as sure holde as they had of hym) was scaped stoutly (naked as he was) from them, that they after al this, dyd they first lay hands upon Jesus" (*EW*, 1404).

19. On the unfinished state of More's text, see *CW* 14.2:738–39. The signed holograph of *De tristitia* was held in the Real Colegio Seminario de Corpus Christi in Valencia, Spain, but "the anglophone academic world" didn't know of its location or existence until Andrés Vázquez de Prada, biographer of More, showed microfilm of the manuscript to Geoffrey Bullough of King's College in December 1963. This discovery meant that Clarence Miller could consult the Valencia manuscript in time for his preparation of the Yale critical edition of *CW* 14, parts 1 and 2. See Frank Mitjans, "The 'Discovery' of the Autograph of Thomas More's *De tristitia Christi* through Andrés Vázquez de Prada," *Moreana* 58, no. 1 (2021): 112–24.

20. Stapleton, 37.

21. *CW* 14.1:565/6–8.

22. "But Lorde howe harde a matter is it to love, and not disclose it. This young man for all he was amongest the thickest of them that mortally maligned Christ, yet by his pase & other his demeanor so bewrayed he him self, that they al might wel perceve, that he whan all the reste had forsaken hym, thus folowed Christe still, not to hurte hym, but meanyng to dooe him service. Wherupon they espyeng at length that al the remant of Christes company wer fled away, upon this yong man in a gret fury began they to take hold, whom they saw al alone so boldelye folowyng him" (*EW*, 1400–1401); cf. *CW* 14.1:581/2–582/1.

23. "the body is lyke a garmente to the soule, whiche the soule putteth on when it first entreth into the worlde, and whan by death it departeth hence, casteth of[f] agayne" (*EW*, 1402; cf. *CW* 14.1:605/8–10).

24. "we shal therewith become fresh and yonge agayne, and so be shortelye caryed up into heaven, where we shall never waxe olde after" (*EW*, 1403; cf. *CW* 14.1:615/4–617/6).

25. Harpsfield, 134–35, also asserts that More's Tower Works were divinely inspired and evidence of More's holiness.

26. Stapleton, 69, writes of More that "sometimes he used to go on pilgrimages to shrines distant as much as seven miles from his home" so that he could "fortify himself" before he "undertook any business of difficulty."

27. See *CW* 6.2:486, where Marc'hadour calls Willesden "a place of frequent resort for More" because "his daughters were married there in 1525 in

the private chapel of his stepchild Alice Alington, and in *the last week of his freedom* we find him writing 'from Willesdon' to his secretary" (my emphasis). Frank Mitjans follows Marc'hadour but posits that the letter was written on Easter Sunday, 5 April; see Mitjans, "Thomas More's Veneration of Images, Praying to Saints and Going on Pilgrimages," in *Thomas More Studies* 3 (2008): 67n7. On Harris, Stapleton calls him "a man of great industry, well versed in literature and a first-rate Patristic scholar" (xv; and see *LL*, 162).

28. As early as 1917, Joseph Delcourt pointed out how More's letter to Harris overturned the assumption that the *Treatise* was a Tower Work, but More scholars favored early modern biographers instead. See J. Delcourt, *Essai sur la langue de Sir Thomas More* (Paris: H. Didier, 1914), 370–71. On Rastell's handling of the letter to Harris, see *CW* 13:xxvii.

29. On the composition date of More's *Answer*, see *CW* 11:lxxxvii, which suggests the "last three of four months of 1533." On 1 February 1534, More informed Cromwell that copies had been sold before Christmas 1533. It is most likely that More began work on the *Treatise* after the holiday. More's letter to Harris is in *SL*, 185–87. On More's arrest shortly after completing the *Treatise*, see Peter Ackroyd, *The Life of Thomas More* (London: Chatto & Windus, 1998), 350. Ackroyd believes these were final corrections that More made "to put his life in order" and before being summoned to take the oath.

30. *EW*, 1351. The printed page number, 1319, is an error. Basset's actual title appears like a section heading in Rastell's edition.

31. *EW*, 1350.

32. *CW* 14.2:740.

33. "This worke in latine hath been by sondrye great clarkes read and wayed, and veary well lyked, and is agayne so sette oute in oure tongue, and goeth so nere sire Thomas Mores own english phrase that the gentlewoman (who for her pastyme translated it) is no nerer to hym in kynred, vertue and litterature, than in his Englishe tongue" (*EW*, 1350).

34. *EW*, 1350.

35. On printing translations to further familial, religious, and political ends, see Brenda M. Hosington, "Translation in the Service of Politics and Religion: A Family Tradition for Thomas More, Margaret Roper and Mary Clarke Basset," in *In between Scylla and Charybdis: Learned Letter Writers Navigating the Reefs of Religious and Political Controversy in Early Modern Europe*, ed. Jeanine De Landtsheer and Henk Nellen (Leiden: Brill, 2010), 93–108.

36. *CW* 14.2:724–35.

37. On Basset's expertise and Rastell's edition, see Brenda M. Hosington, "Translating Devotion: Mary Roper Basset's English Rendering of

Thomas More's 'De tristitia ... Christi," *Renaissance and Reformation*, 35, no. 4 (2012): 63–95.

38. *EW*, 1350.

39. *EW*, 1350.

40. On More giving his manuscript to Margaret in the Tower, see Guy, *A Daughter's Love*, 250. In Guy's depiction, More's "secret"—or the reason why he refused to take the oath—was disclosed with this gift.

41. See *CW* 14.2:748.

42. *CW* 14.2:741.

43. On merchant and lay readers, see Anne F. Sutton, "Merchants," and Mary C. Erler, "The Laity," in *A Companion to the Early Printed Book in Britain, 1476–1558* (Cambridge: D. S. Brewer, 2019), 127–33, and 134–49. Fifty-one of Henry VIII's 112 ambassadors were gentlemen or nobles, according to L. MacMahon, "The Ambassadors of Henry VIII: The Personnel of English Diplomacy, 1500–1550" (PhD thesis, University of Kent, 2000), 116–17.

44. Guy, *Thomas More*, 203. See also More's biographer Richard Marius, "Henry VIII, Thomas More, and the Bishop of Rome," *Albion: A Quarterly Journal with British Studies* (Quincentennial Essays on St. Thomas More) 10 (1978): 95, who claims, "It is clear that in the *Assertio* Henry VIII made much of papal authority and that Thomas More never did." Brian Gogan, *The Common Corps of Christendom: Ecclesiological Themes in the Writings of Sir Thomas More* (Leiden: E. J. Brill, 1982), 341, 365, calls More "a papal moderate" and believes he "remained an unrepentant 'populist' to the end."

45. Henry was already declared "supreme head of the Church of England" with "no superior under God but only your Grace" in the act forbidding payment of Peter's Pence from March 1534, which also attacked the pope for pretending to wield authority in England. The law was passed the same month as More's letter to Cromwell. See *Statues of the Realm*, 3:464–65.

46. I cite Henry from the translation of Richard Rex, "The Religion of Henry VIII," *The Historical Journal* 57, no. 1 (2014): 29. For the original, see Henry VIII, *Assertio septem sacramentorum*, ed. P. Fraenkel (Munster: Aschendorf, 1992), 128 and 130. On the genesis of Henry's *Assertion*, see the introduction to Rex, ed., *Henry VIII and Martin Luther: The Second Controversy, 1525–1527* (Woodbridge: The Boydell Press, 2021), 1–13.

47. *CW* 5.1:141/7–16. Cf. *CW* 5.1:140/5–14: "Cui sedi ut obedienter obtemperem cum illa movent omnia: quae docti sanctique in eam rem collegerunt: tum illud profecto non movet minime: quod toties sumus experti, non modo neminem inimicum fuisse christianae fidei: qui non illi sedi bellum simul indixerit: sed etiam neminem unquam extitisse qui se professus sit eius

sedis inimicum: quin idem paulo post se declararit insigniter, Christique, et religionis nostrae capitaliter hostem, et proditorem esse." The marginal note for these passages at *CW* 5.1:141 highlights the same point: "That no one has resisted the Roman See who did not also throw off the yoke of Christ" (Nullum recalcitrasse Romanae sedi: qui non Christi quoque iugum excusserit).

48. *CW* 5.1:141/25–29.

49. In the interim, beginning in 1528 or 1529, Henry moved toward William Tyndale's position on obedience to princes and fashioned a divine right kingship. See Richard Rex, "The Crisis of Obedience: God's Word and Henry's Reformation," *The Historical Journal* 39, no. 4 (1996): 863–94.

50. *CW* 8.1:131/31–3; 132/1–9.

51. *CW* 8.3:1508, commentary on 132/7–9.

52. More deferred to the same Council of Florence in defining the primacy of the pope in his *Responsio* at *CW* 5.1:138/33–140/3. On the Greek agreement to papal authority, see Deno J. Geanakoplos, "The Council of Florence (1438–1439) and the Problem of Union between the Greek and Latin Churches," *Church History* 24, no. 4 (1955): 324–46.

53. *CW* 13:267, commentary on 88/22–90/14. The additional sections are printed at 88/22–90/14 and at 91/14–22. Rastell included them both. See *EW*, 1308–9, and *CW* 13:xxvii.

54. "I wold not good readers stick so long upon the declaracion of this poynte, (as a thynge wherein some shall peradventure take lyttle savour) savyng that I thought it not a tyme all lost, to lette you knowe that upon the scrypture in this poynte mysse taken, the churche of Greece fell fro the churche of the Latyns in a poynte or twayne" (*CW* 13:88/12–17).

55. *CW* 13:89/19–90/14 and 92/22.

56. Hence, John 13:1–2 refers to Holy Thursday as the day "before" the feast of the paschal lamb because the first day of the Feast of Unleavened Bread, by Jewish custom, began the night before, "as we might call Christmas even the day before the feastful day of Christmas" (*CW* 13:88/5–11). On the conflation of Passover with the Feast of Unleavened Bread, see Luke 22:1.

57. *CW* 13:87/30–32.

58. *CW* 13:92/12–13.

59. Hence, More was no "Conciliarist," according to Paul Akio Sawada, "Was Thomas More a 'Conciliarist'?," in *Thomas More ... and More: Freundesgabe für/Liber Amicorum for Hubertus Schulte Herbrüggen*, ed. Christoph M. Peters and Friedrich-K. Unterweg (Frankfurt am Main: Peter Lang, 2002), 73–88.

60. *CW* 13, 91/28–92/1–3.

61. "But surely the church of Greece was farre over seene in this poynte and dyvers other, in which they partely knowledged their errours after, and were refourmed in general counsailes, and yet retourned of frowardnes to their errours agayne, and in conclusyon we see wherto they be comen" (*CW* 13:91/22–27).

62. "Certe si quis rerum gestarum monumenta revoluat: inveniet iam olim, protinus post pacatum orbem, plerasque omnes christiani orbis ecclesias, obtemperasse Romanae. Quin Graeciam ipsam, quamquam ad ipsos commigrasset imperium: reperiemus tamen: quod ad ecclesiae primatum pertinebat: praeterquam dum schismate laborabat, ecclesiae Romanae cessisse. Beatus vero Hieronymus quantum Romanae sedi censeat deferendum: vel inde luculenter ostendit: quod quum romanus ipse non esset: tamen aperte fatetur, sibi satis esse: si suam fidem, quibusuis improbantibus aliis, comprobaret papa Romanus" (*CW* 5.1:344/20–26). For the translation cited in the text, see 345/24–34.

63. *CW* 13:92/5–6.

64. "If the church which Luther calls papist is not the church of Christ," More asserts, "it necessarily follows either that the church of Christ is nowhere or that it is only in whatever place there are two or three heretics buzzing in a corner about Christ" (*CW* 5.1:119/27–30).

65. Popes Martin V (1369–1431), Alexander VI (1431–1503), Leo X (1475–1521), and Clement VII (1478–1534) all issued similar dispensations. The definitive bull *Deus qui Ecclesiam* by Innocent III (1161–1216) made clear there was no impediment in divine or natural law against a man marrying his brother's widow. For a comprehensive overview of the cases both for and against Henry, see J. J. Scarisbrick, "The Canon Law of the Divorce," in *Henry VIII* (Berkeley: University of California Press, 1968), 163–97.

66. *CW* 13:92/5–6.

67. *CW* 13:112/4–113/6.

68. See Rastell's marginal notes listed in *EW*, 1307–9.

69. Roper, 248.

70. "ffor that primatie is at the leist wise instituted by the corps of Christendom and for a great urgent cause in avoiding of scysmes and corroborate by continuall succession more than the space of a thowsand yere at the liest ffor there are passed almoost a thowsand yere sith the tyme of holy Saynt Gregory" (*Corr.*, 498/227–31).

71. "But surely after that I had redd his Grac*is* boke therin, and so many other thing*is* as I have sene in that point by this continuaunce of these x yere synnys and more have founden in effecte the substaunce of all the holy doctors from Saynt Ignatius, disciple to Saynt John th'Evangelist, unto our awne dayes both Latynis and Grekis so consonaunt and agreing in that point, and the

thing by such generall counsailis so confirmed also, that in good faith I never neither redd nor herd eny thing of such effect on the tother syde, that ever could lede me to thinke that my conscience were well discharged, but rather in right great perell if I shold follow the tother syde and deny the primatie to be provided by God" (*Corr.*, 498/214–25).

72. Elton, *Policy and Police*, 417, calls More's argument for papal primacy in his letter to Cromwell "shaky ground" but thinks the argument at trial was better "if, once again, we may trust Roper." Most recently, Paul, *Thomas More*, 113, writes of More's trial speech: "We might wonder if it was an addition made by Roper, who was writing under the Catholic Mary I."

73. Guy, *Thomas More*, 204.

74. *Corr.*, 498/229–234.

75. *SL*, 212. More also cited Henry with approval against Luther on the question of papal primacy: Luther "distinguishes the church of the pope from the church of Christ, whereas the pope is head of the same church of which Christ is." As a result, Luther "says that the church has invented what she did not invent but received as instituted" (*CW* 5.1:117/31–35). For More, the Catholic Church, under the pope, was the Church instituted by Christ.

76. Roper, *The Life of Sir Thomas More*, *TMSB*, 48. When Luther accused Henry of not writing the *Assertion*, Henry replied: "yet is well known for mine and I for mine part avow it" (Rex, *Henry VIII and Martin Luther*, 79).

77. Wolsey and Henry recognized the diplomatic advantages of papal support and the need to suppress Lutheranism at home by 1520. See Cecilia A. Hatt, introduction to John Fisher, *English Works of John Fisher, Bishop of Rochester (1469–1535): Sermons and Other Writings, 1520–1535*, ed. Cecilia A. Hatt (Oxford: Oxford University Press, 2002), 48–54.

78. Fisher, *English Works of Fisher*, 79, and see 80–83. Erasmus, too, had come to accept papal primacy as a matter of faith; see Harry J. McSorley, "Erasmus and the Primacy of the Roman Pontiff: Between Conciliarism and Papalism," *Archiv für Reformationsgeschichte* 65 (1974): 37–54. Brian Gogan, *The Common Corps of Christendom* (Leiden: E. J. Brill, 1982), 430, notes that what persuaded Erasmus "was his growing awareness of the decrees of the council of Ferrara-Florence. It may well be that he learned of these from More's *Responsio* as well as Fisher's *Confutatio*."

79. Fisher, *English Works of John Fisher*, 52–53. More himself may have been convinced of papal primacy because of Fisher. In More's *Responsio ad Lutherum* (1523), he writes: "Certainly, as far as the primacy of the pope is concerned, the same venerable bishop [John Fisher of Rochester] rendered the matter very clear from the gospels, from the Acts of the Apostles, from the whole body of the Old Testament, from the agreement of all the holy

fathers, not only the Latin but also the Greek, of whose extreme opposition Luther likes to boast, and finally from the fact the Armenians and Greeks were defeated, and admitted themselves defeated, by definition of a general council after the most stubborn resistance" (*CW* 5.1:139–41). More refers here to the Greeks and Armenians who acknowledged the universal authority of the pope as father of all Christians at the Council of Florence.

80. Rex, *Henry VIII and Martin Luther*, 129–31 (my emphasis).

81. Rex, *Henry VIII and Martin Luther*, 119, 183, and see 43 for where Henry started to agree with Luther about the papacy in July 1529, that is, when Cardinal Lorenzo Campeggio halted Henry's canonical tribunal.

82. On Henry's "conversion" to the "truth about royal power," see Richard Rex, "The Religion of Henry VIII," *The Historical Journal* 57, no. 1 (2014): 31.

83. *SL*, 214. To make good on this claim, however, More suppressed publication of his last book against Tyndale, which did support papal primacy. Rastell printed it in his 1557 folio; see *CW* 8.2:993–1011. Thus, More confessed to Cromwell in 1534: "But whereas I had written thereof at length in my *Confutation* before, and for the proof thereof had compiled together all that I could find therefore, at such time as I little expected that there should fall between the King's Highness and the Pope such a breach as is fallen since, when I after that saw the thing likely to draw toward such displeasure between them, *I suppressed it utterly and never put word thereof into my book*, but put out the remnant without it" (*SL*, 214; my emphasis). The "remnant" refused to define the papacy as part of the Church because if the pope were the "necessary head," he would be included already in the definition of the Church "in the name of the whole body" (*CW* 8.2:576–77). In the book that More suppressed, however, he argued for a "known head" of the Church and claimed that those who are "against all the known church and all the known heads thereof from Christ's days to their own" are the same people who "fall from Saint Peter and refuse him for head of the church and so forth down all the remnant of his successors by row" (*CW* 8.2:1010).

84. John M. Headley, ed., *CW* 5.2:771. Headley adds in the same paragraph: "In affirming his obedience to the divinely established See of Peter, More was not promoting the authority of the pope to the detriment or neglect of councils. Nevertheless, he saw that the papacy provided the only satisfactory and continuing touchstone to the visible, well-known church which he had earlier been satisfied to define in terms of agreement achieved through the Holy Spirit."

85. More's Latin writings, however, were another matter. In his *Response to Luther*, More upholds the pope as "ecclesiae caput et primas" for the following reason: "Because of the steadfastness of Peter's faith, Christ made him

the head and primate of His church, as a rock standing in His own place, not as though Peter were immortal and so could hold office forever, but many would successively follow him into that office, and these not all of equal merit" (*CW* 5.1:134/17, 135/17–22). On how England's commitment to orthodoxy wanes in the 1520s, see Richard Rex, "The English Campaign against Luther in the 1520s: The Alexander Prize Essay," *Transactions of the Royal Historical Society* 39 (1989): 85–106.

86. *CW* 13:clxviii.
87. *CW* 12:lvii.
88. *CW* 14.2:737, and 737n4.
89. *CW* 12:lxxxiv.
90. *CW* 12:lxxxv.
91. Haupt (editor) writes: "We have every reason to believe that Rastell was a good editor, and although we cannot know what minor changes he may have made, it seems clear that his major changes were editorial liberties for which he no doubt felt (I believe correctly) that he had More's license. I have therefore chosen 1557 as copy text because it doubtless reflects More's intentions and because it is the text which has already entered the literary tradition" (*CW* 13:xxxvi).
92. The "unanimity of Harpsfield and Stapleton concerning the *Treatise*" as a Tower Work, writes Haupt (editor), "is not without weight, and, of course, Rastell's testimony in *EW* is not to be taken lightly" (*CW* 13:xxxix). But Harpsfield and Stapleton wrote in compliance with Rastell's edition, the very edition Haupt was able to challenge at the time of the Yale critical edition of the *Treatise*.
93. Harpsfield, 100; for his extensive borrowing from the *Works* in attacking heresy, see 114–31.
94. Harpsfield, 132.
95. Stapleton, 37. Piety included More's public defenses of the Church, which Stapleton particularly valued: "It was from his deep religious sentiment that flowed the ardent zeal which animated him for the defense and the exposition of the Catholic faith against the heretics. *He, unaided, did more in this field of labour than all the English clergy of that together.* Layman though he was, and constantly busied with affairs of State, he yet made time for this work; and although he was so high in honour, he did not disdain the ungrateful task" (Stapleton, 69; my emphasis).
96. Chambers, *Thomas More*, 315.
97. E. E. Reynolds, *St. Thomas More: A Great Man in Hard Times* (Post Falls, ID: Mediatrix Press, 2017), 365, which reprints the original Image Books editions of 1958.
98. Marius, *Thomas More*, 483.

99. John Guy, *A Daughter's Love: Thomas & Margaret More* (London: Fourth Estate, 2008), 265–74.

100. See Ackroyd, *The Life of Thomas More*, 348, who accurately dates the *Treatise* as a pre-arrest composition but claims that More wrote it as "a means by which he prepared himself for his own death ... since by meditating upon the torments of Christ More was better able to understand and endure those which he anticipated for himself." Writing as preparation for death are other words for "devotional More."

101. Chambers, *Thomas More*, 313–14.

102. Reynolds, *St. Thomas More*, 321–22.

103. Reynolds's interpretation is echoed as a fact in commentary upon *CW* 12:208/3–11 at 12:415.

104. Elton, "Thomas More," 354–55.

105. See G. R. Elton, "Thomas More and Thomas Cromwell," in *Studies in Tudor and Stuart Politics and Government*, Vol. 4, *Papers and Reviews 1982–1990* (Cambridge: Cambridge University Press, 1992), 144–60; and for a response, see Curtright, *One Thomas More*, 3–10.

106. For criticism of Elton's legacy in the field of Tudor history, see G. W. Bernard, *Who Ruled Tudor England: Paradoxes of Power* (London: Bloomsbury, 2023).

107. Marius, *Thomas More*, 471–72; Ackroyd, *The Life of Thomas More*, 361.

108. Marius, *Thomas More*, 472; Ackroyd, *The Life of Thomas More*, 361.

CHAPTER TWO

1. *Corr.*, 552/66–8.

2. *CW* 13:xxxix. Hereafter cited in-text by volume, page, and, where appropriate, line numbers.

3. As a sign of its scholarly neglect, consider that *CW* 13 in 1976 was the first published edition of the *Treatise* since its original printing in 1557, marking a span of 419 years.

4. The folio edition is cited from *EW*, 1139–1438.

5. This grouping was first suggested by Germain Marc'hadour, *Thomas More et la Bible* (Paris: J. Vrin, 1969), 72–73 and 80, but not without subsequent qualification. Marc'hadour later suggested that by the time of Rastell's printing "1534 may have become a set label to mean all of More's fifteen months in the Tower" (*CW* 13:xxxvii, n2).

6. See John Foxe's editor note in *The Whole works of W. Tyndall, Iohn Frith, and Doct. Barnes, three worthy Martyrs, and principall teachers of this Church of*

England, collected and compliled in one Tome together, being before scattered, and now in print here exhibited to the Church, ed. John Foxe (London: John Daye, 1573), Sig. CC$_5$v.

7. See D. F. McKenzie, "The Book as an Expressive Form," in *Bibliography and the Sociology of Texts* (London: British Library, 1986), 1–21; and see Robert Darnton, "What Is the History of Books?," *Daedalus* (1982): 65–83.

8. For discussion of how polemics, print, and propaganda unfolded in the sixteenth century, see John N. King, "Thomas More, William Tyndale, and the Printing of Religious Propaganda," in *The Oxford Handbook of Tudor Literature, 1485–1603*, ed. Mike Pincombe and Cathy Shrank (Oxford: Oxford University Press, 2009), 105–20.

9. If bibliography "studies texts as recorded forms, and the processes of their transmission, including their production and reception" (McKenzie, "Book as Expressive Form," 12), then the first printing of More's *Treatise* in 1557, which occurred twenty-three years after its composition, must involve reconstruction of More's original aims.

10. On Barton's political prophecies, see Diane Watt, "Reconstructing the Word: The Political Prophecies of Elizabeth Barton (1506–1534)," *Renaissance Quarterly* 50, no. 1 (1997): 136–63.

11. For the *Articles devised by the whole consent of the King's Council, etc.*, see *Records of the Reformation: The Divorce (1527–1533)*, ed. Nicholas Pocock (Oxford: Clarendon, 1870), 2:523–30; on the shift of religious authority from pope to English king, see 2:528–29. Hereafter cited as *Articles*.

12. Cf. *L&P*, vol. 6, no. 1510, 612, where Chapuys writes to Charles V in December 1533: "I forgot to mention that the Council are no longer to call the Pope anything but bishop of Rome." Of course, the pope was "the bishop of Rome," but calling him by that title alone was a purposeful nod to evangelicals in England. During the same period but on how Henry and his advisors are putting general councils above the pope, see *L&P*, vol. 6, nos. 1487–89, 600–603.

13. See Marius, *Thomas More*, 440.

14. Henry's excommunication was finally promulgated in a papal bull that deposed him and absolved his subjects from obedience to him on 17 December 1538. See Scarisbrick, *Henry VIII*, 361, and *L&P*, vol. 13.2, no. 1087, 469.

15. *Articles*, 2:529.

16. *Articles*, 2:530.

17. Henry concluded that he was emperor and pope of England, a separate jurisdiction of Rome, by August 1530, thanks to his study of the *Collectanea satis copiosa*, a manuscript composed to justify his divorce, but it took Parliament years to make his position law. At the same time, Henry still

thought of himself as *Defensor fidei*. See John Guy, *The Public Career of Sir Thomas More* (New Haven, CT: Yale University Press, 1980), 131–33; Scarisbrick, *Henry VIII*, 260–73; Susan Brigden, *London and the Reformation* (London: Faber and Faber, 1989), 182–83.

18. *Statutes of the Realm*, 3:427–28.
19. *Corr.*, 468/15–22.
20. *Corr.*, 468/30–469/67.
21. *Statues of the Realm*, 3:446.
22. *Statutes of the Realm*, 3:428.
23. I follow Scarisbrick, *Henry VIII*, 310–14.
24. *L&P*, vol. 6, no. 541, 235.
25. *L&P*, vol. 6, no. 585, 266.
26. *L&P*, vol. 6, no. 653, 295.
27. *L&P*, vol. 6, no. 738, 332.
28. Not by coincidence, he had received word of his excommunication in Rome at the beginning of that same month (*LL*, Commentary, 135).
29. I follow Dianne Watt, "Barton, Elizabeth," in *ODNB*, 203.
30. Much of the indictment specifies how Barton's accomplices spread news of her prophecies. They heard her "feigned revelations" and spread them "secretly" to the people of the realm and to noblemen in order that the "King's Highness should be brought in a grudge and evil opinion of his people"; their intention was "to make such a division and rebelling in this Realm among the King's subjects whereby the King's Highness should not only have been put to peril of his life but also in jeopardy to be deprived from his Crown and Dignity Royal" (*Statutes of the Realm*, 3:449).
31. There were seven people condemned to death in the Act of Attainder. In addition to Hugh Rich and Richard Risby, who spoke with More about Barton, and Barton herself, there were two secular priests: Henry Gold, the former chaplain to Archbishop Warham, whom Cranmer replaced, and Richard Master, who was pardoned. The last two were Barton's confessor, Dr. Edward Bocking, and John Dering, a fellow monk. For More's account of his conversations with Fathers Rich and Risby, see *Corr.* 481/40–484/199, and commentary from *LL*, 138–39.
32. *Corr.*, 506, 133–38.
33. C. Wriothesley, *A Chronicle of England, Camden New Series XI*, ed. W. D. Hamilton (Westminster: J. B. Nichols and Sons, 1875), 1:24.
34. *TMSB*, 333/5–16.
35. Brigden, *London and the Reformation*, 224. Cf. Rex, "Execution of the Holy Maid of Kent," 218: "Perusal of the original sources, however, reminds us of something entirely overlooked by most of the recent narratives, namely

that the execution of the Holy Maid was planned and timed to encourage acquiescence in the oath to the succession."

36. Rex, "Execution of the Holy Maid of Kent," 220, comments: "The execution of the Holy Maid and her companions was one of the many ways in which judicious use of judicial terror (albeit falling short of tyranny) was employed to secure compliance with the English Reformation." For the Treasons Act and its prohibition against either "express writing or words," see *Statutes of the Realm*, 3:508.

37. "Good Madam, I [doubt] not, but that you remember that in the begynninge of my communicacione with you, I she[wed] you that I neither was, nor wolde be, curious of eny knowledge of other men[nes] matters, and lest of all of eny matter of princes or of the realme, in case [it so] were that God had, as to manye good folkes before tyme he hathe eny thinge[s] reveled unto you suche thinges, I saide unto your ladishop, that I was not onely not desirous to heare of, but allso woulde not heare of" (*Corr.*, 465/19–26).

38. *Corr.*, 466/37–41. Compare More's emphasis on laymen above with Cramner's assertion that "many learned men, but specially divers and many religious men, had great confidence in her, and often resorted unto her and communed with her, to the intent they might by her know the will of God; and chiefly concerning the king's marriage, the great heresies and schisms within the realms, and the taking away the liberties of the church"; in Thomas Cranmer, *The Miscellaneous Writings and Letters of Thomas Cranmer, Parker Society*, ed. John Edmund Cox (Cambridge: Cambridge University Press, 1846), 273. Barton had a following among both lay and religious.

39. For added measure, More shares with Cromwell how he himself dissuaded Barton's associate, Fr. Rich, by letting him know that "these strange tales" or prophecies were "not part of our creed" (*Corr.*, 487/244).

40. "neither good man nor bad, neither m[onk, friar nor] nonne, nor other man or woman in this worlde shall make me digresse frome my trothe and faithe, *either towarde God, or towarde my natural prynce*, by the grace of allmightie God; and as you therin fynde me trew, so I hartelie therin praye you to contynew towarde me your favour and good will, as you shalbe sure of my poore daylye prayor; for other pleasure can I non do you" (*Corr.* 488/270–76; my emphasis).

41. *LL*, 44n46 and commentary at 144.

42. *Corr.*, 489/27–32.

43. *Statutes of the Realm*, 3:446–49. Watt, "Barton," in *ODNB*, 202: "Under the guidance of her [Barton] confessor she learned about the lives and revelations of St. Bridget of Sweden and St. Catherine of Siena, and from the nature of some of her subsequent mystical experiences and visions (and in

particular her intervention in matters of national politics) it is clear that she began to model herself on them."

44. More never believed in Barton. When the king first asked More to read an account of her visions, More found nothing in her words that he could "regard or esteem." See *Corr.* 481/18–26.

45. The letter that supplied More's own to Barton was suppressed, but a second one to Cromwell and More's letter to Henry (also from March of 1534) were doctored by Rastell.

46. See *Corr.*, headnote, 480.

47. *Statutes of the Realm*, 3:450.

48. *L&P*, vol. 6, no. 1501, 606–7. Katherine herself rejected the title "Princess Dowager," which recognized her as widow of Henry's brother, and maintained that she was England's rightful queen. When Henry attempted to strip her of servants by commanding them to take a new oath, they resisted: "for they said, considering their first oath made to her, as Queen, they might not take the second oath without perjury"; see *State Papers of Henry VIII*, vol. 1, no. xxi, 415–16; hereafter abbreviated as *State Papers*.

49. Wriothesley, *A Chronicle of England*, 24.

50. *Corr.*, 489/27–28, and see *EW*, 1423; *Corr.*, 500/291–92, and see *EW*, 1428.

51. "But afterward by ambicion of the priestes, usurpacion and covetice of the kynges, the right order of the makyng or chosing of the byshop was chaunged, and they were put in and put out by the kynges, sometyme for pleasure, somtyme for displeasure, & sometyme for money to, so that in stede of one, now were they waxen many" (*CW* 13:73/2–7).

52. J. J. Scarisbrick, "Appendix 1: Protest of Archbishop William Warham in Defense of the Church on February 24, 1532," *Moreana* 58, no. 2 (2021): 236–37, and Scarisbrick, "Warham, William," in *ODNB*, 414.

53. J. J. Scarisbrick, "Archbishop William Warham's 1532 Defense," *Moreana* 58, no. 2 (2021): 218–35, and cited at 224, 225, 235, and see 241n14.

54. See *CW* 13:146/14–16 for another instance of the same formulation above. For other statements on the Eucharist and Church unity, see 149/21–23; and against Jan Huss, condemned Bohemian reformer, 149/25–150/10; or as the "sacrament of communion" or the "gathering together in one, because that this sacrament doth not only signify that communion but that the very real thing that is in this Blessed Sacrament beside the signification thereof, doth also effectually make it" (154/9–13); and as distinct to "Christ's whole Catholic Church" (174/11–19).

55. "For surely the very best waye were neyther to rede thys book nor theyrs / but rather the people unlerned to occupye them selfe besyde theyr

other busynesse in prayour, good medytacyon, and the redyng of suche englysshe bookes as moste may norysshe and encrease devocyon. Of whyche kynde is Bonaventure of the lyfe of Cryste, Gerson of the folowynge of Cryste, and the devoute contemplatyve booke Scala perfectionis wyth suche other lyke / then in the lernynge what may well be answered unto heretykes" (*CW* 8.1:37/25–33).

56. On this approach and its potential to backfire by way of spreading an opponent's views, see Alexandra Walsham, "The Spider and the Bee: The Perils of Printing for Refutation in Tudor England," in *Tudor Books and Readers*, ed. John King (Cambridge: Cambridge University Press, 2010), 163–91.

57. Elsewhere, More applies this point to the Bible as a whole so long as translations conformed with Catholic Church teaching and approval. For discussion, see Curtright, *One Thomas More*, 124–29, and Eamon Duffy, "'The comen knowen multitude of christen men': *A Dialogue Concerning Heresies* and the Defense of Christendom," in *CCTM*, 191–215, 207–8.

58. *CW* 13:lxxxvi and lxxxvi, n2. For a modern edition, see Nicholas Love, *The mirror of the Blessed Lyf of Jesu Christ / A Translation of the Latin Work Entitled Meditationes Vitae Christi / Attributed to Cardinal Bonaventura*, ed. Lawrence F. Powell (Oxford: Clarendon, 1908).

59. Kempis will be identified by his own name and not by Gerson's in what follows.

60. See *CW* 13:xc–xciv. For More's reference, see *CW* 8.1:37/31; for the text's publication history and circulation, see *CW* 8.3, commentary on 37/31 at 1474; and Walter Hilton, *Walter Hilton: The Scale of Perfection*, ed. John P. H. Clark and Rosemary Dorward (New York: Paulist Press, 1991), 33.

61. Kempis, for example, formulates growth in personal sanctity as correlative to growth in freedom. To achieve "freedom of heart," Christ teaches "forsake thyself and resign thyself wholly to me and thou shalt have great inward peace" and "freedom of spirit." See Richard Whitford, *The Imitation of Christ: From the First Edition of an English Translation Made c. 1530 by Richard Whitford*, ed. Edward J. Klein (New York: Harper & Brothers, 1941), 165. For critical discussion, see also Mathilde van Dijk, José van Aelst, and Tom Gaens, eds., introduction to *Faithful to the Cross in a Moving World: Late Medieval Carthusians as Devotional Reformers*, *Church History and Religious Culture* 96, no.1/2 (2016): 1–129.

62. Whitford, *The Imitation of Christ*, 3. Whitford was a friend of More's, and this edition of the *Imitation* was the probable one to which More referred in the *Confutation*. I have modernized the old forms of verbs and inserted quotation marks but otherwise followed Klein's presentation.

63. I cite from W. H. Hutchings, *The Life of Christ* (London: Rivingtons, 1881), xxix, who translates the Latin edition of 1668. Nicholas Love's translation is substantially the same, which renders the same final question above as: "For where shalt thou find so open example and doctrine of sovereign charity / of perfect poverty / of profound meekness / of patience and other virtues as in the blessed life of Jesu Christ?" (Love, *The Mirror of the Blessed Lyf of Jesus Christ*, 11–12). Despite multiple editions and variants, the overall message remains continuous over the course of centuries. For discussion, see the introduction to Nicholas Love, *The Mirror of the Blessed Life of Jesus Christ: A Full Critical Edition*, ed. Michael Sargent (Abington: Routledge, 2019).

64. Hilton, *Scale of Perfection*, 77. "Him" here refers to God, but Hilton subsequently qualifies: "Nobody can come to the contemplation of the Deity unless by the fullness of humility and charity he is first reformed to the likeness of Jesus in his manhood" (Hilton, *Scale of Perfection*, 160).

65. "Good lorde gyve us thy grace, not to reade or here this gospell of thy bytter passyon with our eyen and our eares in maner of a passetyme, but that it may with compassyon so synke in to our heartes, that it maye streche to theverlastyng profyte of our soules" (*EW*, 1292).

66. *CW* 8.3:1474. On the importance of Hilton to More's earlier writings, see Curtright, *One Thomas More*, 34–37. On how all three works treat More's life of prayer, see James Monti, *The King's Good Servant but God's First: The Life and Writings of Saint Thomas More* (San Francisco: Ignatius, 1997), 65–79.

67. The discovery of the *Treatise*'s organization belongs to Haupt, who notes that "structurally the *Vita* is much closer to More, for although it does not quote the relevant text from a gospel harmony at the beginning of each chapter, as does More, it does make claim to harmonizing the gospels and it follows the biblical narrative with a fullness and regularity not found in the *Meditationes*" (*CW* 13:xcvii).

68. Hilton, *Scale of Perfection*, 108.

69. Kempis, *Imitation of Christ*, 259.

70. On the Eucharist, compare Ludolph of Saxony, *The Life of Jesus Christ*, Part Two, Vol. 1, Chapters 1–57, trans. Milton T. Walsh (Collegeville, MN: Liturgical Press, 2021), 804–20, with More, *CW* 13:140–46, and Kempis, bk. 4, 219–61. Kempis writes to prepare souls to receive the Eucharist in terms of lyrical invocations and heightened sentiments, whereas More and Ludolph draw upon Aquinas in *Summa Theologica*, III, q. 73–84. Other striking differences from vernacular devotional literature include how More's preoccupations stray into philology, the historical circumstances of the Gospels' composition, and extend to the accuracy of his texts.

71. Erasmus, *Erasmus on Literature: His Ratio or System of 1518/1519*, ed. Mark Vessey, trans. Robert D. Sider (Toronto: University of Toronto Press, 2021), 117–18. On the importance of reading early Church Fathers for the cultivation of virtue, More writes to his children's tutor, William Gonnell: "and this your prudent charity will so enforce as to teach virtue rather than reprove vice, and make them love good advice instead of hating. To this purpose nothing will more conduce than to read to them the lessons of the ancient fathers, who, they know, cannot be angry with them; and, as they honor them for their sanctity, they must needs be much moved by their authority" (*SL*, 106).

72. Erasmus to Grimani, 1517 (Letter 710), in *The Correspondence of Erasmus*, Vol. 5, *Letters 594 to 841, 1517 to 1518*, trans. R. A. B. Mynors and D. F. S. Thomson (Toronto: University of Toronto Press, 1979), 196/31–33. This letter is Erasmus's preface to the *Paraphrasis ad Romanos*, and his goal is to make Paul "somewhat more attractive and certainly more accessible" (197/41–3). Mary Jane Barnett, "Erasmus and the Hermeneutics of Linguistic Praxis," *Renaissance Quarterly* 49, no. 3 (1996): 555, explains how these same lines cited above are indicative of the method Erasmus used "in order to help the New Testament *act* more effectively upon its readers." More also wants the scriptures to "act more effectively upon its readers" but in defense of Catholic sacramental theology.

73. More's purpose and tone differed from Erasmus's on the theological points of the Eucharist. "Certainly the apostles consecrated the Eucharist very piously," Erasmus writes in *The Praise of Folly* (1514), but they couldn't have answered questions "about the differences between the body of Christ as it is in heaven, as it was on the cross, and as it is in the Eucharist"; cited from Desiderius Erasmus, *The Praise of Folly*, trans. and intro. Clarence H. Miller (New Haven, CT: Yale University Press, 1979), 91.

74. More's *Treatise*, in other words, is meant to combat Tyndale's efforts at reform through a vernacular printing campaign that intensified in 1534. On Tyndale's efforts, see Jan J. Martin, "The Congregation and Church of England? William Tyndale's Approach to Lexical and Ecclesiological Reform between 1525 and 1535," *Moreana* 59, no. 1 (2022): 66–95.

75. "The thyng of the sacrament that is bothe sygnifyed and conteyned, is the verye bodye and the very bloud of our savioure hym self, therein actuallye and really present. The thing of this Blessed Sacrament that is signified thereby & not conteyned therein, is the unitye or societye of all good holye folke, in the misticall bodye of Christe" (*CW* 13:142/10–15).

76. William Tyndale, *The Obedience of a Christian Man*, ed. with intro. and notes by David Daniell (London: Penguin, 2000), 160, 156.

77. Tyndale, *Obedience*, 115. Tyndale is speaking of penance here and of sacraments in general.

78. *The Independent Works of William Tyndale, An Answer Unto Sir Thomas More's Dialogue*, ed. Anne M. O'Donnell, S.N.D., and Jared Wicks, S.J. (Washington, DC: Catholic University of America Press, 2000), 3:178/11–14 and 164/10–14.

79. Tyndale, *Answer*, 164/14–21.

80. "This is my body" and "this is my blood" were spoken by Christ, according to More in his *Letter against Frith* in 1533, in "the plain open literal sense of Christ's words spoken of the Blessed Sacrament." Reformers such as Frith, therefore, "deny the literal sense" and "forsake the plain common sense" in their rejection of Christ's real presence in bread and wine (*CW* 7:243/10–11, 240/12, and 242/8).

81. The *Supper of the Lord* is from Appendix A in *CW* 11 and cited as *CW* 11 followed by page and line numbers. The passages quoted above are at *CW* 11:336/8 and 325/3–5; 325/21–23; and 306/9–15. More supposed the unnamed author to be either Tyndale or Joye, and scholars are still divided over whether the *Supper* should be attributed to one or the other. For critical review and the argument for Joye as probable author, see Michael Anderegg, "The Probable Author of The Souper of the Lorde: George Joye," in *CW* 11:343–74, appendix B. Anderegg is typical in the sense that he never entertains the idea of coauthorship, but I see no reason why the piece wasn't coauthored by both men. Both Joye and Frith assisted Tyndale in his work up until Frith's death and Tyndale's rift with Joye in 1534. Though the *Supper* derives from Joye's original translation and digest of Zwingli's *On the Lord's Supper* (1526), it could have easily been revised by both men into an attack of More's *Letter against Frith*. Anonymous publication would be advised so as not to lose the support of Henry VIII, who still believed in the Eucharist in the Roman Catholic sense.

82. *CW* 11:307/2–4; 311/6, and compare More's teaching that bread indicates not only Christ's actual body but also the "bread of his godhead," which feeds one before the beatific vision and is realized "in the meanwhile by spiritual doctrine" (*CW* 11:50/32–51/8).

83. *CW* 8.1:298/27–30.

84. *CW* 11:20/10–14.

85. *CW* 11:20/26–30. For More, a literal meaning couldn't contradict any proposed moral, tropological, or anagogical senses; allegorical readings should spring from literal ones. These points were iterated against Frith and in More's *Answer*. See *CW* 7:237/26–31 and *CW* 11:20–23.

86. Thus, the author of the *Supper of the Lord* "goeth about to take away from us the very literal truth of the very eating and bodily receiving of Christ's own very flesh and blood" (*CW* 11:18/30–31). In More's *Answer to a Poisoned Book*, published with his *Letter against Frith*, More calls for figurative readings because there are "diverse other senses spiritual" in scripture, "pertaining to the profit of our manners, and instructions in sundry virtues by means of allegories"; all such senses can provide "inward high sight of God" (*CW* 11:17/34–18/2).

87. "And so thoughe there were in hys blessed bodye and hys bloude gyven theym in the Sacramente before hys passyon, suche a secrete wonderfull glorye of impassibilitie for the tyme, as was in his bodye for the tyme a visyble open glorye at hys marveilous transfyguracion, yet in the sacramentall receyvynge after hys gloryous resurreccion, it hadde that poynte of newenesse, whiche it hadde not actuallye before, that is to wytte, wythout losse, mynishment, or intermyssion, eternall endurynge of impassible and immortall glorye" (*CW* 13:134/28–35).

88. Thomas Aquinas, *Summa Theologica*, 2nd rev. ed., trans. Fathers of the English Dominican Province (London: Burns Oates and Washbourne, 1920–1922), III, q. 81, a. 3, https://www.newadvent.org/summa/4081.htm.

89. *CW* 11:94/21–37.

90. Gerson compiled the *Monotesseron*, a collection of all four Gospels in a single narrative. On Gerson's "harmony" of the four Gospels as resource for More, see *CW* 13:xliv–xlviii. More used the *Monotesseron* in his composition of *A Treatise upon the Passion*, written in English, and for *De tristitia Christi*, written in Latin.

91. The "context of the story" refers to the story's narrative order. Thus, More uses the term "context" in reference to the overall story of the four Gospels taken together. The ultimate author of scripture remains God. More seeks the authorial or divine intention behind all four Gospels.

92. "A warning to the Reader. Here I wil gyve the reader warnyng, that I wyll rehearse the wordes of thevangelistes in this proces of the passion, in latyne, word by word after my copy, as I finde it in the worke of that worshipful father maister Iohn Gerson, whych worke he entitled *Monatessaron*, that is to wit, one of all foure, as I have declared you before in my preface, because I wil not in any worde wyllinglye, mangle or mutulate that honourable mans worke: but so reherse it, that learned whych shal read it here, may have the selfe same comoditie thereby, that they maye have by the reading of the same among his owne other workes, as in considering such doutes as he sometime moveth concerning the context of the stori, and in searching (if their pleasure be) every word in his own proper place, wher it was gathered and taken out

of any of the foure evangelists, and for their owne learning, lyst confer the place and use their owne iudgment in thallowing or in the controllynge of any part of hys context, in the gathering and compylyng of his present woorke" (*CW* 13:50/5–21; cf. *EW*, 1291).

93. See the marginal note at *EW*, 1291. There, the "nota lector"—that is, a note for educated readers—informs one that Mark's Gospel is signified "per litteram R" so that the letter "M" may stand for Matthew alone. More cites scripture from Gerson after this manner in the first chapter of the *Treatise*, and afterward he presents only his English translation from Gerson. If readers had access to Gerson, however, it would be easy enough to follow along or to locate the passages from which More worked.

94. There is an assumption of visual and silent reading practices that accords with Latin language skills and expectations of private study. Unlike liturgical texts and books of prayer, which would be recited aloud, devotional texts such as Gerson's would be read *in silentio* and "with the heart" rather than the mouth, or for the sake of comprehension instead of saying vocal prayers. See Paul Saenger, *Space between Words: The Origins of Silent Reading* (Stanford, CA: Stanford University Press, 1997), 268 and see 256–76.

95. Gerson is quoted from the commentary on 50/15–16 in *CW* 13:255, and Tyndale from *Tyndale's New Testament: Translated from the Greek by William Tyndale in 1534*, ed. David Daniell (New Haven, CT: Yale University Press, 1989), xvi. Here, the loss of narrative context and order gives rise to allegorical readings.

96. A "harmony" also meant "a medicine composed of four ingredients" in English. See commentary on 50/9 in *CW* 13:255.

97. More, in effect, asks, based upon what principle of organization should a harmony be presented to readers? Even the chronological sequencing of events may be different in, for example, John's account than in the other Synoptic Gospels. How does one know which verse should precede another verse from one or another Gospel? Questions such as these are ones that More means to raise here. In doing so, he follows the cautious approach of Gerson. See commentary on 50/29–32 in *CW* 13:255.

98. "But yet wil I not fully folowe the same fashion in the rehersyng of the same thing in englyshe. For if I shoulde, there neyther could any suche fruite growe thereof, and also the context of the story shuld in the eye of the englishe reader, and yet much more in the eare of the english hearer, seme very farre unsavery, by reason of the often interposicion of the iniciall letters, signifying the names of the four evangelists, & som one sentence wyth so litle chaunge so often repeted, & in some place the context so diversly entrycked in his colleccion, that himself with a note in the mergine declareth himselfe to dout and

stand unsure, whether in that place he ioyne & link well in one, the sundry words of thevangelystes or no. And therefore in the rehearsing of hys context in englishe, nothing wil I put in of mine own: but out will I not let to leave, any such thing as I shal think to be unto the english reader, no furtheraunce but a hindraunce, to the cleare progresse of thys holy story, whiche wee shall wyth helpe of God in thys wyse nowe begynne" (*CW* 13:50/21–51/4; cf. *EW*, 1291).

99. On developing literacy and the sixteenth century, see Adam Fox, *Oral and Literature Culture* (Oxford: Clarendon, 2002), 47; and for further discussion with respect to oaths, see David Cressy, *Literacy and the Social Order: Reading and Writing in Tudor and Stuart England* (Cambridge: Cambridge University Press, 1980), 62–66.

100. See Keith Thomas, "The Meaning of Literacy in Early Modern England," in *The Written Word: Literacy in Transition*, ed. Gerd Baumann (Oxford: Clarendon, 1986), 97–131.

101. See the definition of the word "unsavoury | unsavory, adj.," from the *OED*: "Having no savour; not attractive to the taste; tasteless, insipid. *Obsolete*." Definition 2.b., the "figurative" meaning, cites More's text as an example: "The context of the story shuld . . . seme very farre vnsauery, by reason of the often interposicion of the iniciall letters."

102. More's style and theme contrasts to consolation literature because he is interested in the living and ongoing debates of the Reformation, not the passage out of this world, but how people in London consider the scriptures and the sacraments of the Catholic Church in light of recent attacks against the traditional faith. To contrast More with an example of consolation literature, Sir Thomas Elyot's translation of a sermon by St. Cyprian, composed for his stepsister, Susan Kyngeston, emphasized happiness in the next life or acted as *momento mori*. Or, as stated in Elyot's translation, "And yet doest thou delight to tarry long here among the swords of people malicious, when rather thou shouldst covet and desire (death setting thee forward) to haste thee towards Christ." See Thomas Elyot, *A svvete and devote sermon of holy saynt Ciprian of mortalitie of man. The rules of a Christian lyfe made by Picus erle of Mirandula, bothe translated into englyshe by syr Thomas Elyot knyghte* (London: in aedibus Tho. Bertheleti, 1534), B5r. Elyot addresses his sister after Elizabeth Barton, the Nun of Kent, was executed for her prophesies against the king's second marriage, during the same period as More's *Treatise*. For discussion, see Mary C. Erler, *Women, Reading, and Piety in Late Medieval England* (Cambridge: Cambridge University Press, 2002), 85–99.

103. Reading aloud could "unite people around a book," argues Roger Chartier, and book discussion "could attract others—silent auditors—instructed through listening to the exchange of arguments"; see Chartier,

"Leisure and Sociability: Reading Aloud in Early Modern Europe," in *Urban Life in the Renaissance*, ed. Susan Zimmerman and Ronald Weissman (Newark: University of Delaware Press, 1989), 104, 107, 117. Later, Bibles and other books were listed in inventories of public places, an indication of a tradition of communal reading practices. For examples, see Peter C. D. Brears, ed., *Yorkshire Probate Inventories, 1542–1689*, Yorkshire Archaeological Society Record Series 134 (Kendal, UK: Yorkshire Archaeological Society, 1972), 68, 97.

104. "And therefore good reader, here wee maye well consider, that when men are in device about myschiefe, if they bringe theyr purpose properlye to passe, cause have they none to be proude and prayse theyr owne wyttes. For the dyvell it is hymselfe that bringeth theyr matters about, much more a greate deal than thei. Ther was once a yong man fallen in a leud mynde towarde a woman, and she was such, as he coulde conceive none hope to get her, and therefore was fallyng to a good poynt in his own mynde, to let that lewde enterprise passe. He myssehapped nevertheless to shew hys minde to another wretche, whyche encouraged hym to go forward and leave it not. For begynne thou once man the matter quod he, and never feare it, let the dyvel alone with the remnaunt, he shall bringe it to passe in such wyse as thy selfe alone cannest not devise how. I trow that wretch had learned that counsayle of these priestes and these aunciencts, assembled here together against Christ at this counsayl" (*CW* 13:78/1–15).

105. In another instance of referring to kings but in terms resonant of Henry's actions with Anne and the passage above, More ponders the example of Christ, left alone and forsaken by his friends. Since Christ was abandoned, More asks, "If thou were a king, will not all thy realm send thee forth alone and forget thee?" In direct address to such a one, More asks what will happen if he should die in the arms of some "fleshly lover"? In that case, both would suffer together in "wretched burning forever" (*CW* 13:84/12–23).

106. *CW* 9:170/34–171/4; for More's citation of Horace, see the commentary of 170/35.

107. On the rhetorical function of merry tales, see Travis Curtright, "Thomas More on Humor," *LOGOS* 17, no. 1 (2014): 13–35.

108. See *CW* 13:xxviii and xlix; for discussion of MS. Bodleian 431, Bodleian Library, the mid-sixteenth century ms. and source of More's apparent instruction to Rastell, see *CW* 13:xviii–xx.

109. *CW* 11:332/37–8.

110. Quoted from *CW* 13:xxix.

111. *CW* 13:289, commentary on 160/13–20.

112. Compare *EW*, 1343–47, with *CW* 13:160–71. The Yale edition does not represent variegation in font sizes.

113. For rejoinders against the division of More's humanist and apologetical writings, see Curtright, *One Thomas More*, 105–39; Duffy, *Reformation Divided*, 19–49; Paul, *Thomas More*, 1–13.

CHAPTER THREE

1. The *Dialogue* deals with and springs from the occasion of religious conflict that More and his family experienced. See Romuald I. Lakowski, "Thomas More, Protestants, and Turks: Persecution and Martyrdom in a *Dialogue of Comfort*," *The Ben Jonson Journal* 7, no. 1 (2000): 199–223. For More's friends and family as his audience, see *CW* 12:cxxxv–cxlvi.

2. On the persona of Antony as More himself, Stephen Greenblatt, *Renaissance Self-Fashioning: From More to Shakespeare* (Chicago: University of Chicago Press, 1980), 45, calls Antony "More's spokesman"; and A. D. Cousins, "Role-Play and Self-Portrayal in Thomas More's *A Dialogue of Comfort against Tribulation*," *Christianity and Literature* 54, no. 4 (2003): 464, names Antony as More's "conclusive self-presentation." See also Alison V. Scott, "More's Letters and the 'Comfort of the Truth,'" in Cousins and Grace, eds., *A Companion to Thomas More*, 63.

3. See Schmidt, "Thomas More's *Dialogue of Comfort* and the Reformation Debate on Martyrdom," 209–38; and Deiter, "Building Opposition at the Early Tudor Tower of London," 27–55.

4. On the Tower Works, early modern biographies of More, and More's letters, Monika Fludernik, *Metaphors of Confinement: The Prison in Fact, Fiction, and Fantasy* (Oxford: Oxford University Press, 2019), 124, writes, "What we have here is not a contrast between autobiography and fiction but a substantive overlap or interpenetration of the autobiographical, biographical, and fictional elements in More's letters, sixteenth-century biographies of More, and the ex-chancellor's devotional texts." Hence "More the martyr," argues Dillon, *The Construction of Martyrdom*, 45, "was essentially a creation of these and his own texts."

5. *EW*, 1427. For the full letter, see *Corr.*, 491–501; the passage cited is at 497/183–199: "Byside this dyverse other wayes have I so used my selfe, that if I rehersed theym all, it shold well appere that I never have had agaynst his Grac*is* mariage eny maner demeanure, wherby his Highnes myght have eny maner cause or occasion of displeasure toward me, ffor lyke wise as I am not he which either can, or whome it could bycome, to take upon hym the determination or decision of such a waighty mater, nor boldely to afferme this thing or that therin, wherof dyverse point*is* a great way pase my lerning, so am I he that among other his Grac*is* faithfull subgiett*is*, his Highnes being

in possession of his marriage and this noble woman really anoynted Quene, neither murmure at it, nor dispute uppon it, nor never did nor will, but with owt eny other maner medlyng of the mater among his other faithfull subgiett*is* faithfully pray to God for his Grace and hers both, long to lyve and well and theyr noble issue to, in such wise as may be to the pleasure of God, honor and surety to theym selfe, reste, peace, welth and profit unto this noble realme." Rogers prints More's letter from MS. Royal 17D.xiv, a collection of letters and treatises by him and Rastell's own source.

6. Instead of More's support for Anne, Rastell's biographical account of his uncle emphasized that Queen Anne "made the King a great banquet" and "allured there the king with her dalliance and pastime to grant unto her this request, to put the Bishop [Fisher] and Sir Thomas More to death." See *The Rastell Fragments*, in Harpsfield, 235.

7. Peter Marshall writes that More's position was well known: "For him [More] to swear such an oath against his belief to the contrary would have been perjury, not just a legal transgression but a cause of eternal damnation. Everyone understood that this was the position" (Marshall, "The Last Years," in *CCTM*, 122).

8. *Corr.*, 498/200–201, 227–28.

9. *Corr.*, 552/43–44.

10. *Corr.*, 508/1–10.

11. *Corr.*, 509/15–18.

12. "A deadly grief unto me, and moch more deadly than to here of mine owne death, (for the feare therof, I thanke our Lorde, the feare of hel, the hope of heaven and the passion of Christ daily more and more aswage), is that I perceive my good sonne your husband, and you my good doughter, and my good wife, and mine other good children and innocent frendes, in great displeasure and daunger of great harme therby. The let wherof, while it lieth not in my hand, I can no further but commit all unto God" (*Corr.*, 509/19–26; cf. *EW*, 1431).

13. *Corr.*, 509/43–46; cf. *EW*, 1431.

14. Compare More's recommendation to meditate on the Passion with Antony's injunction to do the same: "if we could and would with due compassion, conceive in our mind's right imagination and remembrance of Christ bitter painful passion . . . I verily suppose . . . that we should find ourselves not only content, but also glad and desirous to suffer death for his sake" (*CW* 12:312/11–313/6).

15. *Corr.*, 510–11; cf. *EW*, 1432.

16. Cicero, *Rhetorica ad Herennium*, trans. H. Caplan (Cambridge, MA: Harvard University Press, 1954), 4.53.66. Hereafter cited as *Ad Herennium*.

17. Margaret even named her son after "the hero of the *Dialogue of Comfort*," Antony. See Guy, *A Daughter's Love*, 253.

18. Vincent had come to Antony in "need of some comfortable counsel against tribulation" to be given by one "that have so long lived virtuously, and are so learned in the law of god, as very few be better in this country here" (*CW* 12:3/20–23). Cf. Margaret's letter, where she addresses her father by referring to his Godly conversation, wholesome counsel, and virtuous example (*Corr.*, 510/16–18). Just as Vincent seeks comfort from Antony, so Margaret seeks comfort from her father.

19. "But now my good uncle the world here wexen such / & so gret perilles appere here to fall at hand that me thynketh the gretest comfort that a man can have, ys when he may see that he shall sone be gone. And we that are lykely long to lyve here in wrechidnes, have nede of some comfortable councell agaynst trybulacion / to be gevyn us by such as you be good uncle, that have so long lyvid vertuously, & are so lernyd in the law of god, as very few be better in this countrey here . . . here shall you leve of your kyndred a sort of very comfortles orphanes / to all whom your good help & counsaile & comfort hath longe bene a great staye / not as an uncle unto some, & to some as one ferther of kyn / but as though unto us all, you had bene a naturall father" (*CW* 12:3/16–4/5). Hereafter, cited in-text by page and line numbers.

20. I follow Rivka Zim, "Writing behind Bars: Literary Contests and the Authority of Carceral Experience," *Huntington Library Quarterly* 72, no. 2 (2009), 306: "For any reader aware of the writer's situation—in the first place, More's extended family—these coded references to fatherhood, to 'here,' 'now,' and 'this country,' all signify not Hungary in 1526 but England in 1534 and the situation of More himself, defying Henry VIII's supremacy in the English Church."

21. "But when so ever god take me hens, to reken your selfe then comfortles / as though your chiefe comfort stode in me / therin make ye me thinketh a rekenyng very much like, as though ye wold cast a way a strong staff, & lene upon a rotten rede / for god ys & must be your comfort & not I. And he is a sure comfort" (*CW* 12:4/28–5/3).

22. I have modernized the quotation as found in *The New Testament: The Text of the Worms Edition of 1526 in Original Spelling*, trans. William Tyndale (London: The British Library, 2000), 378.

23. "Margaret's contributions are delivered through the mouth of Vincent" (Guy, *A Daughter's Love*, 238).

24. Margaret writes to More during his imprisonment and calls him "the chief comfort" of her life (*Corr.*, 539/30).

25. Cf. "the dialogue may be seen as taking place in More's own heart" (*CW* 12:lxxxviii, n3).

26. *Corr.*, 549/17–20.

27. "But to fear while the pain is coming, *there is all our lett*" (*CW* 12:319/15–16; my emphasis).

28. For this reason, the *Dialogue* emphasizes the virtue of courage. Courage is necessary not just to follow one's convictions but also to check rebellion against God: "This fault of pusillanimity makes a man in his tribulation ... first impatient and afterward oftentimes drives him by impatience into a contrary affection: making him frowardly stubborn and angry against God and thereby to fall into blasphemy as do the damned souls in hell" (*CW* 12:111/19–23).

29. The full quotation reads: "Every tribulation the devil uses for temptation to bring us to impatience and thereby to murmur and grudge and blasphemy, and every kind of temptation to a good man that fights against it and will not follow it is a very painful tribulation" (*CW* 12:103/17–20).

30. *CW* 12:102/16, 103/22–25.

31. *Corr.*, 542/89–93.

32. "And I thanke our Lorde (Megge) since I am come hether I sett by death every daye lesse than other. For thoughe a man leese of his yeres in this worlde, it is more than manyfolde recompensed by cominge the sooner to heaven. And thoughe it be a paine to die while a man is in health yet see I very fewe that in sickenes dye with ease. And finally, very sure am I that when so ever the tyme shal come that may happe to come, God wote how sone, in which I shoulde lye sicke in my death bed by nature, I shal than thinke that God had done much for me, if he had suffred me to dye before by the colowr of such a lawe. And therefore my reason sheweth me (Margaret) that it wer gret foly for me to be sory to come to that death, which I wolde after wyshe that I had dyed" (*Corr.*, 542/108–543/120). Compare the above point on the pains of a natural death with Antony's on the same at *CW* 12:301/21–302/1–18. See also More's use of the term "reason" from the letter just cited and Antony's definition of "reason" that is "furthered with faith and grace" in *CW* 12:294/6–12.

33. More "speaks of the carrying into Hungary of the blasphemies of Mahomet, but in reality he is referring to the coming into England of the doctrines of the Lutherans, Sacramentarians, and other heretics or schismatics" (Stapleton, 116).

34. The relationship between More's personal anguish, Henry VIII, and the context of More's fictive *Dialogue* is suggested further by annotations such as the kind More made to Psalm 68:7. There, More writes, "to be said in [time of] tribulation by the faithful among the Hungarians when the Turks grow

strong and many Hungarians fall away into the false faith of the Turks." But More is writing (and praying for this) *after* the Turkish invasion and during the months of his imprisonment in the Tower. For annotations on the Turks, see Thomas More, *Thomas More's Prayer Book: A Facsimile Reproduction of the Annotated Pages*, transcribed and trans. Louis L. Martz and Richard S. Sylvester (New Haven, CT: Yale University Press, 1969), sigs. b2v, h7v, i1v, i2v, k1v; the annotation cited is at g4.

35. The Hungarians were defeated after the Battle of Mohács in 1526 but there were no forced conversions. "The threat of enforced conversion is entirely fictional," writes Fludernik, *Metaphors of Confinement*, 129, who thinks "it serves as an extended parable, an allegory of how Christians should behave under adversity." More specifically, though, it addresses how Catholics in England should behave under adversity. For context on the Turk as a visible political threat in the period, see Clare Murphy, "The Turks in More and Tyndale," in *Word, Church, and State: Tyndale Quincentenary Essays*, ed. John T. Day, Eric Lund, and Anne M. O'Donnell (Washington, DC: Catholic University of America Press, 1998), 228–42.

36. Harpsfield, 134.

37. The full title of the *Dialogue* included the additional fiction that it was a translation MADE BY AN HUNGARYEN IN LATEN, & TRANSLATYD OUT OF LATEN INTO FRENCH, & OUT OF FRENCH INTO ENGLYSH (*CW* 12:2). Of such a subterfuge, Chambers, *Thomas More*, 314, comments: "The *Dialogue* had to be kept very secret; it was a denial of the thesis that the head of the State might dictate the religious belief of his subjects."

38. More's use of the lion figure through the *Dialogue* most likely alludes to the king and his tyrannical impulses and practices; see *CW* 12:108/6–25, 110/30–111/3, 317/24–318/17, and the commentary on 108/1–6: "in the medieval-renaissance system of correspondences the lion and king were regarded as analogous since both were the prime representatives of their respective species. Symbolic transfers from one to the other were therefore commonplace" (*CW* 12:380).

39. The implied readership of the *Dialogue* may have indicated More's own plans for wide dissemination across Europe, though. The title already made mention of French, Latin, Hungarian, and English editions, but at the end of the *Dialogue*, Vincent also says, "I purpose, uncle, as my poor wit and learning will serve me, to put your counsel in remembrance not in our own language only but in the Almayne [German] tongue too" (*CW* 12:320/13–15).

40. "Incedent adj. naturally pertaining or attached (to)," from the Glossary in *CW* 12:525.

41. "yf we well consider thes two thynges, temptacion & persecucion we may fynd that eyther of them is incedent to tother / For both by temptacion the devill persecuteth us, & by persecucion the devill also temptith us / and as persecucion is tribulacion to every man, so is temptacion tribulacion to every good man / Now though the devil our spirituall enemye fight agaynst man in bothe, yet this difference hath the comen temptacion from the persecucion, that that temptacion ys as it were the fendes trayne / and persecucion his playne open fight" (*CW* 12:100/12–20).

42. For the definition of "trayne," see Glossary in *CW* 12:541.

43. Commentary on 100/13–22, in *CW* 12:374–75.

44. In the *Dialogue Concerning Heresies*, More writes that all men should "cleave to the faith of the Church as to an undoubted truth" (*CW* 6.1:127/34–35).

45. Antony explicitly designates the Catholic faith as the subject of persecution: as in the "Catholic Church" (*CW* 12:75/10); or in reference to "Catholics" (314/15), who are so named because they belong to "Christ's true Catholic faith" (200/21).

46. "in this temptacion this playne open persecusion for the fayth / he cometh evyn in the very mydd day / that is to witt evyn upon them that have an high light of fayth shynyng in their hart, & openly suffreth hym selfe so playnely be percevid by his fierce maliciouse persecucion agaynst the faythfull christians for hatrid of christes trew catholike fayth / that no man havyng fayth, can doute what he is / for in this temptacion he shewith himselfe such as the prophet nameth hym, *Demonium meridianum* / the midday devil" (*CW* 12:200/16–24).

47. See Dillon, *Construction of Martyrdom*, 23.

48. On Augustine's treatment of the noonday devil, see commentary in *CW* 12 on 201/3–11.

49. On kings and princes and their connection to the metaphorical Turk, see C. A. Patrides, "'The Bloody and Cruell Turke': The Background of a Renaissance Commonplace," *Studies in the Renaissance* 10 (1963): 126–35.

50. Because More saw the devil behind religious persecution, Antony advises Vincent to see the noonday devil with an "inward eye." Whenever the devil roars through "the threats of mortal men" then "let us tell him that *with our inward eye*, we see him well enough, and intend to fight with him even hand to hand" (*CW* 12:318/13–15; my emphasis). To see demons with an inward eye and to fight them "even hand to hand" explains why More's Psalter marginalia, by my count, includes more than forty references to demons and most in the contexts of *contra demones*, prayers to be used against demons. For

a typical example, see More's *Prayer Book*, Sig. f₅, and 196: "Imploracio auxilii contra vel demones vel malos homines" (A plea for help against either demons or evil men), which More applied to Psalm 58:2: "Deliver me from my enemies, O my God; and defend me from them that rise up against me."

51. The "Great Turk is the literal historical figure of Suleiman the Magnificent," or "a veiled reference to Henry VIII," or a "symbolic representation of the Devil himself" (Lakowski, "Thomas More, Protestants, and Turks," 291). In a polyphonic reading here, the "veiled reference" and the "representation of the Devil" combine.

52. More's fuller formulation reads: "From which whosoever shrink away with forsaking his faith, and falls in the peril of everlasting fire: he shall be very sure to repent it ere it be long after . . . he will wish that he had be[en] killed for Christ's sake before" (*CW* 12:319/7–10).

53. Scott, "Comfort of Truth," 63, confirms this point: "To deliberately desert the Catholic church was to desert the truth, a heretical position from which one was either 'saved' or purified of in death."

54. Cf. Dillon, *Construction of Martyrdom*, 24: "Indeed, caution had always epitomized classical and apostolic martyrdom; to die unnecessarily, even carelessly, was not true martyrdom, and the true martyr exercised every option to save themselves from death, other than denial of conscience."

55. In the *Dialogue*, Vincent suggests, "whereas by the forsaking of the faith in the beginning betime and for the time, and yet not but in word neither keeping it still nevertheless in his heart, a man may save himself from that painful death, and after ask mercy, and have it, and live long, and do many good deeds, and be saved as Saint Peter was" (*CW* 12:297/17–21). Compare Vincent's articulation of mental reservation with Rastell's note in *EW*, 1441.

56. On the significance of pain's pinch, Vincent also tells his uncle: "We think it reason what you say and in our minds agree that we should do as you say (yea, and do peradventure think also that we would indeed do as ye say), yet as soon as we should once hear these hellhounds—these Turks—come yelping and bawling upon us, our hearts should soon fall as clean from us as those other harts fly from the hounds" (*CW* 12:295/15–20).

57. *TMSB*, 325/18–27. "Verely, Daughter, I never entend (God being my good lorde) to pynne my soule at a nother mans backe, not even the best man that I know this day living; for I knowe not whither he maye happe to carry it. Ther is no man living, of whom while he liveth, I may make myself sure. Some may do for favour, and some may doe for feare. . . . And some might hap to frame him self a conscience and thinke that while he did it for feare God wolde forgive it. And some may peradventure thinke that they will repent, and be shryven therof, and that so God shall remitt it them. And some may

peradventure of that minde, that if they say one thing and thinke the while the contrary, God more regardeth their harte than their tonge, and that therfore their othe goeth upon that they thinke, and not upon that they say, as a woman resoned once, I trow, Daughter, you wer by. But in good faith, Marg[ar]et, I can use no such wais in so great a matter" (*Corr.*, 521/250–66).

58. *TMSB*, 333/16.

59. *EW*, 1441.

60. Cited from J. J. Scarisbrick, "The Pardon of the Clergy, 1531," *Cambridge Historical Journal* 12, no. 1 (1956): 34.

61. *New Additions*, in Christopher St. German, *Doctor and Student*, ed. T. F. T. Plucknett and J. L. Barton (London: Seldon Society, 1974), 327.

62. "Fynally whan christ spake so often & so playne of the mater, that every man shuld uppon payne of dampnacion, openly confesse his fayth, yf men toke hym & by drede of deth wold drive hym to the contrary / it semeth me in a maner implied therin, that we be bounden condicionally to have evermore that mynd actually some tyme, & evermore habitually, that yf the case so shuld fall, than with goddes helpe so we wold / And thus mich thinketh me necessarye for every man and woman, to be alway of this mynd, and … must they call to mynd & remembre, the greate payne & torment that christ suffred for them, and hartely pray for grace / that yf the case shuld so fall, god shuld give them strength to stand / And thus with exercise of such medytacion, though men shuld never stand full out of feare of fallyng / yet must they percever in good hope / & in full purpose of standyng / And this semeth me cosyn so ferforth the mynd that every christen man and woman must nedes have" (*CW* 12:198/5–22; my emphasis).

63. *Corr.*, 549/17–20.

64. For rhetoric's genera, see *Ad Herennium* 1.2.2.

65. *Ad Herennium* 3.3.5.

66. *Ad Herennium* 4.25.35.

67. *Ad Herennium* 3.3.6.

68. *CW* 12:292/15–22.

69. "Syth all our principall coumforte must come of God, we must first presuppose in hym to whome we shall with anye ghostely counsell geve any effectuall coumfort, one ground to begyn withall: whereuppon all that we shall build must be supported and stand, that is to witte, the ground & foundacion of fayth, without which had ready before, all the spiritual coumfort that any man maye speake of, can never availe a flye" (*CW* 12:12/8–14.)

70. On philosophy's role, see *CW* 12:9/22–11/23.

71. "First must you Cosyn be sure / that you loke well to the marke / & that can you not, but yf ye know what thing tribulacion ys / for sith that is

one of the thinges that we principally speke of / but yf you consider well what thyng that is / you may mysse the marke agayne" (*CW* 12:50/13–17).

72. "The delay in cohabiting," writes Eric Ives of Henry's desire for Anne, was certainly longer "than the king had hoped when he sought her for his mistress," and his passion for Anne was evident in his letters; cited from Ives, *The Life and Death of Anne Boleyn* (Oxford: Blackwell, 2005), 90–91. On a king and his lust for a lover, see *CW* 13:84/12–23.

73. See Beth Blum, "Therapeutic Redescription," in *Literary Studies and Human Flourishing*, ed. James F. English and Heather Love (Oxford: Oxford University Press, 2023), 185–86. Martha Nussbaum, *Therapy of Desire: Theory and Practice in Hellenistic Ethics* (Princeton, NJ: Princeton University Press, 1994), 369, notes how emotions or passions, unlike thirst or hunger, "embody ways of interpreting the world" in Greek thought because "the feelings that go with the experience of emotion are hooked up with and reset upon beliefs or judgments that are their basis or ground, in such a way that the emotion as a whole can appropriately be evaluated as true and false, and also as rational or irrational, according to our evaluation of the grounding belief."

74. Quintilian, *The Orator's Education: Books 6–8*, ed. and trans. Donald A. Russell (Cambridge, MA: Harvard University Press, 2001), 8.4, and see Quentin Skinner, *Reason and Rhetoric in the Philosophy of Thomas Hobbes* (Cambridge: Cambridge University Press, 1996), 144.

75. The teaching is cited from Epictetus, *Epictetus: Discourses and Enchiridion*, trans. Thomas Wentworth Higginson (Roslyn, NY: Walter J. Black, 1944), 289, or section 4.4, which reads: "But if you happen on a crowd, call it one of the public games, a grand assembly, a festival."

76. Antony does hold a place for philosophy because he believes that old moral "philosophers" and natural "wise men" are imperfect physicians, but with "some good drugs" left in their shops. Their "medicines" against "these diseases of tribulation" should be used in accordance with prescriptions of "that high physician," who is Christ (*CW* 12:10–11).

77. "But in this case yf we wilbe good christen men, we shall have greate cause gladly to be content, for the great comfort that we may take therby / while we remember, that in the pacient & glad doyng of our service unto that man for goddes sake, accordyng to his high commaundment by the mowth of saynt paule / *servi obedite dominis* / we shall have our thanke & our reward of god" (*CW* 12:254/14–19).

78. See Marcus Aurelius, *Meditations*, trans. A. S. L. Farquharson (London: J. M. Dent & Sons, 1961), 61–62, who associated a philosophical mindset with observation of the world's happenings rather than immersion in them, an exercise in detachment. More's last meditation on detachment was called "A

godly meditation" that began "Give me thy grace good Lord / to set the world at naught" (*EW*, 1416).

79. Antony employs Stoic distinctions between good, bad, and indifferent things in address of wealth, fame, glory, and offices at *CW* 12:223/6–225/17. The aim here is to teach how everything on earth should be loved for God's sake and not desired for its own sake.

80. For More's definition of meditation and how reason lead by faith transcends reason, see *CW* 12:204/28–205/14, 294/5–12; and with reference to the passion of Christ at 198/15–17, 312/10–313/7.

81. John Guy, *The Public Career of Sir Thomas More* (New Haven, CT: Yale University Press, 1980), 203, writes of the *Dialogue* that More "stood for moral crusade, and Henry VIII was adroitly cast in this work as the Great Turk."

82. The original note of Rastell reads: "Within a while after sir Thomas More was in prison in the towre, his daughter maistress Margaret Rop[er] wrote and sent unto him a letter, wherein *she semed somewhat to labour to perswade hym to take the othe (though she nothing so thought)* to winne thereby credence with maister Thomas Cromwell, that she might the rather gette libertye to have free resort unto her father (which she only had for the most tyme of hys imprisonment) unto which letter her father wrote an answer. The copy whereof here followeth" (*EW*, 1431; my emphasis).

83. See Guy, *A Daughter's Love*, 236–37.

CHAPTER FOUR

1. On connections between More's *Utopia* and his later theological polemics, see Julianne Sandberg, "Utopian Literality: Thomas More and the Faith of Catholic Reading," *Studies in Philology* 117, no. 2 (2020): 261–84. On More's self-presentation in *Utopia*, see Greenblatt, *Renaissance Self-Fashioning*, 11–73. For More's letters and his self-presentation, see Scott, "More's Letters and 'the Comfort of the Truth,'" 53–76; Guy, *Thomas More*, 175; McCutcheon, "Decoding the Alice Alington–Margaret More Roper Letters," 144–70.

2. For an analysis of the argument between Morus and Hythlodaeus, see George Logan, *The Meaning of More's Utopia* (Princeton, NJ: Princeton University Press, 1983), 32–130; Dominic Baker-Smith, *More's Utopia* (Toronto: University of Toronto Press, 2000), 104–50; and Gerard Wegemer, *Thomas More on Statesmanship* (Washington, DC: Catholic University of America Press, 1996), 109–27.

3. The "dialogue of counsel" refers to the majority of *Utopia*'s first book. On the composition of *Utopia*, see *CW* 4:xv–xxiii. For an introduction to the

problem or question of counsel in the period, see John Guy, "The Henrician Age," in *The Varieties of British Political Thought, 1500–1800*, ed. J. G. A. Pocock, Gordon J. Schochet, and Lois G. Schwoerer (Cambridge: Cambridge University Press, 1996), 13–22. On "counsel" and More's own life and career, see J. H. Hexter, "Thomas More and the Problem of Counsel," *Albion: A Quarterly Journal Concerned with British Studies* 10 (1978): 55–66.

4. More claims to play secretary to Hythlodaeus. He writes to Peter Giles in a letter published with *Utopia*: "I had only to repeat what in your company I heard Raphael relate" (*CW* 4:39/8). On More's narrative hoax, see Baker-Smith, *More's Utopia*, 75–93.

5. On the verisimilitude of *Utopia* as a function of More's rhetorical design, see Travis Curtright, "Thomas More and the 'genius' of *Utopia*," *Moreana* 54, no. 1 (2017): 1–18.

6. More had taken fictional liberties before in his letters. See Lisa Jardine, *Erasmus, Man of Letters: The Construction of Charisma* (Princeton, NJ: Princeton University Press, 1993), 17–18; on *Utopia* at 40–41.

7. I cite from an already modernized version of the correspondence between Alice Alington and Margaret Roper in August 1534 from *TMSB*, 316–35 (hereafter cited in-text by page and line numbers). The charge of scrupulosity is introduced at 318/1; More first calls Margaret "mistress Eve" at 320/5. The original texts with Rastell's commentary are in *Corr.*, 511–32.

8. "Everything in the book," Beatus Rhenanus reports of a "trained" theologian's comment upon *Utopia*, "came from the mouth of Hythloday; all More did was write it down. And for that More deserved no more credit than attaches to making a good transcript." Beatus Rhenanus's letter of 23 February 1518 to Willibald Pirckheimer is quoted from Thomas More, *Utopia*, 3rd ed., trans. Robert M. Adams, ed. George Logan (Cambridge: Cambridge University Press, 2016), 132. For Rastell's comment, see *Corr.*, 514.

9. The question of Margaret's authorship remains vexing. For recent discussion, see Stephen M. Foley, "Virtual and Absolute: The Voices of the 'Letter to Alington,'" in *A Companion to Margaret More Roper Studies: Life Records, Essential Texts, and Critical Essays*, ed. William Gentrup and Elizabeth McCutcheon (Washington, DC: Catholic University of America Press, 2022), 222–52; Nancy E. Wright, "The Name and the Signature of the Author of Margaret Roper's Letter to Alice Alington," in *Ashgate Critical Essays on Women Writers in England*, Vol.1, *Early Tudor Women Writers*, ed. Elaine V. Beilin (Burlington, VT: Ashgate, 2009), 27–45. Many argue for coauthorship of some kind: "The speeches of More are absolute More, and the speeches of Margaret are absolute Margaret"; writes R. W. Chambers, *On the Continuity of English Prose from Alfred to More and His School* (London: Early English

Text Society, 1932), clxii. Walter M. Gordon updates and adjusts the assessment by Chambers: "More's thought so dominates the dialogue and Margaret's feelings so color it that the participation of neither can be safely ruled out"; Gordon, "Tragic Perspective in Thomas More's Dialogue with Margaret in the Tower," *Cithara* 17 (1978): n2. Other versions of collaboration are less equal. Jaime Goodrich, for example, writes that "Roper acts as More's mouthpiece and so reifies his retreat from the world while mediating his participation in it"; Goodrich, "Thomas More and Margaret More Roper: A Case for Rethinking Women's Participation in the Early Modern Public Sphere," *The Sixteenth Century Journal* 39, no. 4 (2008): 1038. Alvaro DeSilva cites and answers Rastell's original concern: "But it is quite clear that it was written by Thomas More" (*LL*, 166).

10. Compare: "The methods and concepts of textual criticism can establish a definitive text of the letter to Alice Alington but cannot definitely attribute it to either More or Margaret on the basis of external evidence or extant sixteenth-century texts: two manuscript copies contained in Bodleian MS. Ballard 72 and B. L. MS. Royal 17D xiv, and the printed text in More's *Works*" (Wright, "Roper's Letter to Alice Alington," 29). Such textual criticism does not admit comparative rhetorical analyses between and among More's other works as decisive evidence.

11. See *EW*, 1434.

12. Louis L. Martz, *Thomas More: The Search for the Inner Man* (New Haven, CT: Yale University Press, 1992), 58–59.

13. More discusses heresy cases such as that of Thomas Bilney with intimate knowledge of events and legal precision in More, *A Dialogue Concerning Heresies*, in *CW* 6.1:264–80. On liberal learning and faith, see *CW* 6.1:130–32. On More's Star Chamber investigation into whether Bilney recanted, see Guy, *Thomas More*, 121. For discussion of the Bilney case in terms of More's wedding of humanism with his defense of the church, see Curtright, *One Thomas More*, 105–17.

14. On William Roper as the messenger, see *CW* 6.2:491–94.

15. Cf. Lewis, *English Literature in the Sixteenth Century Excluding Drama*, 172, who called More's *Dialogue* a "great Platonic dialogue, perhaps the best written in English."

16. Louis L. Martz, "The Tower Works," in *St. Thomas More: Action and Contemplation*, ed. Richard S. Sylvester (New Haven, CT: Yale University Press, 1972), 66, summarizes: "The general subject of this dialogue-letter and the *Dialogue of Comfort* is basically the same: how should the Christian behave when persecutors test his strength to endure for what he believes, in his conscience, to be the true faith?"

17. "Indeed Margaret," More tells his daughter in regard to her arguments for him to take the oath, "for the part you are playing, you are not doing a bad job" (*TMSB*, 328/34–35).

18. On the various members of the family who make a disguised appearance in the *Dialogue of Comfort*, see *CW* 12:cxxxv–cxlvii.

19. See Guy, *Thomas More*, 175–77.

20. I cite An Act for the Establishment of the King's Succession, 1534, from G. R. Elton, *The Tudor Constitution*, 2nd ed. (Cambridge: Cambridge University Press, 1982), 12. See *Statues of the Realm*, 3:471–74, for the complete legislation.

21. Elton, *Tudor Constitution*, 7–8. See *Statutes of the Realm*, 3:472.

22. Elton, *Tudor Constitution*, 11. See *Statutes of the Realm*, 3:474.

23. "If any person or persons," the new law read, "by any words without writing or any exterior deed or act, maliciously and obstinately publish, divulge or utter any thing or things to the peril of your Highness, or to the slander or prejudice of the said matrimony solemnised ... or to the slander or disherison of the issue and heirs of your body begotten and to be gotten of the said Queen Anne ... that then every such offense shall be taken and adjudged for misprision of treason" (Elton, *Tudor Constitution*, 11; cf. *Statutes of the Realm*, 3:474).

24. More designated Margaret as his proxy, and Ackroyd, *Thomas More*, 365, observes that "it is also likely that she smuggled out letters or pieces of his work and provided him with any books he required for his devotional writings." Martz believes Rastell's copy of *The Dialogue of Comfort* derives from More's original holograph, "which may have remained in the possession of Margaret Roper until her death in 1544" (*CW* 12:xlv). For the case that Margaret employed John Harris, More's secretary, in preparation of a collected works editions of her father's writings, see Guy, *A Daughter's Love*, 266–67; 271–73; Guy calls Rastell's *Workes* "Margaret Roper's project" at 271.

25. We can be certain the letter circulated because of Rastell's suggestion that More authored the letter: "Rastell was using a copy and not the original, for the handwriting would have told him by whom the letter was actually written down"; E. E. Reynolds, *Margaret Roper: Eldest Daughter of St. Thomas More* (New York: P. J. Kenedy & Sons, 1960), 76.

26. *Corr.*, 508/11–509/14.

27. *Corr.*, 510/15–16.

28. Stapleton, 114.

29. *EW*, 1431.

30. Stapleton, 114.

31. Elaine V. Beilin, *Redeeming Eve: Women Writers of the English Renaissance* (Princeton, NJ: Princeton University Press, 1987), 27–28.

32. Jonathan V. Crewe, "The 'Encomium Moriae' of William Roper," *ELH* 55, no. 2 (1988): 301–2. See also Wright, "Roper's Letter to Alice Alington," 37.

33. Guy, *A Daughter's Love*, 239.

34. Guy, *A Daughter's Love*, 239.

35. Reynolds, *Margaret Roper*, 76.

36. For critical discussion of Margaret's scholarly accomplishment, see Elizabeth McCutcheon, "'A Young, Virtuous, and Well-Learned Gentlewoman': Margaret More Roper in the Republic of Letters" (123–57), and Patricia Demers, "Margaret Roper and Erasmus: The Relationship of Translator and Source" (158–71), both in McCutcheon, ed., *A Companion to Margaret More Roper*. On Margaret's intellectual independence from her father, see Peter Iver Kaufman, "Absolute Margaret: Margaret More Roper and 'Well Learned' Men," *Sixteenth Century Journal* 20, no. 3 (1989): 443–56; and Gerard Wegemer, "The 'secret of his heart': What Was Thomas More's?," *Moreana* 52, no. 199–200 (2015): 45–60. Cf. Goodrich, who writes: "Margaret Roper was essential to More's cultivation of a private identity precisely because of her limitation to the domestic sphere, a circumstance arising from the inability of women to have a directly public voice during the Tudor period" (Goodrich, "Thomas More and Margaret More Roper," 1027).

37. *State Papers*, Vol. 1, no. xxxii, 435.

38. A judicial case is "based on legal controversy [*controversia*], and comprises criminal prosecution or civil suit, and defense" (quoted from *Ad Herennium* 1.2.2).

39. For an introduction to familiar letters, see Elbert N. S. Thompson, *Literary Bypaths of the Renaissance* (New Haven, CT: Yale University Press, 1924), 91–126; and for critical discussion and analysis, see Kathy Eden, *The Renaissance Rediscovery of Intimacy* (Chicago: University of Chicago Press, 2012). Erasmus, *De conscribendis epistolis*, trans. Charles Fantazzi, in the *Collected Works of Erasmus*, ed. J. K. Sowards (Toronto: University of Toronto Press, 1985), 25:20, defines the epistolary form as "mutual conversation between absent friends," which "favours simplicity, frankness, humour, and wit."

40. Cicero, *Letters to Atticus*, Vol. 2, trans. E. O. Winstedt (New York: The Macmillan Co., 1913), 9.4.1. Even as Cicero characterizes his correspondence in terms of *familiaritas*, his letter rehearses arguments over how one should deal with a tyrant. The letter is not a violation of *familiaritas* between the two men but an illustration of it during a time of crisis. Erasmus puts forward Cicero's letters to Atticus as a standard in *De conscribendis epistolis*, 14.

41. *Desiderius Erasmus of Rotterdam to Beatus Rhenanus of Sélestat, 1521*, in the *Collected Works of Erasmus*, trans. R. A. B. Mynors (Toronto: University of Toronto Press, 1988), 8:220.

42. Erasmus, *De conscribendis epistolis*, 20 (my emphasis).

43. Erasmus, *De ratione studii*, trans. Brian McGregor, in *Collected Works of Erasmus*, ed. Craig R. Thompson (Toronto: University of Toronto Press, 1978), 24:680.

44. The possible exceptions above define "the familiar" as a fourth type of letter in *De conscribendis epistolis*, 71. Erasmus's teaching, however, is not uniform. See *Conficiendarum epistolarum formula*, trans. Charles Fantazzi, in *Collected Works of Erasmus*, 25:262: "Since there are three kinds of causes in which the orator engages, the demonstrative, the deliberative, and the judicial, as Cicero and Quintilian inform us, *all the various types of letters* must be reduced to these three" (my emphasis). In *De ratione studii*, 680, all kinds of letters derive from the three categories of classical oratory. For basic definitions of the epideictic or demonstrative (*demonstrativum*), deliberative, and judicial, see *Ad Herennium* 1.2.

45. See *Ad Herennium* 1.3.4; and Cicero, *De inventione*, in *De inventione, De optimo genere oratorum, Topica*, trans. Harry Mortimer Hubbell (Cambridge, MA: Harvard University Press, 1949), 1.22.31. *Divisio* and *confutatio* are replaced by the terms *partitio* and *reprehensio* in the latter, but the function of both remains the same.

46. *De conscribendis epistolis*, 65.

47. *De conscribendis epistolis*, 20, 50.

48. For an overview and discussion of More's use of formal rhetorical, see R. J. Schoeck, "On the Letters of Thomas More," *Moreana* 4, no. 15–16 (1967): 193–203.

49. On the structure and style of More's humanist letters, see *CW* 15:xciii–cxviii; the oratorical partitioning of the *Letter to Dorp* is described at xciv.

50. Forensic debate makes up the most influential sections of the *Ad Herennium*. Quentin Skinner traces the humanist dissemination of the *Ad Herennium* from Venetian printings in 1470 in Skinner, *Forensic Shakespeare* (Oxford: Oxford University Press, 2014), 29.

51. *Ad Herennium* 1.4.6. *De inventione* 1.15.20: "An exordium is a passage which brings the mind of the auditor into a proper condition to receive the rest of the speech. This will be accomplished if he becomes well-disposed, attentive, and receptive." Within the fiction of a correspondence, Margaret allies herself with Alice from the start, but the introduction piques the curiosity of any and all subsequent readers to discover the reasons why More will remain in prison.

52. *Ad Herennium* 1.16.26. Formally, the *quaestio iudicii* forms the *constitutio* of the case. In the letter, the *constitutio* is juridical by definition: "An Issue is Juridical when there is agreement on the act [the facts of the case], but the right or wrong of the act is in question" (*Ad Herennium* 1.14.24). The controversy, thus, addresses the question of whether or not it was just or unjust of More to refuse the oath. "A proper beginning," adds Erasmus, "is determined according to precisely those principles which writers on rhetoric have handed down concerning the judicial class, but these teachings, which they correctly applied to speeches in the courtroom, should be modified to suit the peculiar characteristics of a letter" (*De conscribendis epistolis*, 76). Erasmus's later doubts about the letter's form for "determining of the [judicial] matter at issue" illustrate why More may have felt the need to insert a dramatic dialogue (*De conscribendis epistolis*, 76).

53. *Ad Herennium* 1.8.13.

54. *Ad Herennium* 1.8.13.

55. Erasmus, *De copia: Foundations of the Abundant Style*, trans. Betty I. Knott, in *Collected Works of Erasmus*, ed. Craig R. Thompson (Toronto: University of Toronto Press, 1978), 24:649.

56. The *divisio* is at 321/1–12; the *refutatio* from 321/33 to 328/17; the *confirmatio* from 328/18 to 334/21; the *peroratio* from 334/22 to 335/36. Page and line references are to *TMSB*.

57. Louis L. Martz observes that "More could have no doubt that every letter he wrote might be carefully read by his keepers, perhaps even sent to Cromwell himself" (*CW* 12:lix).

58. "The fictional letter pretends that it is not fiction and thus imitates the conventions of ordinary correspondence"; cited from Claudio Guillen, "Notes toward the Study of the Renaissance Letter," in *Renaissance Genres: Essays on Theory, History, and Interpretation*, ed. Barbary Kiefer Lewalski (Cambridge, MA: Harvard University Press, 1986), 85.

59. The treatment of *sermocinatio* in Erasmus, *De copia*, includes when "Homer, in *Iliad* 22, makes old Priam try to dissuade Hector from taking part in the duel, and in *Iliad* 6 makes Hector's wife Andromache try to deter him from battle, and shows Hector replying to them, in all of which he demonstrates a wonderful mastery of what is appropriate to each character." *Sermocinatio* makes "the historical writers" also "particularly worthy of admiration, for everyone accepts that they are allowed to put speeches into the mouths of their characters" (649).

60. See *Ad Herennium* 3.2.3. On the use of deliberative rhetoric in *Utopia*, see George Logan "*Utopia* and Deliberative Rhetoric," *Moreana* 31, no. 118–19 (1994): 103–20. Though More had represented Henry before 1518, Guy

rightly notes that More did not think of himself as a "fully-fledged councilor" until he "entered the King's Council in March 1518" (Guy, *Thomas More*, 51).

61. Aristotle, *Rhetoric*, trans. W. Rhys Roberts (New York: Modern Library, 1954), put the distinction between deliberative and forensic speech this way: "The political orator is concerned with the future: it is about things to be done hereafter that he advises, for or against. The party in a case at law is concerned with the past; one man accuses the other, and the other defends himself, with reference to things already done" (1358b14–18).

62. *Corr.*, 512/18–513/29: "There was a countrey in the which there were almoste none but foolys, savynge a fewe which were wise. And thei by their wisedome knewe, that there shoulde fall a greate rayne, the which shoulde make theym all fooles, that shoulde so be fowled or wette therewith. Thei seing that, made theym caves under the grounde till all the rayne was paste. Than thei came forthe thinkinge to make the fooles to doe what thei liste, and to rule thym as thie woulde. But the fooles woulde none of that, but would have the rule theimselfes for all their crafte. And whan the wisemen sawe thei coulde not obteyne their purpose, thei wished that thei had bene in the rayne, and had defoyled their clothes with theim."

63. *CW* 4:103/16–23. "Quam ob rem pulcherrima similitudine declarat Plato, cur merito sapientes abstineant a capessenda Republica. Quippe quum populum videant in plateas effusum assiduis imbribus perfundi, nec persuadere queant illis, ut se subducant pluviae, tectaque subeant. Gnari nihil profuturos sese si exeant, quam ut una compluantur, semet intra tecta continent habentes satis, quando alienae stultitiae non possunt mederi, si ipsi saltem sint in tuto" (*CW* 4:102/13–20).

64. *CW* 4:87/11–13 and 19–22.

65. On Hythlodaeus's use of the term "philosophy," see the definition from Erasmus, *The Education of a Christian Prince*, trans. Lester K. Born (New York: W. W. Norton, 1968), 133–34: "By 'philosophy' I do not mean that which disputes concerning the first beginnings, of primordial matter, of motion and infinity, but that which frees the mind from the false opinions and the vicious predilections of the masses and points out a theory of government."

66. *CW* 4:101/1–4.

67. "You must not abandon the ship in a storm because you cannot control the winds" (*CW* 4:99/34–35).

68. *CW* 4:87/37–89/18.

69. *CW* 4:91/21–30. "Praeterea si ostenderem omnes hos conatus bellorum, quibus tot nationes eius causa tumultuarentur, quum thesauros eius exhausissent, ac destruxissent populum, aliqua tandem fortuna frustra cessuros tamen, proinde auitum regnum coleret, ornaret quantum posset, &

faceret quam florentissimum. Amet suos & ametur a suis, cum his una vivat, imperetque suaviter, atque alia regna valere sinat, quando id quod nunc ei contigisset, satis amplum superque esset, hanc orationem quibus auribus mi More, putas excipiendam?" (*CW* 4:90/14–22).

70. On the dates of More's composition of the epigrams, see *CW* 3.2:10–17.

71. "Princeps pius nunquam carebit liberis. / Totius est regni pater. / Princeps abundat ergo felicissimus, / Tot liberis, quot ciuibus" (No. 111, *CW* 3.2:162); translation from *CW* 3.2:163. On *liberis* as a pun in the epigrams, see Cathy Curtis, "'The Best State of the Commonwealth': Thomas More and Quentin Skinner," in *Rethinking the Foundations of Modern Political Thought* (Cambridge: Cambridge University Press, 2006), 103.

72. Thomas More, *De bono rege et populo*, No. 112, *CW* 3.2:164: "Totum est unus homo regnum, idque cohaeret amore"; translation at *CW* 3.2:165. Compare with *CW* 4:95/16–19: "It belongs to the king to take more care for the welfare of his people than for his own, just as it is the duty of a shepherd, insofar as he is a shepherd, to feed his sheep rather than himself."

73. Thomas More, *De cupiditate regnandi*, no. 243, *CW* 3.2:256: "Regibus e multis regnum cui sufficit unum, / Vix Rex unus erit, sit tamen unus erit. / Regibus e multis regnum bene qui regat unum, / Vix tamen unus erit, si tamen unus erit"; translation from *CW* 3.2:257.

74. Military expenditures are given in de Silva's commentary, *LL*, 168.

75. *CW* 4:99/36–100/2. "At neque insuetus & insolens sermo inculcandus, quem scias apud diversa persuasos pondus non habiturum, sed obliquo ductu conandum est, atque adnitendum tibi, uti pro tua virili onmia tractes commode. & quod in bonum nequis vertere, efficias saltem, ut sit quam minime malum" (*CW* 4:98/28–100/2).

76. For the typologies of *ductus* theory, see John Monfasani, *George of Trebizond: A Biography and a Study of His Rhetoric and Logic* (Leiden: E. J. Brill, 1976), 280. For critical discussion, see Lucia Calboli Montefusco, "*Ductus* and *color*: The Right Way to Compose a Suitable Speech," *Rhetorica: A Journal of the History of Rhetoric* 21, no. 2 (2003): 113–31. The classical origin of purposeful, rhetorical deceit is from Quintilian's discussion of *figuratae controversiae* in Quintilian, *The Institutio Oratoria of Quintilian*, trans. H. E. Butler (Cambridge, MA: Harvard University Press, 1980), 9.2.66. One condition for the use of deceit is "if it is unsafe to speak openly" and applies to living under tyrants. More's contribution to the *Letter to Alington* could fall under Quintilian's category of *figuratae controvesiae* because "we may speak against tyrants in question as openly as we please without loss of effect, provided always that what we say is susceptible of a different interpretation, since it is only danger

to ourselves, and not offence to them, that we have to avoid. And if the danger can be avoided by any ambiguity of expression, the speaker's cunning will meet with universal approbation" (9.2.66–67).

77. On the humanist genealogy and development of *ductus* as a rhetorical term, see Virginia Cox, "Rhetoric and Humanism in Quattrocento Venice," *Renaissance Quarterly* 56, no. 3 (2003): 657–68.

78. Virginia Cox, "Dialogue," in *A Guide to Neo-Latin Literature*, ed. Victoria Moul (Cambridge: Cambridge University Press, 2017), 305–6.

79. On More's indirect approach in this same letter, see Curtright, *One Thomas More*, 189–92.

80. More's Tower letters are "art in every sense of that word, for they show the most artful regard for the presence of two or three or more different audiences" (*CW* 12:lix).

81. *CW* 4:99/22–25. On the comparison of plays and commonwealths, Morus claims: "Whatever play is being performed, perform it as best you can, and do not upset it all simply because you think of another which has more interest. So it is in the commonwealth. . . . If you cannot pluck up wrongheaded opinions by the root . . . you must not on that account desert the commonwealth" (*CW* 4:99/27–34).

82. Thomas More, *Utopia: Latin Text and English Translation*, ed. George M. Logan, Robert M. Adams, and Clarence H. Miller (Cambridge: Cambridge University Press, 2006), 96–97; cf. *CW* 4:98/36–38.

83. *Corr.*, 524/371–378: "But Father, they that thinke you shoulde not refuse to swere the thinge, that you see so many so good men and so well learned swere before you, meane not that you shoulde sweare to beare them fellowship, nor to passe with them, for good cumpany: But that the credence that you may with reason geve to their persons for their aforsayd qualities, shoulde well move you to thinke the oath such of it selfe, as every man may well swere without peryll of their soule." In this context, Margaret adds that since the oath is commanded by a law of Parliament, More is "bound" to change his conscience to conform it to others (*Corr.*, 524/382–85).

84. "As for such thinges as some men woulde happely saye, that I might with reason the lesse regard their chaunge, for any sample of them to be taken to the chaunge of my conscience, because that the kepinge of the princes pleasure, and the avoyding of his indignacion, the feare of the losing of their worldly substaunce, with regarde unto the discomfort of their kynrede and their frendes, might happe make some men either swere otherwise than they thinke, or frame their conscience afreshe to thinke other wise than they thought, any such opinion as this, wil I not conceive of them" (*Corr.*, 527, 495–504).

85. More contrasts the worldly gains of those who took the oath with his status: "I counted, Margaret, you can be very sure, during many a restless night, while my wife slept and thought that I did too, all the perils that could possibly come upon me. I went so far that I am sure there can come nothing more than what I thought. And in thinking this through, daughter, I did have a heavy heart" (*TMSB*, 334/1–5).

86. See the Act of Succession, in Elton, ed., *The Tudor Constitution*, 6–8; cf. *Statutes of the Realm*, 3:471–72. For discussion, see Wright, "Roper's Letter to Alice Alington," 35.

CHAPTER FIVE

1. All citations from *De tristitia* are from *CW* 14.1. Hereafter cited in-text by volume, page, and line numbers. Introduction, commentary, and index constitute *CW* 14.2.

2. Stapleton, 140.

3. For More's use of the *Catena* and the quotes above about his "basic tools," see *CW* 13–xliii–xlviii; Haupt is cited at xlviii. See also Sr. Mary Thecla, "S. Thomas More and the Catena Aurea," *Modern Language Notes* 61 (1946): 523–29. On the importance of Gerson's *Monotesseron*, see Katherine Gardiner Rodgers, "The Lessons of Gethsemane: De Tristitia Christi," in *CCTM*, 243–45.

4. Miller, in *CW* 14.2:781.

5. For representative comments on More's work as devotional literature, see Louis L. Martz, *Thomas More: The Search for the Inner Man* (New Haven, CT: Yale University Press, 1992); and Frank Mitjans, *Thomas More's Vocation* (Washington, DC: Catholic University of America Press, 2023), 237–39; and Guy, *A Daughter's Love*, 250.

6. As martyr literature, see *CW* 12:cxvii–cxx.

7. Tracey A. Sowerby, "'All Our Books Do Be Sent into Other Countreys and Translated': Henrician Polemic in Its International Context," *English Historical Review* 121, no. 494 (2006): 1271–99, and at 1276–77 on the *Glass*.

8. I follow Sowerby, "All Our Books," 1277–81, who adds that Henry's *Articles devised by the King's council* (1533) was distributed to foreign ambassadors residing in England. Edward Foxes's *De vera differentia regiae potestatis et ecclesiae* (1534) was written in Latin and to abolish the papacy; it aimed at educated and foreign readers.

9. "The state of the world demanded vigorous action and urgency," writes Duffy, *Reformation Divided*, 31, because as early as 1529, "More was not the only rational man in Europe who believed that the Protestant reformation

threatened the intellectual and moral coherence of Christendom as he (and for that matter Erasmus) understood it." For More's fear of what could happen in England, see *CW* 6.1:427/28–428/1.

10. The overlap between the *Dialogue of Comfort* and *De tristitia* is most clear on "the great horror & the fear that our saviour had in his own flesh against his painful passion" (*CW* 12:245/18–19). See also and compare *CW* 14.1:233–37 with *CW* 12:245/18–20 and *CW* 14.1:61–67 with *CW* 12:246/5–18.

11. *CW* 14.1:341/5–6; 213/5; 259/8.

12. "Surely as to swere to the succession I see no perill, but I thought and thinke it reason, that to mine owne othe I loke well my self, and be of counsaile also in the fashion, and never entended to swere for a pece, and set my hande to the whole othe. How be it (as helpe me God), as touchinge the whole othe, I never withdrewe any man from it, nor never advised any to refuse it, nor never put, nor will, any scruple in any mannes hedde, but leave every man to his owne conscience. And me thinketh in good faith, that so were it good reason that every man shoulde leave me to myne" (*Corr.*, 507/150–59).

13. On Cromwell's perspective on events from 1534–35, see Diarmaid MacCulloch, *Thomas Cromwell: A Revolutionary Life* (New York: Viking, 2018), 260–97.

14. See the Act of Succession on treason at section 5 in *Statutes of the Realm*, 3:473, and on misprision of treason at section 6, 3:474; and on consequences for obstinate refusal of the oath at section 9, 3:474.

15. *Corr.*, 505/106–7.

16. *Corr.*, 541/34–36, 43–46, 60–62.

17. The 1966 movie *A Man for All Seasons* popularized the idea of More's silence as a pretense. In the film, More tells Cromwell: "You must construe that I consented, not that I denied." In Hilary Mantel, *Wolf Hall* (New York: Henry Holt and Co.), 2009, 465, Cromwell says of More: "If he indicates anything, he is done for. Silence is his only hope, and it is not much of a hope at that."

18. The Guildhall report of More's trial in Henry Ansgar Kelly, Louis W. Karlin, and Gerard Wegemer, eds., *Thomas More's Trial by Jury* (Rochester, NY: Boydell Press, 2011), 189, reads: "Then More replied, 'But if it is true what universal law says, 'One who keeps silent seems to consent,' then that silence of mine gave approval to that statute of yours more than it weakened it." The legal precept—*Qui tacet consentire videtur*—is from the *regulae juris* issued by Pope Boniface VIII in his *Liber Sextus* from 1298. See *Sext*, book 5, *De regulis juris*, no. 43: "*Qui Tacet consentire videtur*," in Emil Friedberg, ed., *Corpus Iuris Canonici* (Leipzig, 1879–81), 2:1123.

19. On Warham's earlier usage, see Henry Ansgar Kelly, "A Procedural Review of Thomas More's Trial," in Kelly, Karlin, and Wegemer, eds., *Thomas More's Trial by Jury*, 23.

20. The consensus view of the trial stems from J. Duncan M. Derrett, "The Trial of Sir Thomas More," *English Historical Review* 79, no. 312 (1964): 449–77, but for corrections of Derrett, see Kelly, "Procedural Review," 1–52.

21. *Corr.* 502/16–17.

22. For this same reason, More wouldn't have confessed his opposition to the king's title to Richard Rich. Therefore, Kelly, "Procedural Review," 52, concludes: "More succeeded, I believe, in his attempt to remain silent about the king's supremacy, and therefore he did not come close to uttering words that, if spoken maliciously, could be declared to fall under the act."

23. Cranmer, *Miscellaneous Writings and Letters*, 285–86. Cranmer surmises the grounds of More's refusal of the oath because More's views were known already.

24. *Statutes of the Realm*, 3:472.

25. More "declared his mind" both to the king and to Cromwell "from the beginning" both by "mouth and by writing" (*Corr.* 552/41–44).

26. Roper, 240.

27. *Rastell Fragments*, in Harpsfield, *Life of More*, 228/9–11.

28. Cranmer, *Miscellaneous Writings and Letters*, 287.

29. Harpsfield, *Life of More*, 166/1–8. There, Harpsfield refers to the "statute for the oath of the supremacy and matrimony." See also Jonathan Michael Gray, *Oaths and the English Reformation* (Cambridge: Cambridge University Press, 2013), 122.

30. *Rastell Fragments*, in Harpsfield, *Life of More*, 228/11–14.

31. *Statutes of the Realm*, 3:492.

32. *Statutes of the Realm*, 3:493.

33. A point Bishop Fisher didn't grasp. Fisher was tricked into giving his opinion about the king's new title with the promise that the king himself desired to hear it and that Fisher would suffer no harm for doing so. After Fisher complied, he was accused of treason. At his trial, Fisher was convicted because his judges maintained that "none could spe[ak against the] king's supremacy by any manner of means but that the speaking against it [was treason]"; see *The Rastell Fragments*, in Harpsfield, *Life of More*, 239/27–34.

34. *Statutes of the Realm*, 3:493.

35. As a sign that Henry's desire to secede from the Church was clear in the *Articles*, see Bishop Cuthbert Tunstall's argument against them on the basis that the Council of Constance had condemned the proposition that the

pope of Rome did not have preeminence over other churches in Andrew Allan Chibi, *Henry VIII's Bishops: Diplomats, Administrators, Scholars and Shepherds* (Cambridge: James Clarke & Co., 2003), 162.

36. *Statutes of the Realm*, 3:492.

37. *Statutes of the Realm*, 3:508.

38. It was the Treasons Act that was used in the indictment of More at his trial and that carried the day against him based on Richard Rich's testimony. Rastell explains that this act made it "high treason to do or speak against the king's supremacy and other things." The bill couldn't pass unless the speech was qualified as "malicious." "And yet afterwards," Rastell concludes, "in putting the act in execution against Bishop Fisher, Sir Thomas More, the Carthusians, and others, the word 'maliciously,' plainly expressed in the act, was adjudged by the king's commissioners, before whom they were arraigned, to be void" (*Rastell Fragments*, in Harpsfield, *Life of More*, 228–29).

39. *Corr.*, 504/64–65, 505/74–85, 505/89–91.

40. *Statutes of the Realm*, 3:528. Compare More's indictment with the Treasons Act, which specified any "wish, will, or desire, by words or writings, or by craft imagine" that indicated a desire to deprive the king of his title was high treason (*Statutes of the Realm*, 3:508).

41. "Henry VIII's Order to Publicize the Guilt of Fisher and More, June 25, 1535," in Kelly, Karlin, and Wegemer, eds., *Thomas More's Trial by Jury*, 171; calendared in *L&P*, vol. 8, no. 921, 362.

42. For the search of Chelsea and More's solitary confinement, see *Corr.*, 540.

43. *Corr.*, 539/11–16.

44. Antonio Bonvisi, a friend who sent More gifts of wine and food three times a week, stopped delivery in February 1535, which was the same month the Treasons Act became effective; see *L&P*, vol. 8, no. 856, 329. For More's farewell letter to Bonvisi, see *EW* 1454–57. Rastell placed it as More's last letter and claimed it was one of the last things More ever wrote, but More probably wrote it when the Treasons Act took effect in February and Bonvisi stopped sending gifts.

45. *L&P*, vol. 8, no. 661, 247–48. On the point of how many actually believed what they swore: "I dare even say all this kingdom, although the smaller part holds with you, for I am sure the larger part is at heart of our opinion, although outwardly, partly from fear and partly from hope, they profess to be of yours" (248). For Roper's account of Margaret's visit, see Roper, 242.

46. The words of the executed also indicate that More's position wasn't as singular as is sometimes fancied today; his stance also belonged to Fisher

and to the Carthusian monks. Robert Bolt's *A Man for All Seasons* focuses on More as a hero, and Hilary Mantel's *Wolf Hall* presents More as a villain, but others who held the same positions, such as Fisher, are an afterthought in both fictional accounts.

47. *L&P*, vol. 8, no. 661, 248–49.

48. From "Account in a Paris Newsletter," in *TMSB*, 355 (my emphasis). The phrase is rendered "and God's first" instead of "but God's first," as is commonly reported. See Germain Marc'hadour, "Latin Lives of Thomas More," in Cousins and Grace, eds., *A Companion to Thomas More*, 31.

49. "Wherunto I answerd that in good fayth I had well trusted that the Kyng*is* Hyghnesse woulde never have commaunded eny such questyon to be demaunded of me, consydryng that I ever from the begynnyng well and trewely from tyme to tyme declared my mynde unto hys Hyghnesse" (*Corr.*, 552/38–42).

50. *Corr.*, 556/22–27.

51. *CW* 12:292/15–22.

52. *CW* 12:292/15–22; *Corr.*, 557/62–73.

53. Gogan, *Christendom*, 336, writes of the "divine right of the papacy" in England during More's lifetime and before Henry claimed to be "vicar" of England: "Indeed, it was so much part of established ecclesiastical thought in England, that not merely was papal jurisdiction over the church fully recognized both in canonical theory and practice, but recognition of the papacy was regarded as a test of doctrinal orthodoxy by the state."

54. *Corr.*, 558/91. On More's treatment of heretics, see Henry Ansgar Kelly, "Thomas More and Inquisitorial Due Process," *English Historical Review* 123 (2008): 847–94.

55. *Corr.*, 557/74–558/94.

56. More emphasized agreement about the papacy in his 1529 argument in *CW* 6.1, 204/18–22. There, the Catholic Church is "all the Christian people whom we call the church under obedience of the Pope" (20–21).

57. At his trial, More "declared that this realm, being but one member and small part of the Church, might not make a particular law disagreeable with the general law of Christ's universal Catholic Church, no more than the City of London, being but one poor member in respect of the whole realm, might make a law against an act of Parliament to bind the whole realm" (Roper, 248). Compare Roper's account with *Corr.*, 558/96–105.

58. *Corr.*, 552/53–68.

59. *Corr.*, 558/110–11: "I answered," More reports to Margaret, "that verily I never purposed to swear any book oath more while I lived."

60. *Corr.*, 559/135–41.

61. For a different account of *De tristitia*'s genesis, see House, "Endgame," 50, which argues for "some point" between More's "mid-January admission that force might be used to persuade him to swear" and the 12 June date of his books' removal.

62. For More's exchange of letters with Margaret during the likely period of writing *De tristitia* up until 2 or 3 May 1535, see *Corr.*, 538–47; 550–54.

63. *Corr.*, 527/507.

64. See *A Short Debate Concerning the Distress Alarm, and Sorrow of Jesus (Disputatiuncula de Taedio, Pavore, Tristicia Jesu)*, in *Spiritualia and Pastoralia*, trans. Michael J. Heath, in *Collected Works of Erasmus*, vol. 70 (Toronto: University of Toronto Press, 1998), 13–67. I refer and cite this text by the short title of *De taedio Iesu*.

65. Erasmus, *De taedio Iesu*, 15–16.

66. On the significance of Christ's human nature, More writes: "It was by His own marvelous arrangement that His divinity moderated its influence on His humanity for such a time and in such a way that He was able to yield to the passions of our frail humanity and to suffer them with such terrible intensity" (*CW* 14.187/6–189/1).

67. Erasmus, *De taedio Iesu*, 39.

68. Erasmus, *De taedio Iesu*, 54–56. In contrast with Erasmus, More hypothetically grants that there are those, after Christ, who suffered physical harms and tortures greater than his own. Yet "tortures which to all appearances may be considerably less fierce," More writes, "actually caused Christ to suffer more excruciating pain than someone might feel from tortures that seem much more grievous." As Christ envisions his coming passion, he becomes "overwhelmed by mental anguish *more bitter than any other mortal has ever experienced* from the thought of coming torments" (233/1–235/2; my emphasis). On Christ's inner torment, More asks, "For who has ever felt such bitter anguish that a bloody sweat broke out all over his body and ran down in drops in blood?" More, therefore, estimates the intensity of "actual pain" by the following standard: "I see that even the presentiment of it before it arrived was more bitter to Christ than such anticipation has ever been to anyone else" (235/3–7). Christ did not just suffer inner torments but the degree of that suffering was such that other forms of physical torture, no matter how severe, cannot compare to how Christ's sensitivity magnifies pain.

69. Erasmus, *De taedio Iesu*, 20, and see 20n30.

70. On Erasmus's recapitulation of representative scholastic doctrine, see James D. Tracy, "Humanists among the Scholastics: Erasmus, More, and

Lefevre d'Etaples on the Humanity of Christ," in *Erasmus of Rotterdam Society Yearbook* (Oxon Hill, MD: Erasmus of Rotterdam Society, 1985), 5:30–42.

71. John W. O'Malley, introduction to Erasmus, *Spiritualia and Pastoralia*, xii.

72. For Aquinas's position on the pain of Christ's passion, see any edition of the *Summa Theologica* III, q.46, a. 6. More may have known Aquinas's teaching. Stapleton reports a story of John Harris, More's secretary, that shows how More had read Aquinas with such care that he could recognize when and where others quoted Aquinas out of context. See Stapleton, 38.

73. Erasmus, *De taedio Iesu*, 22.

74. In Erasmus, *The Correspondence of Erasmus: Letters 1122 to 1251, 1520 to 1521*, trans. R. A. B. Mynors (Toronto: University of Toronto Press, 1988), 238/467–480, Erasmus writes of another dispute he had with John Colet: "But to Thomas [Aquinas] he was for some reason more unfair than to Scotus. *When I once praised Thomas in his hearing as no negligible figure among recent philosophers, because he did seem to have read both sacred literature and the old authors (so I had come to suspect from what they call the "Catena aurea") and showed some sensibility in what he wrote, Colet concealed his feelings two or three times and said nothing.* But on another occasion when I made the same remarks with more emphasis, he looked carefully at me, as though to see whether I meant it seriously or was pretending; and when he saw that I meant what I said, he broke out as though some spirit inspired him: 'How can you praise that man in front of me? Had he not been most arrogant, he could never have been so rash and so self-confident as to lay down definitions for everything; and had he not been touched by the spirit of this world, he would not have mixed up the whole of Christ's teaching with a gentile philosophy of his own'" (my emphasis). Erasmus then comments that he treated Aquinas with more skepticism because of Colet's outburst. This letter was dated 13 June 1521.

75. Tracy, "Humanists among the Scholastics," 36.

76. Erasmus, *De taedio Iesu*, 66.

77. *CW* 14.2, commentary on 45/2–47/1.

78. See Germain Marc'hadour, *The Bible in the Works of St. Thomas More*, Part 2, *The Four Gospels* (Nieuwkoop: B. De Graaf, 1969), 70.

79. Damascene and Origen are cited from Thomas Aquinas, *Catena aurea*, Vol. 1, *St. Matthew*, ed. John Newman (Exeter: The Saint Austin Press, 1997), 907–8. Theophylactus is from the *Catena*, 2:293. For the same passages in Latin, reproducing biblical verses in bold, see S. Thomae Aquinatis, *Catena aurea in quatuor Evangelia, I: Expositio in Matthaeum et Marcum*, ed. Angelico Guarienti O.P. (Romae: Marietti, 1953), 390 and 545. For More's earlier

and extensive use of the *Catena* on Matthew 26, see *CW* 13:126/27–127/2; 127/13–29; 128/25–29; 128/33–129/1; 133/27–134/7; and 136/4–18.

80. See Jerome in the *Catena*, 1:908.

81. Though More agrees in doctrine with Erasmus's treatise, his presentation differs from Erasmus's dispute with Colet. *De taedio Iesu* addresses Christological controversy, but eschews questions of rhetorical nuance and tone. Erasmus himself explains the difference in genre, stating how commentaries emphasize the thoughts of others, whereas his "battle" against Colet will be by "logic against logic, theory against theory, argument against argument" (*De taedio Iesu*, 17). More's own "manner" in both *The Treatise upon the Passion* and *De tristitia* "is free from scholastic divisions and disquisitions; his whole aim is to draw the spiritual, the moral meaning from the letter" (Martz, *Inner Man*, 91). Yet Erasmus's approach in *De taedio Iesu* contradicts his *philosophia Christi*, "located as it is more truly in the disposition of the mind than in syllogisms," and wherein "life means more than debate, inspiration is preferable to erudition, transformation is a more important matter than intellectual comprehension." See Erasmus, *Paraclesis*, in *Christian Humanism and the Reformation: Selected Writings of Erasmus*, 3rd ed., ed. John C. Olin (New York: Fordham University Press, 1987), 97–108, and for the lines cited, 104.

82. "Etenim moles immensa molestiarum tenerum piumque sanctissimi servatoris corpus insedit. Imminere iam iam / et tantum non adesse sensit / infidum traditorem / infensos hostes / vincula / Calumnias / blasphemias / verbera / spinas / clavos / crucem / et dira per horas multas continuata supplicia. Super hec angebat eum discipulorum terror / perditio Iudeorum / quin ipsius quoque perfidi proditoris interitus / indicibilis denique dilectae genetricis dolor" (*CW* 14.1:47/1–49/2).

83. Heath notes that Jerome lists four causes for Christ's sadness: they are "concern for Judas, for the apostles, for the Jews, and for the fate of Jerusalem" (Erasmus, *De taedio Iesu*, 17n20); none of these causes include the position of More; Erasmus identifies Colet with Jerome at 17; cf. Miller's comment on 47/3–49/2 in *CW* 14.2, which notes how More "combines the positions of Colet and Erasmus." Erasmus does not deny Colet's explanation that Christ grieves for the "destruction of the Jews and the desertion of the disciples" but "would go further" in *De taedio Iesu*, 50.

84. Hilary is cited from the *Catena*, 1:906. Erasmus, however, cites a general objection from Hilary in *De taedio Iesu*, 19–20, which argues that it is "impious folly to maintain that it was for himself that Christ dreaded his death."

85. *CW* 14.2, commentary on 53/4–6.

86. "Sed hic fortassis obiicias / desino mirari quod potuit / at non mirari nequeo quod voluit. Nam qui convenire potest ut qui discipulos docuit eos

non timere qui tantum corpus possunt occidere / et post hoc non habent ultra quod faciant / eosdem nunc pertimescat ipse / idque quum nec in corpus eius possint quicquam / nisi quatinus ipse permitteret" (*CW* 14.1:53/2–7).

87. Hilary is cited from the *Catena*, 1:906.

88. See Miller's commentary in *CW* 14.2 on 55/8–57/4.

89. More could follow Bede's gloss on Mark 14, which says of Christ that "He here represses the rash, who think that they can compass whatever they are confident about. But in proportion as we are confident from the ardour of our mind, so let us fear from the weakness of our flesh. For this place makes against those, who say that there was but one operation in the Lord and one will. For He shows two wills, one human, which from the weakness of the flesh shrinks from suffering; one divine, which is most ready" (*Catena*, 2:295). Erasmus, *De taedio Iesu*, 27, concurs but in another sense: "to be insensible to things that are dangerous and hostile to nature" is "inhuman" rather than "brave"; instead, "the brave are all the braver since they have had to overcome a natural desire to flee." Erasmus, next, discusses heroes from poets such as Virgil and Homer to make his case about how brave men may experience fear. More, however, does not make the "two wills" argument in this instance. For More's own later discussion about Christ's two natures, see *CW* 14.1:183/9–187/6. Erasmus's point, finally, is first anthropological and, eventually, analogical with respect to the person of Christ. More explicitly and immediately ties the fearful to Christ's own example.

90. *Corr.*, 502/16–17.

91. Compare More's treatment of the fearful martyr with Erasmus, *De taedio Iesu*, 46–50: "Is it not true that the more he took on the disabilities of our condition, the more he loved us? And is not the worst of all humanity's woes our dread of death?" (50). Erasmus argues how Christ's fear is "the clearest proof of his love" because "he did not grant himself the same eager joy he bestowed on his members." Yet Christ, Erasmus hastens to add, undergoes death in the manner of both his "more robust members," or brave followers, and his "weaker members," and the latter by "apprehending death in his mind before it was inflicted upon his body" (49).

92. "The implied argument of such popular works as the *Legenda aurea*," Katherine Rodgers reminds us, "is that martyrs possess heroic courage and bravery and thus are fearless in the face of death," yet More makes the "opposite argument" (*CCTM*, 255). More's poetic approach, therefore, differs from "the heritage of late medieval devotion" (*CW* 13:clxxviii).

93. A point that Marian Catholics would recognize. See Anne Dillon's formulation in Dillon, *Michelangelo and the English Martyrs*, 287: "More's writings on the nature of martyrdom and his own example were officially adopted

and disseminated in text and manuscript as part of the programme devised by the Marian regime to restore Catholicism, and more importantly ... to use as a polemical tool against the Protestant reformers who were seen to have been responsible for his death."

94. Matthew 5:11 is quoted from, and this same point is made by, Walsham, *Charitable Hatred*, 2–3.

95. "As More notes, Christ himself had recounted his own trials in the Garden to the disciples ... for the sake of future generations of martyrs who would hear the account and take heart" (House, "Endgame," 34). By recounting his own trials in the Tower, More does the same.

96. On true and false martyrs, see More's preface to his *Confutation of Tyndale's Answer* (1532) in *CW* 8.1:3–40 and 29/37 for the quotation cited above.

97. Martz, *Inner Man*, 92.

98. *Corr.*, 542/94–97 (my emphasis).

99. *Corr.*, 549/17–20 and 559/136–141.

100. "Confortare pusillanimis et noli desperare. Times tristaris tedio et pavore concuteris crudeliter intentati supplicii. Confide. Ego vici mundum qui plus supra modum timui / plus tristatus sum plus affectus tedio plus ad contuitum appetentis tam dirae passionis inhorrui. Habeat fortis / quos imitari se gaudeat magnanimos martyres mille. Tu timidula et imbecillis ovicula / uno me contenta pastore me ducem sequere / de te diffidens in me spera. En ego te in via ista tam formidolosa precedo" (*CW* 14.1:101/10–105/1).

101. Rodgers demonstrates that the paradox of reluctant martyrs functions in tandem with More's style. Miller's sense of how More's style breaks from parallel constructions and includes shifting viewpoints, in other words, relates to More's subject of martyrdom. See *CCTM*, 257, and *CW* 14.2:770.

102. *CW* 14.2:774.

103. On the pseudomartyr debate and More, see Dillon, *The Construction of Martyrdom in the English Catholic Community*, 18–71.

104. *CW* 6.1:427/29–35.

105. *CW* 8.1:11/37–12/1. More condemns schism with heresy because "never shall that country long abide without debate and ruffle where *schisms and factious heresies* are suffered a while to grow" (*CW* 8.1:29/27–9; my emphasis).

106. More, in a famous example, calls Thomas Hitton "the devil's stinking martyr of whose burning Tyndale makes boast" (*CW* 8.1:17/1–2).

107. *CW* 8.1:34/3–7.

108. Bilney's recantation is disputed, but Duffy, *Reformation Divided*, 89, comments: "Whatever the facts about Bilney's end, More's skillful handling of the episode is designed to balance and contrast with his previous portraits of the unrepentant heretics."

109. *CW* 8.1:25/26–34.

110. On religious persecution as "charitable hatred" in the period, a position derived primarily from Augustine's thought, see Walsham, *Charitable Hatred*, 1–105; on More's understanding of combating heresy, see Curtright, *One Thomas More*, 103–39.

111. For Duffy's assessment that More's position on heresy, rather than a "murderous panic," was "rational," see Duffy, *Reformation Divided*, 30–34. On why More thought heresy led to anarchy, see Paul, *Thomas More*, 98–99.

112. *CW* 6.1:480/36–481/3.

113. *CW* 6.1:206/24–28.

114. Dillon, *Michelangelo and the English Martyrs*, 34–35.

115. Eustace Chapuys, the Spanish ambassador, reported that the Carthusians were "put to death for no other cause than their having said and maintained that the Pope was the true chief and sovereign of the universal Christian Church." More's position was identical. For Chapuys's comment, see Gustav A. Bergenroth et al., eds., *Calendar of Letters, Despatches and State Papers, Relating to the Negotiations between England and Spain* (London, 1862–1954), vol. 5, no. 156.

116. Rastell would have known the point from Harpsfield, 214/3–16, who stipulated that there are "those that suffered because they would not deny and refuse the holy faith of Christ," but there is also martyrdom "to preserve the unity of the Church." In the first case, "a man dies to save his own soul"; in the second, "he dies for the whole Church." Hence, the latter form of martyrdom, an effect of the Reformation, Harpsfield suggests is superior, and he places More in this category.

117. More's last prayer is cited from *CW* 13:229/20–24; on its dating see cl–cli.

118. "An non in hac disparitate traditoris et apostolorum nobis iam inde succedentium ad nostram usque aetatem temporum / velut in speculo quodam figura non minus clara quam tristis et horrenda relucet? Cur non hic contemplentur episcopi sompnolentiam suam qui sicut in apostolorum succedunt locum sic utinam virtutes eorum perinde nobis referrent ut et authoritatem libenter amplectuntur / et ignauam istam illorum dormitantiam representant" (*CW* 14.1:259/5–261/1).

119. More's Christ teaches: "But this hour and this power of darkness are not only given to you *now* [*nunc*] against me, but such an hour and such a brief power of darkness will also be given to other governors and other caesars against other disciples of mine" (At non in me dumtaxat vobis nunc / sed et in discipulos meos aliis adversus alios / presidibus dabitur et cesaribus hora similis et potestas tenebrarum brevis / potestas vere tenebrarum inquam) (*CW* 14.1:543/3–5, 4–7;

my emphasis). I draw attention to "now" and "nunc" because "this interlined word implies that future rulers, in persecuting Christ's disciples, will also be persecuting Him, as they are now" (*CW* 14.2:977).

120. More resigned as chancellor on 16 May 1532, the day after the Submission of the Clergy and hours after representative prelates and abbots "duly subscribed the articles of Submission." See John Guy, *The Public Career of Sir Thomas More*, 200–201.

121. As an early example of More's confidence in clerical magistrates, he writes of heresy proceedings in his *Dialogue*: "And finally the law binds not the judge so precisely to the words of the witness but that it leaves many things to be pondered and weighed by his wisdom. For it is in a judge as it is in a physician, to whom there be many good books written able to give good light and instruction" (*CW* 6.1:261/31–36). After he resigned as chancellor, More continued to defend the conduct of bishops. In reply to the charge that many innocents were wrongly condemned as heretics, More writes, "For though I might think that this harm and this harm might happen: yet since I have well since it proved, that the spiritual judges have used themselves in these matters, not only so truly, but over that also so favorably that no man can prove in this realm such harms to have happened yet" (*CW* 10:183/34–184/5).

122. Even More's defense included sharp criticism in the *Apology* (1533). After More condemns Christopher St. German for rebuking prelates "before the people" by writing in the vernacular, More does the same thing by attacking prelates for their failure to reform themselves (*CW* 9:60/12–20; 144/33–145/6).

123. More was commissioned to respond to heretical writings in 1529, an assignment the bishops approved in their provincial statues. There, More's *Dialogue Concerning Heresies* is listed as *Responsio Johannis Tindall ad dialogum Thomae Mori militis, in sermo Anglicano*. See David Wilkins, *Concilia Magnae Britanniae et Hiberniae* (London: 1737), 3:720.

124. *CW* 6.1:341/9–16.

125. *CW* 6.1:344/18–19, 25–28.

126. More writes, "And thus may the bishop order the scripture in our hands with as good reason as the father doth by his discretion appoint which of his children may for his sadness keep a knife to cut his meat and which shall for his wantonness have his knife taken from him for cutting of his fingers" (*CW* 6.1:344/9–13).

127. *Corr.*, 527/476–79.

128. Edward Hall, *Hall's Chronicle* (London: Johnson, Rivington, et al., 1809), 788. Henry's transformation of the Church in England was helped by the fact that eleven bishops were dead or dying by 1535 and the Italians were

deprived of their Sees by him. In all, there were fourteen late bishops replaced. See Chibi, *Henry VIII's Bishops*, 159–60.

129. J. J. Scarisbrick, *The Conservative Episcopate in England, 1529–1535* (PhD thesis, University of Cambridge, 1955), 270–318. In 1535, conservative bishops were made to preach in favor of the schismatic doctrines that they once deemed *anathema*. See Brigden, *London and the Reformation*, 233.

130. For brief biographies of all of Henry's bishops, see Chibi, *Henry VIII's Bishops*, 287–314.

131. Andrew A. Chibi, "Standish, Henry," *ODNB*, 95.

132. "Sicut ignauus gubernator naius ad fragorem tempestatis animo concidens temonem deserit atque in angulum quempiam tristis semet abiiciens puppim permittit fluctibus / sic episcopus mesticiae suae sompno superatus ea relinquat infecta quae in salutem gregis officii sui locus efflagitat / hanc ego certe tristiciam / conferre et comparare non dubitem cum ea tristicia que ducit ut ait ad inferum / immo adeo longe postposuerim quoniam in re divina speciem quondam habet animi desperantis de deo" (*CW* 14.1:265/1–8).

133. *CW* 4:98/27–28.

134. On More's frequent use of this metaphor, see Gerard Wegemer, *The Young Thomas More and the Arts of Liberty* (New York: Cambridge University Press, 2011), 20.

135. *CW* 14.1:265/7–8.

136. Roper, 240.

137. Though most died before Mary's reign and the publication of Rastell's *EW*, there were others who made contrary confessions of faith, including not only Tunstall, but also bishops William Barlow (d. 1568), John Bird (d. 1558), Edmund Bonner (ca. 1500–1569), Paul Bush (1490–1558), John Capon (d. 1559), Nicholas Heath (ca. 1501–78), and Anthony Kitchin (1477–1566).

138. By 1529, More believed without a strong defense against Lutheranism by the prelates and his king, heresy would have brought the end of law and reason to the realm of England; see *CW* 6.1:428/1–19. Once Henry and the bishops changed, More foresaw the consequences; see Duffy, *Reformation Divided*, 34.

139. More: "If anyone is brought to the point where he must either suffer torment or deny God, he need not doubt that it was God's will for him to be brought to this crisis" (*CW* 14.1:69/2–4).

CONCLUSION

1. Robert Bolt, *A Man for All Seasons* (New York: Random House, 1962), 158.

2. We here recall representative statements of exaggerated biographical divisions based upon More's canon: "The schizophrenia created by More's dual roles as author of *Utopia* and inquisitor in heresy cases will never be dispelled" (Guy, *Thomas More*, 122); "the Thomas More of the 'Tower Works,' and of those last letters to Margaret Roper is, on the face of it, *a very different person from the persecutor of protestants*" (Elton, "Thomas More," 354; my emphasis); and Clebsch, *England's Earliest Protestants*, 304, who claims that More, against heretics, exchanged "humaneness for harshness," but "at the end, finding a merciful God, More received a gift that transcended humaneness and humanism, for he became serenely human."

3. On disparaging the "controversial More," see Ridley, *Statesman and Saint*, i, 133, 238, who calls More an "intolerant fanatic" and "persecuting bigot" whose answer to Luther "reads like the scribblings of a dirty-minded schoolboy on a lavatory wall," and sees the "fanatical eyes and mouth of the heretic-baiter" in the Holbein portrait of More with his family; and Marius, *Thomas More*, 345, who writes of More's "rigid affirmation" of the Church that it might have been "an expression of a trait we know well enough in our own time from the clinical observation of people under stress." Such people repeat assertions before "discovering that life as they have meticulously built it up dissolves into nothing." This figure disappears, wholly transformed, after More's arrest. On "devotional More," see Ridley, *Statesman and Saint*, 276, and Marius, *Thomas More*, 472, who writes that "so much of More's consolation lies in his serene confidence that God has His own purposes and that Christians must yield themselves to those purposes in trust and hope."

4. J. H. Baker, *The Legal Profession and the Common Law: Historical Essays* (London: Hambledon Press, 1986), 9. Moots were pervasive in legal training.

5. According to Wilfrid R. Prest, *The Inns of Court under Elizabeth I and the Early Stuarts, 1590–1640* (London: Longman, 1972), 116, mooting was the "formulation and debate of a hypothetical case or set of circumstances involving one or more controversial questions of law."

6. "moot," in *OED*, adj. 1.

7. "moot," in *OED*, 4.

8. Samuel E. Thorne and J. H. Baker, eds., *Readings and Moots at the Inns of Court in the Fifteenth Century* (London: Selden Society, 1990), 2:lxxii–lxxiii.

9. On More's own practice of and understanding of moots, see Edward Berry, "Thomas More and the Legal Imagination," *Studies in Philology* 106, no. 3 (2009): 316–40.

10. "More's Indictment," in Kelly, Karlin, and Wegemer, eds., *Thomas More's Trial by Jury*, 184–85.

11. Elton, *Policy and Police*, 415, wonders if More, "beguiled by memories of 'putting cases' with other lawyers, said something concerning the Act of Supremacy" because "he had always regarded putting his view hypothetically to be a perfect safeguard." On More's lawyerly and imaginative practice of posing hypothetical situations, see Greenblatt, *Renaissance Self-Fashioning*, 32–33.

12. Roper, 246.

13. *Statutes of the Realm*, 1:320 and 3:508.

14. *Corr.*, 557/70–73.

15. *Statutes of the Realm*, 3:474 (my emphasis).

16. *Statutes of the Realm*, 3: 508 (my emphasis).

17. Roper, 245 (my emphasis).

18. Roper writes of Rich's testimony: "Upon whose only report was Sir Thomas More indicted of treason upon the statute whereby it was made treason to deny the king to be Supreme Head of the Church. Into which indictment were put these heinous words, '*maliciously*, traitorously, and diabolically'" (Roper, 245; my emphasis).

19. According to More, the Catholic Church is "all the Christian people whom we call the church *under obedience of the Pope*" (*CW* 6.1, 204/20–21; my emphasis).

20. *Corr.*, 553/87–92; 556/24–29, 556/43–557/2.

21. Walker, *Comedy and Survival in Tudor England*, 182.

22. Walker, *Comedy and Survival in Tudor England*, 183.

23. Roper, 249–50.

24. Roper, 250.

25. I follow Walker, *Comedy and Survival in Tudor England*, 185: "When 'malice' became politicized in defence of the new Henrician order, so 'merriness' was claimed by its opponents and critics as a shield for their own convictions and a badge of honour for their cause."

BIBLIOGRAPHY

Ackroyd, Peter. *The Life of Thomas More.* London: Chatto and Windus, 1998.

Ahnert, Ruth. "Writing in the Tower of London during the Reformation, ca. 1530–1558." *Huntington Library Quarterly* 72, no. 2 (2009): 168–92.

Altman, Joel. *The Tudor Play of Mind: Rhetorical Inquiry and the Development of Elizabethan Drama.* Berkeley: University of California Press, 1978.

Aquinas, Thomas. *Catena aurea.* Vol. 1, *St. Matthew.* Edited by John Newman. Exeter: Saint Austin Press, 1997.

———. *Catena aurea in quatuor Evangelia, I: Expositio in Matthaeum et Marcum.* Edited by Angelico Guarienti, O.P. Rome: Marietti, 1953.

———. *The Summa Theologica.* 2nd and rev. ed. Translated by the Fathers of the English Dominican Province. London: Burns, Oates and Washbourne, 1920–1922. Online edition: https://www.newadvent.org/summa/.

Aristotle. *Rhetoric.* Translated by W. Rhys Roberts. New York: The Modern Library, 1954.

Aurelius, Marcus. *Meditations.* Translated by A. S. L. Farquharson. London: J. M. Dent & Sons, 1961.

Baker-Smith, Dominic. *More's "Utopia."* Toronto: University of Toronto Press, 2000.

Barnett, Mary Jane. "Erasmus and the Hermeneutics of Linguistic Praxis." *Renaissance Quarterly* 49, no. 3 (1996): 542–72.

Baumann, Uwe. "The Humanistic and Religious Controversies and Rivalries of Thomas More (1477/78–1535): A Typology of Religious Forms and Genres?" In *Forms of Conflict and Rivalries in Renaissance Europe*, edited by David A. Lines, Jull Kraye, and Marc Laureys, 79–108. Göttingen: V&R unipress BmbH, 2015.

Beilin, Elaine V. *Redeeming Eve: Women Writers of the English Renaissance.* Princeton, NJ: Princeton University Press, 1987.

Bernard, G. W. *The King's Reformation: Henry VIII and the Remaking of the English Church.* New Haven, CT: Yale University Press, 2005.

———. *Who Ruled Tudor England: Paradoxes of Power*. London: Bloomsbury, 2023.

Billingsley, Dale B. "The Editorial Design of the 1557 *English Works*." *Moreana* 23, no. 89 (1986): 39–48.

Blum, Beth. "Therapeutic Redescription." In *Literary Studies and Human Flourishing*, edited by James F. English and Heather Love, 185–206. Oxford: Oxford University Press, 2023.

Bolt, Robert. *A Man for All Seasons*. New York: Random House, 1962.

Bradshaw, Brendan. "The Controversial Sir Thomas More." *Journal of Ecclesiastical History* 36, no. 4 (1985): 535–69.

Brears, Peter C. D., ed. *Yorkshire Probate Inventories, 1542–1689*. Edited by Peter C. D. Brears. Yorkshire Archaeological Society Record Series 134. Kendal, UK: Yorkshire Archaeological Society, 1972.

Brewer, J. S., J. Gairdner, and R. S. Brodie, eds. *Letters and Papers, Foreign and Domestic, of the Reign of Henry VIII*. Vols. 1–21 (London: Longman, Green, Longman and Roberts, 1862–1932).

Brigden, Susan. *London and the Reformation*. London: Faber and Faber, 1989.

Chambers, R. W. *On the Continuity of English Prose from Alfred to More and His School*. London: Early English Text Society, 1932.

———. *Thomas More*. London: Jonathan Cape, 1935. Reprint, Ann Arbor: University of Michigan Press, 1958.

Chartier, Roger. "Leisure and Sociability: Reading Aloud in Early Modern Europe." In *Urban Life in the Renaissance*, edited by Susan Zimmerman and Ronald Weissman, 103–20. Newark: University of Delaware Press, 1989.

Chibi, Andrew Allan. *Henry VIII's Bishops: Diplomats, Administrations, Scholars and Shepherds*. Cambridge: James Clarkes & Co., 2003.

Cicero, Marcus Tullius. *De inventione*. In *De inventione, De optimo genere oratorum, Topica*, translated by Harry Mortimer Hubbell, 1–348. Cambridge, MA: Harvard University Press, 1949.

———. *Letters to Atticus*. Vol. 2. Translated by E. O. Winstedt. New York: The Macmillan Co., 1913.

———. *Rhetorica ad Herennium*. Translated by H. Caplan. Cambridge, MA: Harvard University Press, 1954.

Clebsch, William A. *England's Early Protestants, 1520–1535*. New Haven, CT: Yale University Press, 1964.

Cousins, A. D. "Role-Play and Self-Portrayal in Thomas More's *A Dialogue of Comfort against Tribulation*." *Christianity and Literature* 54, no. 4 (2004): 457–70.

Cousins, A. D., and Damian Grace, eds. *A Companion to Thomas More*. Madison, NJ: Fairleigh Dickinson University Press, 2009.

Cox, Virginia. "Dialogue." In *A Guide to Neo-Latin Literature*, edited by Victoria Moul, 305–6. Cambridge: Cambridge University Press, 2017.

———. "Rhetoric and Humanism in Quattrocento Venice." *Renaissance Quarterly* 56, no. 3 (2003): 652–94.

Cranmer, Thomas. *The Miscellaneous Writings and Letters of Thomas Cranmer*. Edited by John Edmund Cox. Cambridge: Cambridge University Press, 1846.

Cressy, David. *Literacy and the Social Order: Reading and Writing in Tudor and Stuart England*. Cambridge: Cambridge University Press, 1980.

Crewe, Jonathan V. "'The Encomium Moriae' of William Roper." *ELH* 55, no. 2 (1988): 287–307.

Curtis, Cathy. "'The Best State of the Commonwealth': Thomas More and Quentin Skinner." In *Rethinking the Foundations of Modern Political Thought*, edited by Annabel Brett and James Tully, with Holly Hamilton-Bleakley, 93–112. Cambridge: Cambridge University Press, 2006.

Curtright, Travis. "From Thomas More's Workshop: *De tristitia Christi* and the *Catena aurea*." *LOGOS: A Journal of Catholic Thought and Culture* 18, no. 4 (2015): 100–126.

———. "The Making of a Martyr and Loss of a Poet: Richard Tottel, Reginald Pole, and Thomas More in 1556–57." *Moreana* 55, no. 1 (2018): 1–23.

———. *The One Thomas More*. Washington, DC: Catholic University of America Press, 2012.

———. "Sir Thomas More and His Opposition to Henry VIII in 1533." In *Thomas More: Why Patron of Statesmen?*, edited by Travis Curtright, 111–31. Lanham, MD: Lexington Books, 2015.

———. "Thomas More and the 'genius' of *Utopia*." *Moreana* 54, no. 1 (2017): 1–18.

———. "Thomas More as Author of Margaret Roper's Letter to Alice Alington." *Moreana* 56, no. 1 (2019): 1–27.

———. "Thomas More on Humor." *LOGOS: A Journal of Catholic Thought and Culture* 17, no. 1 (2014): 13–35.

———, ed. *Thomas More: Why Patron of Statesmen?* Lanham, MD: Lexington Books, 2015.

Cyprian, Bishop of Carthage. *A svvete and devote sermon of holy saynt Ciprian of mortalitie of man. The rules of a Christian lyfe made by Picus erle of Mirandula, bothe translated into englyshe by syr Thomas Elyot knyghte*. London: in aedibus Tho. Bertheleti, 1534.

Darnton, Robert. "What Is the History of Books?" *Daedalus* 111, no. 3 (1982): 65–83.

Deiter, Kristen. "Building Opposition at the Early Tudor Tower of London: Thomas More's *Dialogue of Comfort.*" *Renaissance and Reformation* 38, no. 1 (2015): 27–55.
Delacourt, J. *Essai sur la langue de Sir Thomas More.* Paris: H. Didier, 1914.
Demers, Patricia. "Margaret Roper and Erasmus: The Relationship of Translator and Source." In *A Companion to Margaret More Roper Studies: Life Records, Essential Texts, and Critical Essays*, edited by William Gentrup and Elizabeth McCutcheon, 158–71. Washington, DC: Catholic University of America Press, 2022.
Derrett, J. Duncan M. "The Trial of Sir Thomas More." *English Historical Review* 79, no. 312 (1964): 449–77.
Dillon, Anne. *The Construction of Martyrdom in the English Catholic Community.* Burlington, VT: Ashgate, 2002.
———. *Michelangelo and the English Martyrs.* Burlington, VT: Ashgate, 2012.
Duffy, Eamon. "'The comen knowen multitude of christen men': *A Dialogue Concerning Heresies* and the Defense of Christendom." In George Logan, ed., *The Cambridge Companion to Thomas More*, 191–215.
———. *Fires of Faith: Catholic England under Mary Tudor.* New Haven, CT: Yale University Press, 2009.
———. *Marking the Hours: English People and Their Prayers, 1240–1570.* New Haven, CT: Yale University Press, 2006.
———. *Reformation Divided: Catholics, Protestants and the Conversion of England.* New York: Bloomsbury, 2017.
———. "Writing the Reformation: Fiction and Faction." In *A People's Tragedy: Studies in Reformation*, 196–228. London: Bloomsbury, 2021.
Eden, Kathy. *The Renaissance Rediscovery of Intimacy.* Chicago: University of Chicago Press, 2012.
Eire, Carlos M. N. *Reformations: The Early Modern World, 1450–1650.* New Haven, CT: Yale University Press, 2016.
Elton, G. R. *Policy and Police: The Enforcement of the Reformation in the Age of Thomas Cromwell.* Cambridge: Cambridge University Press, 1972.
———. "The Real Thomas More." In *Studies in Tudor and Stuart Politics and Government*, Vol. 3, *Papers and Reviews, 1973–1981*, 344–55. Cambridge: Cambridge University Press, 2002.
———. Review of *The Complete Works of St. Thomas More. English Historical Review* 93, no. 367 (1978): 399–404.
———. "Thomas More and Thomas Cromwell." In *Studies in Tudor and Stuart Politics and Government*, Vol. 4, *Papers and Reviews, 1982–1990*, 144–60. Cambridge: Cambridge University Press, 1992.

———, ed. *The Tudor Constitution*. 2nd ed. Cambridge: Cambridge University Press, 1982.

Epictetus. *Epictetus: Discourses and Enchiridion*. Translated by Thomas Wentworth Higginson. Roslyn, NY: Walter J. Black, 1944.

Erasmus, Desiderius. *The Collected Works of Erasmus*. 86 vols. Toronto: University of Toronto Press, 1974–2021.

———. *Conficiendarum epistolarum formula*. Translated by Charles Fantazzi. In *The Collected Works of Erasmus*, edited by J. K. Sowards, 25:255–67. Toronto: University of Toronto Press, 1985.

———. *The Correspondence of Erasmus: Letters 594 to 841, 1517 to 1518*. Translated by R. A. B. Mynors and D. F. S. Thomson. In *The Collected Works of Erasmus*, Vol. 5. Toronto: University of Toronto Press, 1979.

———. *The Correspondence of Erasmus: Letters 1122 to 1251, 1520 to 1521*. Translated by R. A. B. Mynors. In *The Collected Works of Erasmus*, Vol. 8. Toronto: University of Toronto Press, 1988.

———. *De conscribendis epistolis*. Translated by Charles Fantazzi. In *The Collected Works of Erasmus*, edited by J. K. Sowards, 25:12–254. Toronto: University of Toronto Press, 1985.

———. *De copia: Foundations of the Abundant Style*. Translated by Betty I. Knott. In *The Collected Works of Erasmus*, edited by Craig R. Thompson, 24:290–659. Toronto: University of Toronto Press, 1978.

———. *De ratione studi*. Translated by Brian McGregor. In *The Collected Works of Erasmus*, edited by Craig R. Thompson, 24:661–91. Toronto: University of Toronto Press, 1978.

———. *Desiderius Erasmus of Rotterdam to Beatus Rhenanus of Sélestat, 1521*. Translated by R. A. B. Mynors. In *The Collected Works of Erasmus*, 8:217–21. Toronto: University of Toronto Press, 1988.

———. *The Education of a Christian Prince*. Translated by Lester K. Born. New York: W. W. Norton, 1968.

———. *Erasmus on Literature: His Ratio or System of 1518–1519*. Translated by Robert D. Sider. Edited by Mark Vessey. Toronto: University of Toronto Press, 2021.

———. *Paraclesis*. In *Christian Humanism and the Reformation: Selected Writings of Erasmus*, 3rd ed., edited by John C. Olin, 97–108. New York: Fordham University Press, 1987.

———. *The Praise of Folly*. Translated by Clarence Miller. New Haven, CT: Yale University Press, 1979.

Erasmus, Desiderius, and John Colet. "A Short Debate Concerning the Distress Alarm, and Sorrow of Jesus." In *Spiritualia and Pastoralia*, translated by Michael J. Health, in *The Collected Works of Erasmus*, 70:1–67. Toronto: University of Toronto Press, 1998.

Erler, Mary C. "The Laity." In *A Companion to the Early Printed Book in Britain, 1476–1558*, edited by Vincent Gillespie and Susan Powell, 127–49. Cambridge: D. S. Brewer, 2019.

———. *Women, Reading, and Piety in Late Medieval England*. Cambridge: Cambridge University Press, 2002.

Fisher, John. *English Works of John Fisher, Bishop of Rochester (1469–1535): Sermons and Other Writings, 1520–1535*. Edited by Cecilia A. Hatt. Oxford: Oxford University Press, 2002.

Fludernik, Monika. *Metaphors of Confinement: The Prison in Fact, Fiction, and Fantasy*. Oxford: Oxford University Press, 2019.

Fox, Adam. *Oral and Literature Culture in England, 1500–1700*. Oxford: Clarendon, 2002.

Fox, Alistair. *Thomas More: History and Providence*. New Haven, CT: Yale University Press, 1985.

Friedberg, Emil, ed. *Corpus Iuris Canonici*. 2 vols. Leipzig, 1879–81.

Geanakopolos, Deno J. "The Council of Florence (1438–1439) and the Problem of Union between the Greek and Latin Churches." *Church History* 24, no. 4 (1955): 324–46.

Gee, John Archer. "Margaret Roper's English Version of Erasmus' *Precatio Dominica* and the Apprenticeship behind Early Tudor Translation." *Review of English Studies* 13 (1937): 257–71.

Gentrup, William, ed. *A Companion to Margaret More Roper Studies: Life Records, Essential Texts, and Critical Essays*. Edited by William Gentrup and Elizabeth McCutcheon. Washington, DC: Catholic University of America Press, 2022.

Gogan, Brian. *The Common Corps of Christendom*. Leiden: E. J. Brill, 1982.

Goodrich, Jaime. "Thomas More and Margaret More Roper: A Case for Rethinking Women's Participation in the Early Modern Public Sphere." *The Sixteenth Century Journal* 39, no. 4 (2008): 1021–40.

Gray, Jonathan Michael. *Oaths and the English Reformation*. Cambridge: Cambridge University Press, 2013.

Greenblatt, Stephen. *Renaissance Self-Fashioning: From More to Shakespeare*. Chicago: University of Chicago Press, 1980.

Gregory, Brad S. *Salvation at Stake: Christian Martyrdom in Early Modern Europe*. Cambridge, MA: Harvard University Press, 1999.

Guillen, Claudio. "Notes toward the Study of the Renaissance Letter." In *Renaissance Genres: Essays on Theory, History, and Interpretation*, edited by

Barbara Kiefer Lewalski, 70–101. Cambridge, MA: Harvard University Press, 1986.

Guy, John. *A Daughter's Love: Thomas and Margaret More*. London: Fourth Estate, 2008.

———. "The Henrician Age." In *The Varieties of British Political Thought, 1500–1800*, edited by J. G. A. Pocock, Gordon J. Schochet, and Lois G. Schwoerer, 13–46. Cambridge: Cambridge University Press, 1996.

———. *The Public Career of Sir Thomas More*. New Haven, CT: Yale University Press, 1980.

———. *Thomas More*. London: Arnold, 2000.

———. *Thomas More: A Very Brief History*. London: Society for Promoting Christian Knowledge, 2017.

Hall, Edward. *Hall's Chronicle*. London: Johnson, Rivington, et al., 1809.

Harpsfield, Nicolas. *The Life and Death of Sir Thomas More, Knight*. Edited by Elsie Vaughan Hitchcock. London: Early English Text Society, 1932.

Henry VIII. *Assertio septem sacramentorum adversus Martinum Lutherum*. Edited by P. Fraenkel. Munster: Aschendorf, 1992.

Hexter, J. H. "Thomas More and the Problem of Counsel." *Albion: A Quarterly Journal concerned with British Studies* 10 (1978): 55–66.

Hilton, Walter. *Walter Hilton: The Scale of Perfection*. Edited by John P. H. Clark and Rosemary Dorward. New York: Paulist Press, 1991.

Hosington, Brenda M. "'Quid Dormitis?': More's Use of Sleep as a Motif in *De tristitia*." *Moreana* 26, no. 100 (1989): 55–69.

———. "Translating Devotion: Mary Roper Basset's English Rendering of Thomas More's 'De tristitia . . . Christi.'" *Renaissance and Reformation* 35, no. 4 (2012): 63–95.

———. "Translation in the Service of Politics and Religion: A Family Tradition for Thomas More, Margaret Roper and Mark Clarke Basset." In *In between Scylla and Charybdis: Learned Letter Writers Navigating the Reefs of Religious and Political Controversy in Early Modern Europe*, edited by Jeanine De Landtsheer and Henk Nellen, 93–108. Leiden: Brill, 2010.

House, Seymour Baker. "Endgame: The Genesis of More's *The Sadness of Christ*." *Moreana* 45, no. 174 (2008): 33–53.

———. "'The Filed Is Won': An Introduction to the Tower Works." In *A Companion to Thomas More*, edited by A. D. Cousins and Damian Grace, 225–42. Madison, NJ: Fairleigh Dickinson University Press, 2009.

Hutchings, W. H. *The Life of Christ*. London: Rivingtons, 1881.

Ives, Eric. *The Life and Death of Anne Boleyn*. Oxford: Blackwell, 2005.

Jardine, Lisa. *Erasmus, Man of Letters: The Construction of Charisma*. Princeton, NJ: Princeton University Press, 1993.

Kaufman, Peter Iver. "Absolute Margaret: Margaret More Roper and 'Well Learned' Men." *Sixteenth Century Journal* 20, no. 3 (1989): 443–56.

Kelly, Henry Ansgar. "Thomas More and Inquisitorial Due Process." *English Historical Review* 123 (2008): 847–94.

Kelly, Henry Ansgar, Louis W. Karlin, and Gerard Wegemer, eds. *Thomas More's Trial by Jury: A Procedural and Legal Review with a Collection of Documents*. Rochester, NY: Boydell Press, 2011.

King, John N. "Thomas More, William Tyndale, and the Printing of Religious Propaganda." In *Oxford Handbook of Tudor Literature, 1485–1603*, edited by Mike Pincombe and Cathy Shank, 105–20. Oxford: Oxford University Press, 2009.

Lakowski, Romuald I. "Thomas More, Protestants, and Turks: Persecution and Martyrdom in *A Dialogue of Comfort*." *The Ben Jonson Journal* 20, no. 1 (2000): 199–223.

Lewis, C. S. *English Literature in the Sixteenth Century Excluding Drama*. Oxford: Clarendon, 1954.

Logan, George, ed. *The Cambridge Companion to Thomas More*. Cambridge: Cambridge University Press, 2011.

———. *The Meaning of More's Utopia*. Princeton, NJ: Princeton University Press, 1983.

Love, Nicholas. *The Mirror of the Blessed Lyf of Jesus Christ / A Translation of the Latin Work Entitled Meditationes Vitae Christi / Attributed to Cardinal Bonaventura*. Edited by Lawrence F. Powell. Oxford: Clarendon, 1908.

———. *The Mirror of the Blessed Life of Jesus Christ: A Full Critical Edition*. Edited by Michael Sargent. Abington: Routledge, 2019.

Lowenstein, David. "Religious Demonization, Anti-Heresy Polemic, and Thomas More." In *Treacherous Faith: The Specter of Heresy in Early Modern English Literature and Culture*, 23–68. Oxford: Oxford University Press, 2013.

Ludolph of Saxony. *The Life of Jesus Christ*. Part Two, Vol. 1, *Chapters 1–57*. Translated by Milton T. Walsh. Collegeville, MN: Liturgical Press, 2021.

MacCulloch, Diarmaid. *Thomas Cromwell: A Revolutionary Life*. New York: Viking, 2018.

MacMahon, L. "The Ambassadors of Henry VIII: The Personnel of English Diplomacy, 1500–1550." PhD thesis, University of Kent, 2000.

Mantel, Hilary. *Wolf Hall*. New York: Henry Holt and Co., 2009.

Marc'hadour, Germain. *The Bible in the Works of St. Thomas More*. Part 2, *The Four Gospels*. Niuswkoop: B. De Graaf, 1969.

———. "Latin Lives of Thomas More." In Cousins and Grace, eds., *A Companion to Thomas More*, 21–38.

Marius, Richard. "Henry VIII, Thomas More, and the Bishop of Rome." *Albion: A Quarterly Journal with British Studies* (Quincentennial Essays on St. Thomas More) 10 (1978): 89–107.

———. *Thomas More: A Biography*. New York: Vintage Books, 1985.

Marshall, Peter. *Heretics and Believers: A History of the English Reformation*. New Haven, CT: Yale University Press, 2017.

———. "The Last Years." In George Logan, ed., *Cambridge Companion to Thomas More*, 116–38.

Martin, Jan J. "The Congregation and Church of England? William Tyndale's Approach to Lexical and Ecclesiological Reform between 1525 and 1535." *Moreana* 59, no. 1 (2022): 66–95.

Martz, Louis L. *Thomas More: The Search for the Inner Man*. New Haven, CT: Yale University Press, 1992.

———. "The Tower Works." In *St. Thomas More: Action and Contemplation*, edited by Richard S. Sylvester, 59–83. New Haven, CT: Yale University Press, 1972.

McConica, James K. "The Recusant Reputation of Thomas More." In *Essential Articles for the Study of Thomas More*, edited by Richard S. Sylvester and Germain Marc'hadour, 136–49. Hamden, CT: Archon Books, 1977.

McCutcheon, Elizabeth, ed. *A Companion to Margaret More Roper Studies: Life Records, Essential Texts, and Critical Essays*, edited by William Gentrup and Elizabeth McCutcheon. Washington, DC: Catholic University of America Press, 2022.

———. "Decoding the Alice-Alington-Margaret More Roper Letters." *Moreana* 57, no. 2 (2020): 144–70.

———. "'This Prison of the Yerth': The Topos Immurement in the Writings in St. Thomas More." *Cithara* 25 (1985): 37–46.

———. "'A Young, Virtuous, and Well-Learned Gentle-woman': Margaret More Roper in the Republic of Letters." In Gentrup and McCutcheon, eds., *A Companion to Margaret More Roper Studies*, 123–57.

McGrath, Alister E. *The Intellectual Origins of the Reformation*. 2nd ed. Oxford: Blackwell, 2004.

McKenzie, D. F. "The Book as an Expressive Form." In *Bibliography and the Sociology of Texts*, 1–21. London: British Library, 1986.

McSorley, Harry J. "Erasmus and the Primacy of the Roman Pontiff: Between Concilarism and Papalism." *Archiv für Reformationsgeschichte* 65 (1974): 37–54.

Miller, Clarence H. "More's Biblical Exegesis in *De tristitia Christi*: Original Interpretations and Applications." *Moreana* 45, no. 174 (2008): 17–32.

Mitjans, Frank. "The 'Discovery' of the Autograph of Thomas More's *De tristitia Christi* through Andrés Vázquez de Prada." *Moreana* 58, no. 1 (2021): 112–24.

———. "Thomas More's Veneration of Images, Praying to Saints and Going on Pilgrimages." *Thomas More Studies* 3, no. 7 (2008): 64–69.

———. *Thomas More's Vocation*. Washington, DC: Catholic University of America Press, 2022.

Monfasani, John. *George of Trebizond: A Biography and a Study of His Rhetoric and Logic*. Leiden: E. J. Brill, 1976.

Montefusco, Lucia Calboli. "*Ductus* and *color*: The Right Way to Compose a Suitable Speech." *Rhetorica: A Journal of the History of Rhetoric* 21, no. 2 (2003): 113–31.

Monti, James. *The King's Good Servant but God's First: The Life and Writings of Saint Thomas More*. San Francisco: Ignatius, 1997.

More, Thomas. *The Correspondence of Sir Thomas More*. Edited by Elizabeth Frances Rogers. Princeton, NJ: Princeton University Press, 1947.

———. *The Essential Works of Thomas More*. Edited by Gerard B. Wegemer and Stephen W. Smith. New Haven, CT: Yale University Press, 2020.

———. *The Last Letters of Thomas More*. Annotated ed. Edited by Alvaro De Silva. Grand Rapids, MI: Wm. B. Eerdmans, 2001.

———. *St. Thomas More: Selected Letters*. Edited by Elizabeth Frances Rogers. New Haven, CT: Yale University Press, 1961.

———. *Thomas More's Prayer Book: A Facsimile Reproduction of the Annotated Pages*. Transcribed and translated by Louis L. Martz and Richard S. Sylvester. New Haven, CT: Yale University Press, 1969.

———. *A Thomas More Source Book*. Edited by Gerard B. Wegemer and Stephen W. Smith. Washington, DC: Catholic University of America Press, 2004.

———. *Utopia*. 3rd ed. Translated by Robert M. Adams. Edited by George Logan. Cambridge: Cambridge University Press, 2016.

———. *Utopia: Latin Text and English Translation*. Edited by George M. Logan, Robert M. Adams, and Clarence H. Miller. Cambridge: Cambridge University Press, 2006.

———. *The Works of Sir Thomas More, Knight, Sometime Lord Chancellour of England, Written by him in the English Tongue* (1557). 2 Vols. Edited by William Rastell. London: Scholar Press, 1978.

———. *The Yale Edition of the Complete Works of St. Thomas More.* Vol. 1, *English Poems, Life of Pico, The Last Things.* Edited by Anthony S. G. Edwards, Katherine Gardiner Rodgers, and Clarence Miller. New Haven, CT: Yale University Press, 1997.

———. *The Yale Edition of the Complete Works of St. Thomas More.* Vol. 2, *The History of King Richard III.* Edited by Richard S. Sylvester. New Haven, CT: Yale University Press, 1963.

———. *The Yale Edition of the Complete Works of St. Thomas More.* Vol. 3, Part I, *Translations of Lucian.* Edited by Craig R. Thompson. New Haven, CT: Yale University Press, 1974.

———. *The Yale Edition of the Complete Works of St. Thomas More.* Vol. 3, Part II, *The Latin Poems.* Edited by Clarence H. Miller, Leicester Bradner, Charles A. Lynch, and Revilo P. Oliver. New Haven, CT: Yale University Press, 1984.

———. *The Yale Edition of the Complete Works of St. Thomas More.* Vol. 4, *Utopia.* Edited by Edward Surtz and J. H. Hexter. New Haven, CT: Yale University Press, 1965.

———. *The Yale Edition of the Complete Works of St. Thomas More.* Vol. 5, *Responsio ad Lutherum.* Edited by J. M. Headley. New Haven, CT: Yale University Press, 1969.

———. *The Yale Edition of the Complete Works of St. Thomas More.* Vol. 6, *A Dialogue Concerning Heresies.* Edited by Thomas Lawler, Germain Marc'hadour, and Richard Marius. New Haven, CT: Yale University Press, 1981.

———. *The Yale Edition of the Complete Works of St. Thomas More.* Vol 6., Part II, *A Dialogue concerning Heresies.* Edited by Thomas Lawler, Germain Marc'hadour, and Richard Marius. New Haven, CT: Yale University Press, 1981.

———. *The Yale Edition of the Complete Works of St. Thomas More.* Vol. 7, *Letter to Bugenhagen, Supplication of Souls, Letter against Frith.* Edited by Frank Manley, Germain Marc'hadour, Richard Marius, and Clarence H. Miller. New Haven, CT: Yale University Press, 1990.

———. *The Yale Edition of the Complete Works of St. Thomas More.* Vol. 8, Part I, *The Confutation of Tyndale's Answer.* Edited by Louis A. Schuster, Richard C. Marius, James P. Lusardi, and Richard J. Schoeck. New Haven, CT: Yale University Press, 1973.

———. *The Yale Edition of the Complete Works of St. Thomas More.* Vol. 8, Part II, *The Confutation of Tyndale's Answer.* Edited by Louis A. Schuster, Richard C. Marius, James P. Lusardi, and Richard J. Schoeck. New Haven, CT: Yale University Press, 1973.

———. *The Yale Edition of the Complete Works of St. Thomas More*. Vol. 8, Part III, *The Confutation of Tyndale's Answer*. Edited by Louis A. Schuster, Richard C. Marius, James P. Lusardi, and Richard J. Schoeck. New Haven, CT: Yale University Press, 1973.

———. *The Yale Edition of the Complete Works of St. Thomas More*. Vol. 9, *The Apology*. Edited by J. B. Trapp. New Haven, CT: Yale University Press, 1979.

———. *The Yale Edition of the Complete Works of St. Thomas More*. Vol. 10, *The Debellation of Salem and Bizance*. Edited by John Guy, Ralph Keen, Clarence H. Miller, and Ruth McGugan. New Haven, CT: Yale University Press, 1987.

———. *The Yale Edition of the Complete Works of St. Thomas More*. Vol. 11, *The Answer to a Poisoned Book*. Edited by Stephen Merriam Foley and Clarence H. Miller. New Haven, CT: Yale University Press, 1985.

———. *The Yale Edition of the Complete Works of St. Thomas More*. Vol. 12, *A Dialogue of Comfort against Tribulation*. Edited by Louis L. Martz and Frank Manley. New Haven, CT: Yale University Press, 1976.

———. *The Yale Edition of the Complete Works of St. Thomas More*. Vol. 13, *Treatise on the Passion, Treatise on the Blessed Body, Instructions and Prayers*. Edited by Garry E. Haupt. New Haven, CT: Yale University Press, 1976.

———. *The Yale Edition of the Complete Works of St. Thomas More*. Vol. 14, Part I, *De tristitia Christi*. Edited and translated by Clarence H. Miller. New Haven, CT: Yale University Press, 1976.

———. *The Yale Edition of the Complete Works of St. Thomas More*. Vol. 14, Part II, *De tristitia Christi*. Edited and translated by Clarence H. Miller. New Haven, CT: Yale University Press, 1976.

———. *The Yale Edition of the Complete Works of St. Thomas More*. Vol. 15, *In Defense of Humanism*. Edited by Daniel Kinney. New Haven, CT: Yale University Press, 1986.

Murphy, Clare. "The Turks in More and Tyndale." In *Word, Church and State: Tyndale Quincentenary Essays*, edited by John T. Day, Eric Lund, and Anne M. O'Donnell, 228–42. Washington, DC: Catholic University of America Press, 1998.

Nussbaum, Martha. *Therapy of Desire: Theory and Practice in Hellenistic Ethics*. Princeton, NJ: Princeton University Press, 1994.

O'Malley, John W. Introduction to *Spiritualia and Pastoralia*. In *Collected Works of Erasmus*, 70:ix–li. Toronto: University of Toronto Press, 1998.

Patrides, C. A. "'The Bloody and Cruell Turke': The Background of a Renaissance Commonplace." *Studies in the Renaissance* 10 (1963): 125–35.

Paul, Joanne. *Thomas More.* Cambridge: Polity Press, 2016.
Pettegree, Andrew. "Printing and the Reformation: The English Exception." *The Beginning of English Protestantism*, edited by Peter Marshall and Alex Ryrie, 157–79. Cambridge: Cambridge University Press, 2002.
Pineas, Rainer. *Thomas More and Tudor Polemics.* Bloomington: Indiana University Press, 1968.
Pocock, Nicholas, ed. *Records of the Reformation: The Divorce (1527–1533).* Oxford: Clarendon, 1870.
Quintilian. *The "Institutio Oratoria" with an English Translation by H. E. Butler.* Translated by H. E. Butler. London: William Heinmann, 1921.
———. *The Orator's Education, Books 6–8.* Edited and Translated by Donald A. Russell. Cambridge, MA: Harvard University Press. 2001.
Reed, A. W. *Early Tudor Drama: Medwall, the Rastells, Heywood, and the More Circle.* London: Methuen & Co. Ltd, 1926.
———. "William Rastell and More's English Works." In *The English Works of Sir Thomas More*, edited by W. E. Campbell; introduction and philological notes by A. W. Reed, 1:1–12. London: Eyre and Spottiswoode, 1931.
Rex, Richard. "The Crisis of Obedience: God's Word and Henry's Reformation." *The Historical Journal* 39, no. 4 (1996): 863–94.
———. "The English Campaign against Luther in the 1520s: The Alexander Prize Essay." *Transactions of the Royal Historical Society* 39 (1989): 85–106.
———. "The Execution of the Holy Maid of Kent." *Historical Research* 64, no. 154 (1991): 216–20.
———, ed. *Henry VIII and Martin Luther: The Second Controversy, 1525–1527.* Woodbridge: The Boydell Press, 2021.
———. *Henry VIII and the English Reformation.* 2nd ed. New York: Palgrave Macmillan, 2006.
———. "The Religion of Henry VIII." *The Historical Journal* 57, no. 1 (2014): 1–32.
———. "Thomas More and the Heretics: Statesman or Fanatic?" In George Logan, ed., *Cambridge Companion to Thomas More*, 93–115.
Reynolds, Ernest Edwin. *Margaret Roper: Eldest Daughter of St. Thomas More.* New York: P. J. Kenedy & Sons, 1960.
———. *St. Thomas More: A Great Man in Hard Times.* Post Falls, ID: Mediatrix Press, 2017.
Ridley, Jasper. *Statesman and Saint: Thomas Wolsey and Thomas More.* New York: Viking, 1982.
Rodgers, Katherine Gardiner. "The Lessons of Gethsemane: *De tristitia Christi.*" In George Logan, ed., *Cambridge Companion to Thomas More*, 239–62.

Rogers, William J. "Thomas More's Polemical Poetics." *English Literary Renaissance* 38, no. 3 (2008): 387–408.

Roper, William. "Life of Sir Thomas More." In *A Thomas More Source Book*, edited by Gerard B. Wegemer and Stephen W. Smith, 16–65. Washington, DC: Catholic University of America Press, 2004.

Roper, William, and Cavendish, George. *Two Early Tudor Lives: "The Life and Death of Cardinal Wolsey" by George Cavendish and "The Life of Thomas More" by William Roper.* Edited by Richard S. Sylvester and Davis P. Harding. New Haven, CT: Yale University Press, 1962.

Ryrie, Alec. *The English Reformation: A Very Brief History.* London: Society for Promoting Christian Knowledge, 2020.

Saenger, Paul. *Space between Words: The Origins of Silent Reading.* Stanford, CA: Stanford University Press, 1997.

Sandberg, Julianne. "Utopian Literality: Thomas More and the Faith of Catholic Reading." *Studies in Philology* 117, no. 2 (2020): 261–84.

Sawada, Paul Akio. "Was Thomas More a 'Conciliarist'?" In *Thomas More . . . and More: Freundesgabe für/Liber Amicorum for Hubertus Schulte Herbrüggen*, edited by Christoph M. Peters and Friedrich-K. Unterweg, 73–88. Frankfurt am Main: Peter Lang, 2002.

Scarisbrick, J. J. "Appendix 1: Protest of Archbishop William Warham in Defense of the Church on February 24, 1532." *Moreana* 58, no. 2 (2021): 236–37.

———. "Archbishop William Warham's 1532 Defense," *Moreana* 58, no. 2 (2021): 218–35.

———. "The Canon Law of the Divorce." In Scarisbrick, *Henry VIII*, 163–97.

———. "The Conservative Episcopate in England, 1529–1535." PhD thesis, University of Cambridge, 1955.

———. *Henry VIII.* Berkeley: University of California Press, 1968.

———. "The Pardon of the Clergy, 1531." *Cambridge Historical Journal* 12, no. 1 (1956): 22–39.

———. "Warham, William." In *Oxford Dictionary of National Biography*, edited by H. C. G. Matthew and Brian Harrison, 57:411–15. Oxford: Oxford University Press, 2004.

Schmidt, Gabriela. "'This Turk's persecution for the faith': Thomas More's *Dialogue of Comfort* and the Reformation Debate on Martyrdom." *Moreana* 45, no. 175 (2008): 209–38.

Schoeck, R. J. "On the Letters of Thomas More." *Moreana* 4, no. 15–16 (1967): 193–203.

———. "Thomas More's *Dialogue of Comfort* and the Problem of the Real Grand Turk." *An English Miscellany* 20 (1969): 23–37.
Scott, Alison V. "More's Letters and the 'Comfort of the Truth.'" In *A Companion to Thomas More*, edited by A. D. Cousins and Damian Grace, 53–76. Madison, NJ: Fairleigh Dickinson University Press, 2009.
Sheils, William. "1535 in 1935: Catholic Saints and English Identity: The Canonization of Thomas More and John Fisher." In *Reformation Reputations: The Power of the Individual in English Reformation History*, edited by David J. Crankshaw and George W. C. Gross, 159–88. Cham, Switzerland: Palgrave Macmillan, 2021.
Simpson, James. "Rhetoric, Conscience, and the Playful Positions of Sir Thomas More." In *The Oxford Handbook of Tudor Literature 1485–1603*, edited by Mike Pincombe and Cathy Shank, 121–36. Oxford: Oxford University Press, 2009.
Skinner, Quentin. *Forensic Shakespeare*. Oxford: Oxford University Press, 2014.
———. *Reason and Rhetoric in the Philosophy of Thomas Hobbes*. Cambridge: Cambridge University Press, 1996.
Sowerby, Tracey A. "'All Our Books Do Be Sent into Other Countreys and Translated': Henrician Polemic in Its International Context." *English Historical Review* 121, no. 494 (2006): 1271–99.
Stapleton, Thomas. *The Life and Illustrious Martyrdom of Sir Thomas More*. Translated by Philip E. Hallet. New York: Benziger Brothers, 1928.
State Papers. Vol. 1, *King Henry VIII*. London: John Murray, 1831.
St. German, Christopher. *Doctor and Student*. Edited by T. F. T. Plucknett and J. L. Barton. London: S. Richardson and C. Lintot, 1761.
———. *New Additions*. In *Doctor and Student*, edited by T. F. T. Plucknett and J. L. Barton, 315–40. London: S. Richardson and C. Lintot, 1761.
Sutton, Anne F. "Merchants." In *A Companion to the Early Printed Book in Britain, 1476–1558*, edited by Vincent Gillespie and Susan Powell, 127–49. Cambridge: D. S. Brewer, 2019.
Sylvester, Richard S. "Roper's Life of More." *Moreana* 36 (1972): 47–59.
———. "'Si Hythlodaeo Credimus': Vision and Revision in Thomas More's *Utopia* as a Dialogue." In *Essential Articles for the Study of Thomas More*, edited by Richard S. Sylvester and Germain Marc'hadour, 290–301. Hamden, CT: Archon Books, 1977.
Taylor, Andrew W. "'In stede of harme inestimable good': *A Dialogue of Comfort against Tribulation*." In George Logan, ed., *The Cambridge Companion to Thomas More*, 216–38.

Thecla, Sr. Mary. "St. Thomas More and the *Catena aurea*." *Modern Language Notes* 61 (1946): 523–29.

Thomas, Keith. "The Meaning of Literacy in Early Modern England." In *The Written Word: Literacy in Transition*, edited by Gerd Baumann, 97–131. Oxford: Clarendon, 1986.

Thomas, Morely. "Tunstal—Trimmer or Martyr?" *Journal of Ecclesiastical History* 24, no. 4 (1973): 337–55.

Thompson, Elbert N. S. *Literary Bypaths of the Renaissance*. New Haven, CT: Yale University Press, 1924.

Tomlins, T. E., et al., eds., *Statutes of the Realm*. 11 Vols. London: Dawsons, 1810–1828.

Torrell, Jean-Pierre. *Saint Thomas Aquinas*. Vol. 1, *The Person and His Work*. Translated by Robert Royal. Washington, DC: Catholic University of America Press, 1996.

Tracy, James D. "Humanists among the Scholastics: Erasmus, More, and Lefevre d'Etaples on the Humanity of Christ." In *Erasmus of Rotterdam Society Yearbook*, 5:30–42. Oxon Hill, MD: Erasmus of Rotterdam Society, 1985.

Tyndale, William. *An Answere Unto Sir Thomas Mores Dialoge*. Edited by Anne M. O'Donnell and Jared Wicks. Washington, DC: Catholic University of America Press, 2000.

———, trans. *The New Testament: The Text of the Worms Edition of 1526 in Original Spelling*. Edited by W. R. Cooper. London: The British Library, 2000.

———. *The Obedience of a Christian Man*. Edited with introduction and notes by David Daniell. London: Penguin, 2000.

Tyndall, William, Iohn Frith, and Doctor Barnes. *The Whole works of W. Tyndall, Iohn Frith, and Doct. Barnes, three worthy Martyrs, and principall teachers of this Church of England, collected and compiled in one Tome together, being before scattered and now in print here exhibited to the Church*. Edited by John Foxe. London: John Daye, 1573.

Van Dijk, Mathilde, José van Aelst, and Tom Gaens. Introduction to *Faithful to the Cross in a Moving World: Late Medieval Carthusians as Devotional Reformers*. *Church History and Religious Culture* 96, no. 1 (2016): 1–129.

Von Habsburg, Maximilian. *Catholic and Protestant Translations of the "Imitatio Christi": 1425–1660*. Farnham: Ashgate, 2011.

Walker, Greg. *John Heywood: Comedy and Survival in Tudor England*. Oxford: Oxford University Press, 2000.

Walsham, Alexandra. *Charitable Hatred: Tolerance and Intolerance in England, 1500–1700*. Manchester: Manchester University Press, 2006.

———. "The Spider and the Bee: The Perils of Printing for Refutation in Tudor England." In *Tudor Books and Readers: Materiality and the Construction of Meaning*, edited by John King, 163–91. Cambridge: Cambridge University Press, 2010.

Wandel, Lee Palmer. *The Eucharist in the Reformation*. New York: Cambridge University Press, 2006.

Warner, Christopher J. *Henry VIII's Divorce: Literature and the Politics of the Printing Press*. Rochester, NY: The Boydell Press, 1998.

Watt, Diane. "Barton, Elizabeth." In *Oxford Dictionary of National Biography*, edited by H. C. G. Matthew and Brian Harrison, 4:201–4. Oxford: Oxford University Press, 2004.

———. "Reconstructing the Word: The Political Prophecies of Elizabeth Barton (1506–1534)." *Renaissance Quarterly* 50, no. 1 (1997): 136–63.

Wegemer, Gerard. "The 'secret of his heart': What Was Thomas More's?" *Moreana* 52, no. 199–200 (2015): 45–60.

———. *Thomas More on Statesmanship*. Washington, DC: Catholic University of America Press, 1996.

———. *The Young Thomas More and the Arts of Liberty*. Cambridge: Cambridge University Press, 2011.

Whitford, Richard. *The Imitation of Christ: From the First Edition of an English Translation Made c. 1530 by Richard Whitford*. Edited by Edward J. Klein. New York: Harper and Brothers, 1941.

Wilkins, David. *Concilia Magnae Britanniae et Hiberniae*. Vol. 3. London: Sumptibus R. Gosling, 1737.

Wright, Nancy E. "The Name and the Signature of the Author of Margaret Roper's Letter to Alice Alington." In *Ashgate Critical Essays on Women Writers in England*, Vol. 1, *Early Tudor Women Writers*, edited by Elaine V. Beilin, 27–45. Burlington, VT: Ashgate, 2009.

Wriothesley, C. *A Chronicle of England*. Edited by W. D. Hamilton. Camden New Series XI, Vol. 1. Westminster: J. B. Nichols and Sons, 1875.

Zim, Rivka. "Writing behind Bars: Literary Contests and the Authority of Carceral Experience." *Huntington Library Quarterly* 72, no. 2 (2009): 291–311.

INDEX

A

Ackroyd, Peter, 29–31, 158n29, 165n100, 190n24
Act in Restraint of Appeals, 34–36, 112
Act of Succession, 15, 60–61, 138
   Margaret More Roper on, 62, 72–73, 83–84, 88, 102–3, 196n83
   oath to, 1, 8, 15, 37–38, 66, 69–74, 88–92, 98, 102–5, 108–14, 124, 131, 137
Act of Supremacy. *See* Supremacy Act
Act of Treasons. *See* Treasons Act
Act Ratifying the Oath to Succession, 111–13
Aesop, 96–97, 100, 103
Ahnert, Ruth, 154n36
Alexander VI, pope, 161n65
Alington, Alice, 7, 84, 90–92, 94–96, 157n27, 188n7, 189n10, 192n51. See also *Letter to Alington*
Ambrose (Church Father), 57–58
Anderegg, Michael, 173n81
Answer to a Poisoned Book, The (More), 1, 11–12, 15, 33, 35, 158n29, 173n85
   on the Eucharist, 49–51, 174n86
Antony (*Dialogue of Comfort* character), 59, 63–83, 88, 178n2, 179n14, 180nn17–18, 181n32, 183n45, 183n50
   on philosophy, 186n76, 187n79

Apology of Sir Thomas More, Knight, The, 1, 11, 55, 130, 208n122
apostles, 14, 118, 122–23, 129–33, 141, 157n18, 204n83
   Eucharist and, 49–50, 172n73
Aquinas, Thomas, 46, 119–20, 122, 203n72
   Catena aurea, 106–7, 120–22, 125, 134, 203n74, 203n79, 205n89
   on the sacraments, 50, 171n70
Aragon, 98
Aristotle, 194n61
Armenia, 162n79
Arthur, prince of Wales, 23
Articles devised by the whole consent of the King's Council, etc. (English law), 34–35, 39, 43, 112, 197n8, 199n35
Assertio septem sacramentorum (*Assertion of the Seven Sacraments*) (Henry VIII), 24–25, 57, 159n44, 162n76
Audley, Thomas, 90–91, 95–98, 100–102
Augustine (Church Father), 57–58, 69, 207n110
Aurelius, Marcus, 186n78

B

Barnett, Mary Jane, 172n72

Barton, Elizabeth, 34–40, 42–43, 55, 167nn30–31, 167n35, 168n36, 168nn38–39, 168n43, 169nn44–45, 176n102
Basil (Church Father), 56
Basset, Mary, 5, 13–14, 16–18, 158n30, 158n37
Beckett, Thomas, 41
Bede, 122, 205n89
Beilin, Elaine V., 90
Bernard of Clairvaux, 44–45
Bible, 43, 56, 64, 106, 131, 162n79, 170n57, 174n91, 176n103
  Acts of the Apostles, 141–42, 162n79
  Deuteronomy, 19, 23
  Erasmus and, 172n72
  Leviticus, 23
  Psalms, 69, 181n34, 183n50
  See also Gospels
Billingsley, Dale B., 5
Bilney, Thomas, 127, 189n13, 206n108
bishops, 7, 41–42, 107, 116, 129–33, 141, 149n1, 208n121, 208n128, 209n129
Bocking, Edward, 167n31
Bohemia, 169n54
Boleyn, Anne, 36–38, 55, 60–61, 79, 84, 112, 116, 138, 177n105, 186n72
  Rastell on, 179n6
Bolt, Robert, 135, 137, 200n46
Bonaventure, 43–44, 122, 169n55
Bonvisi, Antonio, 200n44
Bridget of Sweden (Saint), 168n43
Brigden, Susan, 38, 167n35
Britain, 152n29. *See also* England; Scotland; Wales
Bullough, Geoffrey, 157n19

C
caesaropapism, 103, 112
Caiaphas, 40

Campeggio, Lorenzo, cardinal, 163n81
Canterbury, 39
Carthusians, Order of, 2, 45, 114–15, 117, 128, 200n38, 200n46, 207n115
Castile, 86, 98–99
Catherine of Siena (Saint), 168n43
Catholicism
  Barton and, 40
  Church councils and, 95, 103, 141
  De tristitia Christi on, 107, 128, 130, 134
  Dialogue of Comfort on, 74, 77, 83, 131
  in England, 2–3, 7, 10, 47, 133, 155n41, 182n35
  Eucharist and, 33, 44, 47–48
  Henry VIII and, 6–7, 39–41, 67–70, 77, 105, 112, 114–16, 131, 141, 155n41, 199n35
  historiography of, 150n6
  Letter to Alington on, 88, 105
  martyrdom and, 127, 134, 205n93, 207n116
  Mary I and, 150n11, 162n72
  monarchy and, 41–42
  More's defense of, 2, 18–23, 30, 34, 37, 39–40, 56, 87, 112, 115, 211n19
  papacy and, 162n75, 211n19
  persecution of, 59, 63, 67–70, 77, 183nn45–46, 183n50, 207n115
  theology of, 172n72
  Tower Works and, 9, 139–40, 153n32
  unity of, 6–7, 37, 42, 47, 67, 83, 108, 125, 150n8, 169n54, 201n57
  See also Latin Church
Cawod, John, 3
Chambers, R. W., 28–30, 182n37, 188n9
Chapuys, Eustace, 37, 166n12, 207n115

Charles V, holy Roman emperor, 86, 150n11, 166n12
Chartier, Roger, 176n102
Chelsea, 1
Christ
  Catholicism and, 42, 128, 133, 150n8, 162n75, 169n54
  De tristitia Christi on, 16, 107–8, 117, 120–26, 128–29, 132–134, 136, 140, 198n10
  Dialogue of Comfort on, 65, 71, 73–75, 80, 139, 198n10
  Erasmus on, 118–20, 136, 202n68, 203n74, 204n81, 204nn83–84, 205n89, 205n91
  Eucharist and, 47–49, 51, 172n75, 173n80, 173n82
  imitation of, 43–45
  Kempis on, 170n61
  at the Last Supper, 21, 49–50
  martyrdom and, 7, 15, 120–26, 132, 206n95
  Mirror of the Blessed Life of Jesu Christ on, 171n63
  in More's writings, 2, 13–14, 44–45, 55, 117–20, 157n18, 157n22, 161n64, 177n105, 202n66, 202n68, 207n119
  Passion of, 14–16, 32, 49, 51–53, 62, 108, 117, 125–26, 128–34, 179n12, 179n14, 198n10, 203n72
  Responsio ad Lutherum on, 19, 163n85
  Resurrection of, 48–50
  Stapleton on, 28
  Treatise upon the Passion on, 44, 56–57, 165n100
Christianity
  De tristitia Christi on, 130, 133
  Dialogue of Comfort on, 65–67, 69–70, 73, 77, 81–82, 182n35, 189n16
  in England, 10, 13, 26
  More's views of, 2, 11, 21–22, 56, 61, 105, 117, 127, 139–41, 211n19
  papacy and, 19–20, 116, 128, 163n83, 207n115, 211n19
  sacraments in, 48
  in the Tower Works, 6, 31
  unity of, 25, 61, 107, 127, 150n7, 169n54
Christian Sentence, A (Frith), 33
Christmas, 158n29, 160n56
Christology, 108, 118–20, 125, 204n81
Chrysostom (Church Father), 58
Church Fathers, 45–46, 57–58, 69, 106–7, 119, 172n71
Church law, 116–17
  Henry VIII and, 1, 23
  More's views of, 24
Cicero, Marcus Tullius, 63, 75–76, 78, 80, 92–93, 191n40, 192n44
Clebsch, William A., 210n2
Clement VII, pope, 161n65
Clement VIII, pope, 23, 34, 36
Colet, John, 118–122, 136, 203n72, 204n81, 204n83
Communion. *See* Eucharist
Complete Works of St. Thomas More, The, 4, 26–29, 149n2, 157n19, 164n92, 177n112
confession (sacrament), 114
Confutation of Tyndale's Answer, The (More), 3, 20, 43, 45, 56, 163n83, 170n62, 206n96
  on the sacraments, 49
Constance, Council of, 199n35
Constantinople, Sixth Council of, 119
controversial literature
  De tristitia Christi as, 134
  Dialogue of Comfort as, 59–60, 74, 154n36
  Letter to Alington as, 89, 96

controversial literature (*continued*)
   by More, 9, 43–47, 49, 56–69,
     132–36, 141, 176n102
   Tower Works as, 3, 8, 12, 29, 31,
     135–36, 153n32
   Treatise upon the Passion as, 43–44,
     46–47, 51–52, 56, 58
   See also polemics
Corinthians, Second Epistle to, 64
County London, 15
Cox, Virginia, 101
Cranmer, Thomas, 36–37, 41, 167n31,
   168n38, 199n23
Cromwell, Thomas, 34–35, 37–40, 84,
   108, 113–17, 125, 140, 163n83
   De tristitia Christi on, 130
   historiography of, 30
   More's letters to, 24–25, 60–61, 93,
     105, 150n7, 159n45, 162n72,
     169n45
Cyprian, bishop of Carthage (saint),
   176n102

D
Debellation of Salem and Bizance, The
   (More), 1, 11, 130
Deiter, Kristen, 150n6
Delcourt, Joseph, 158n28
Dering, John, 167n31
DeSilva, Alvaro, 188–89n9
De tristitia Christi (More), 3–4, 23,
   26–29, 130, 141, 154n35
   on Christ, 16, 107–8, 117, 120–26,
     128–29, 132–34, 136, 140, 198n10
   date of, 6, 108, 117
   on English bishops, 131–34
   manuscript of, 17, 120, 152n21,
     157n19
   on martyrdom, 123–26, 128, 134,
     140, 142
   publication of, 13–15, 17–18, 27
   translation of, 16–18
   Treatise upon the Passion and, 32–33,
     42, 56
   writing of, 106–8, 114, 117, 136,
     174n90
devotional literature, 33, 43–46, 74, 89,
   171n70, 175n94
   De tristitia Christi and, 107, 136,
     154n35
   More and, 11–13, 23, 27–29, 51,
     56–57, 60, 127, 129, 139, 141–42
   Tower Works as, 2, 6, 9, 18
   Treatise upon the Passion as, 34,
     42–43, 58, 165n100
Dialogue concerning Heresies, A (More),
   55, 87–88, 130, 183n44, 189n13,
   208n123
*Dialogue of Comfort against Tribulation,
A* (More), 4, 6–7, 11–12, 15, 18,
   26–29, 63–74, 152n21, 180n17
   autobiographical elements in, 59,
     63, 83–84, 87–90, 107, 154n35,
     181n34, 190n18
   on Church law, 116–17
   on Henry VIII, 110, 136, 139,
     154n36, 180n20, 181n34, 184n51,
     187n79, 187n81
   on the Passion, 198n10
   on persecution, 124, 189n16
   rhetoric of, 74–82
   smuggling of, 190n24
   See also Antony; Vincent
Dillon, Anne, 7, 128, 156n6, 178n4,
   184n54, 205n93
divorce, 23, 35–36, 60, 107, 166n17
Duffy, Eamon, 10, 153n32, 156n6,
   197n9, 206n108, 207n111

E
editing, of More's works, 4–5, 12,
   26–28, 33, 58, 86, 164n91

education, of readers, 51–53
Edward VI, king, 10, 133, 155n4
Elton, Sir Geoffrey, 30–31, 151n16, 190n23, 210n2, 211n11
Elyot, Sir Thomas, 176n102
England, 5, 17, 54, 85–86, 98–100, 151n12, 159n45, 166n17
   Catholicism in, 2–3, 10, 13, 26, 67, 155n41, 182n35, 201n53, 201n57
   clergy in, 36, 129–33, 149n1, 208nn121–23, 208n128, 209n129, 209n137
   law in, 137–39, 141
   More's views of, 2, 59, 64, 140–141, 180n20, 181n33, 197n9, 209n138
   politics of, 1, 34–37, 169n48
   Reformation in, 150n6, 153n32
   religious conflict in, 6–7, 34, 47–48, 50, 103, 105, 107, 110–13
England, Church of, 23, 25, 60, 73, 103, 112, 116, 135–36, 140–41, 159n45
   Act of Succession and, 88, 109–10
   Catholicism and, 155n41
   De tristitia Christi and, 107
English language, 5, 10, 13, 26–28, 52–53, 174n90, 182n39
   Bible in, 43, 56, 130–31, 170n57
   translation into, 16–17, 19, 33, 45, 57, 67, 175n93
Ephesians, Epistle to the, 82
Epictetus, 81, 186n75
Erasmus, 46, 172nn72–73, 194n65
   on Christ, 118–22, 136, 202n68, 203n74, 204n81, 204nn83–84, 205n89, 205n91
   De taedio Iesu, 118–19, 122–23, 202n64, 202n68, 204n81, 204nn83–84, 205n89, 205n91
   on rhetoric, 92–95, 191n40, 192n44, 193n52, 193n59

Eucharist, 11, 26, 32–33, 35, 45–48, 58, 169n54, 171n70, 172n75, 174nn86–87
   Erasmus on, 172n73
   Henry VIII on, 173n81
   Reformation and, 153n33
   Treatise upon the Passion and, 5–6, 32, 42–47, 49–51, 54, 56
Europe, 18, 98, 108, 140, 150n6, 182n39, 197n9
Evangelical Christianity, 50, 54, 127, 166n12
Exposition of the Passion, An (More). See *De tristitia Christi*

F
Feast of Unleavened Bread, 20–21, 28, 160n56
Fisher, John, 25, 35, 114, 131, 162n79, 179n6, 199n33, 200n38
   historiography of, 200n46
   imprisonment of, 111
Florence, Council of, 20, 22, 115, 139, 160n52, 162n78, 162n79
Fludernik, Monica, 178n4, 182n35
Foxe, Edward, 197n8
Foxe, John, 33, 165n6
France, 98–100
French language, 107, 182n39
Frith, John, 33, 55, 173nn80–81, 173n85. See also *Letter against Frith*

G
Gardiner, Stephen, 131
George of Trebizond, 101
Germany, 127
Gerson, Jean Charlier de, 43–44, 51–54, 106–7, 169n55, 174n92, 175nn93–95, 175n97
   Monotesseron, 51–52, 106, 120, 174n90

Gethsemane, garden of, 118, 121, 124, 129, 155n38, 206n95
God
  De tristitia Christi on, 122–25, 132
  Dialogue of Comfort on, 77–82, 181n28, 187n79
  Erasmus on, 119
  Hilton on, 171n64
  Kempis on, 45
  Letter to Alington on, 94–95, 105
  love of, 15
  Margaret More Roper on, 62–63
  More's views of, 2, 38–39, 61–66, 72–74, 109, 115, 117, 137, 140, 181n32, 209n139, 210n2
  papacy and, 19, 24
  prayers to, 10
  protection of, 31
  Rastell on, 17
  sacraments and, 47
  scripture and, 174n91
  service to, 12
Gogan, Brian, 159n44, 162n78, 201n53
Gold, Henry, 38, 167n31
Gonnell, William, 172n71
Goodrich, Jaime, 188n9, 191n36
Gordon, Walter M., 188n9
Gospels, 14, 45, 52–54, 106, 129–30, 133, 171n70, 174nn90–91
  Fisher on, 162n79
  Haupt on, 171n67
  of John, 16, 21–23, 49, 160n56, 175n97
  of Luke, 16, 21, 160n56
  of Mark, 14, 16, 21, 120, 175n93, 205n89
  of Matthew, 16, 21, 120, 122, 175n93, 203n79, 206n94
  Synoptic, 21, 175n97
  See also Bible
Greece, 22
Greek language, 54, 186n73

Greek Orthodox Church, 20–24, 35, 40–41, 139, 160n52, 160n54, 161n61, 162n79
Gregory, Brad S., 154n35
Gregory, saint, 24, 161n70
Guy, John, 18–19, 24–25, 29, 154n37, 159n40, 193n60, 210n2
  on the *Letter to Alington*, 90
  on More's canonization, 152n29
  on St. German, 149n4

H
Harpsfield, Nicholas, 12–13, 27–28, 67, 152n21, 156n11, 157n25, 164n92, 207n116
  Life and Death of Sir Thomas More, Knight, 10, 28, 156n6, 199n29
Harris, John, 15, 20, 158n27, 159nn28–29, 190n24, 203n72
Haupt, Gary, 4, 26–27, 107, 164nn91–92, 171n67
Headley, John M., 26, 163n84
heaven, 6, 13, 30, 35, 124, 172n73
  Dialogue of Comfort on, 66, 80
  More's writings on, 15, 30, 62, 105, 127, 142, 181n32
Hebrew language, 54
Henry VIII, king
  ambassadors of, 18, 159n43
  Catholicism and, 6–7, 39–41, 67–70, 77, 105, 112, 114–16, 131, 141, 155n41, 199n35
  clergy and, 41, 73, 131, 133, 208n128
  Dialogue of Comfort on, 110, 136, 139, 154n36, 180n20, 181n34, 184n51, 187n79, 187n81
  divorce of, 23, 35–37, 60, 166n17
  Eucharist and, 173n81
  foreign policy of, 100
  Letter to Alington on, 85, 88, 94
  marriages of, 169n48, 186n72
  Mary I and, 40

More and, 1–3, 5–7, 25, 30, 33–39, 42, 60–61, 107, 112–17, 137, 193n60
in More's works, 55, 59–60, 67, 79, 83, 125, 129–30, 139–40, 177n105
papacy and, 19, 25, 34–41, 112, 116, 128–31, 134, 149n1, 159n44, 162n75, 162n77, 163nn81–82, 166n14
Roper on, 150n11
St. German and, 149n4
Tower Works on, 19, 39
Utopia on, 96
views of monarchy, 160n49, 166n17
writings of, 24, 57, 107, 162n76, 197n8
heresy, 2–3, 10, 13, 43, 116
More's views of, 29, 56, 127, 130, 156n6, 206n108, 207n111, 209n138, 210nn2–3
persecution of, 127, 136, 189n13, 208n121, 210n2
schism and, 61, 69, 126, 155n39, 206n105
Treatise on the Passion on, 6, 33, 43, 47, 51
Hesychius (Church Father), 57
Hilary, 122–123, 126, 204n84
Hilton, Walter, 44–45, 171n64, 171n66
Scala perfectionis, 43–44, 169n55
Hitton, Thomas, 206n206
Holbein (Hans Holbein the Younger), 210n3
Holy Spirit, 51, 163n84
Horace, 55
House, Seymour Baker, 153n31, 155n38, 202n61, 206n95
House of Lords, 41. *See also* Parliament
humanism, 85–86, 93, 101, 192n50
More and, 2, 58, 83, 136, 150n9, 155n2, 156n6, 189n13, 210n2

Hungary, 67, 180n20, 181nn33–34, 182n35
Huss, Jan, 169n54
Hutchings, W. H., 171n63

I
Ignatius, saint, 24, 161n71
Imitation of Christ, The, 44–45, 170n62
Innocent III, pope, 161n65
irony, 55, 87, 97–98, 100–101, 142
Islam, 67
Italy, 98–99
Ives, Eric, 186n72

J
James, apostle, 120
Jerome, saint, 22, 58, 118–21, 204n83
John, apostle, 120. *See also* Gospels: of John; John the Evangelist
John Chrysostom, 22
John Damascene, 120–121, 203n79
John the Evangelist, 24, 161n71. *See also* Gospels: of John; John, apostle
Joye, George, 33, 57, 173n81
Judaism, 20–21, 41, 118, 120, 160n56
Judas Iscariot, 51, 121, 129–130, 204n83
Julius II, pope, 23

K
Katherine of Aragon, 23, 37, 39–40, 60–61, 169n48
Kempis, Thomas à, 44–45, 170n59, 170n61, 171n70
King's College, 157n19
Kyngeston, Susan, 176n102

L
Lambeth Palace, 16, 41, 89
Last Supper, 20–22, 47, 49–50
Latin Church, 20–21, 23–24, 112, 162n79. *See also* Catholicism

Latin language, 25, 33, 52–54, 56–58, 67, 93, 107, 120, 175n94, 182n39, 197n8
   More's writings in, 13, 16, 18, 27, 51, 54, 132–34, 158n33, 163n85, 174n90
   translation of, 5, 149n2, 171n63
Leo X, pope, 161n65
Letter against Frith (More), 35, 173nn80–81, 174n86
Letter to Alington (Roper and More), 6–7, 88, 90–91, 97–98, 100, 103–4, 110, 139–41
   authorship of, 86–87, 89, 91, 93, 154n37, 188n9, 189n10
   rhetoric of, 85–86, 89, 92–96, 101–2, 136, 192n51, 195n76
Letter to Dorp (More), 93
lions, 182n38
literacy, 53–54, 58
London, 4, 17, 33, 37–38, 42, 46, 50, 201n57
   public opinion in, 40, 150n11, 176n102
   readers in, 54–55
Longland, John, 131
Louvain, 4
Love, Nicholas, 171n63
Ludolph of Saxony
   Vita Christi, 45–46, 171n67, 171n70
Luther, Martin, 19, 25, 44, 115, 161n64, 162nn75–76, 162n79, 210n3
   Henry VIII and, 19, 162n75, 163n81
Lutheranism, 25, 88, 116, 127, 155n2, 162n77, 181n33, 209n138

M
Magna Carta, 141
Man for All Seasons, A (film), 135, 198n17, 200n46
Manley, Frank, 27

Mantel, Hilary, 135, 137, 198n17, 200n46
Marc'hadour, Germain, 157n27, 165n5
Marius, Richard, 29–31, 159n44, 210n3
marriage, 23, 35–36, 60–61, 99, 116, 139, 161n65, 168n38
Marshall, Peter, 153n31, 155n41, 179n7
Martin V, pope, 161n65
martyrdom, 40, 42, 184n54, 206n95, 206n101
   De tristitia Christi on, 123–26, 128, 134, 140, 142
   of More, 5–7, 10, 13–15, 69, 108, 115, 125–29, 142, 152n29, 156n6, 207n116
   More's views of, 77, 106–8, 117–18, 120–28, 132–34, 140, 154n35, 205nn91–93
martyr literature, 6, 10
Martz, Louis L., 27, 87, 125–26, 189n16, 190n24, 193n57, 204n81
Mary I, 3, 5, 9–10, 24, 39–40, 61, 89, 133, 150n11, 162n72, 205n93
Master, Richard, 167n31
Maundy Thursday, 20–21
Meditationes vitae Christi, 44, 171n63, 171n67
Miles, Leland, 154n35
Miller, Clarence, 16, 18, 27, 107, 120, 132, 154n35, 157n19
   on Erasmus, 204n83
   on martyrdom, 122–23, 126–27, 206n101
Mirror of the Blessed Life of Jesu Christ, 44, 171n63, 171n67
Mitjans, Frank, 157n27
Mohács, Battle of, 182n35
More, Alice, 30, 93, 120
More, Thomas
   advice to Margaret More Roper, 59, 62–65, 70–74, 78, 83, 90, 103–4, 111

allegory and, 173n85, 174n86
Anne Boleyn and, 179n6
arrest of, 37, 60, 210n3
audiences for writings of, 52–56, 156n10, 182n39
Barton and, 38, 167n31, 168n39, 169nn44–45
on the Bible, 170n57, 174n91, 175n93, 175n97, 181n34
on Christ, 118–26, 150nn7–8, 177n105, 179n14, 202n66, 202n68, 204n81, 204n83, 205n89
controversial literature of, 43–46, 51–52, 56–69, 74, 89, 96, 132–36, 141, 176n102
on English bishops, 129–33, 208nn121–23
on the Eucharist, 46–47, 49–51, 56, 171n70, 172nn72–73, 173n80, 173n82
Gerson and, 51–53, 174n90
Gogan on, 159n44
Guy on, 152n29, 159n40
Harpsfield on, 157n25
on heaven, 15, 30, 62, 105, 127, 142, 181n32
Henry VIII and, 33–39, 60–61, 107, 110, 112–17, 180n20, 193n60
Hilton and, 171n66
historiography of, 3, 9–10, 15, 18–19, 26–31, 135–36, 150n9, 151n13, 151n16, 155n2, 198n17, 200n46, 210nn2–3
imprisonment of, 2, 10–13, 25, 30, 62, 64, 74, 97, 106, 111, 137, 181n34
on the Last Supper, 20–21, 49–50
letters to Margaret More Roper, 62–63, 66, 72–74, 89–90, 109, 113, 125, 131
Letter to Alington and, 86–98, 102–5, 110, 188n9, 189n10, 190n25, 192n51

martyrdom of, 5–7, 10, 13–15, 69, 108, 115, 125–29, 142, 152n29, 156n6, 207n116
on martyrdom, 77, 106–8, 117–18, 120–28, 132–34, 140, 154n35, 205nn91–93
on monarchy, 42, 85–87, 96–102, 104–5, 109, 111, 115, 138, 182n38
on the persecution of Catholics, 67–69, 71, 77, 124, 134, 141, 155n38, 183n50
pilgrimages of, 157n26
polemics of, 2–3, 11–13, 18, 23, 43–44, 58, 107, 136, 140–42, 150n9, 151n13, 155n2
prosecution of, 34, 112–17, 135–42, 199nn22–23, 200n38, 211n11, 211n18
on Protestantism, 197n9, 209n138
Rastell and, 164n91
resignation of, 1, 149n4, 208n120
rhetoric of, 74–82, 86, 92–96, 101–5, 136, 188nn4–5, 195n76
Roper on, 12, 24, 156n6
on schism, 6–7, 19, 22–26, 39–40, 61–62, 77, 115–16, 126–28, 139, 155n39, 206n105
Stapleton on, 164n95
support of the papacy, 5–7, 18–26, 39–40, 60–61, 110, 141, 155n41, 160nn52–53, 162n72, 162n75, 162n79, 163nn83–85, 211n19
on virtue, 172n71, 181n28
Walker on, 151n12
Whitford and, 170n62
writing of *De tristitia Christi*, 106–8, 114, 117, 136, 174n90
writing of the *Treatise upon the Passion*, 32–34, 42–45, 57–58, 106–7, 152n21, 158nn28–29, 165n100, 171n67, 174n90

More, Thomas (*continued*)
  writings of, 1–8, 11–13, 16–17, 26–28, 31–32, 178n4, 190n24, 200n44

N
Nix, Richard, 131
Norwich, 127
Nussbaum, Martha, 186n73

O
O'Malley, John W., 119
oratory, 53, 75–76, 78, 80–81, 85, 92–95, 192n44, 194n61. *See also* rhetoric
Origen, 120–21, 203n79
Orthodox Church. *See* Greek Orthodox Church
Ottoman Empire, 30, 67, 75, 81–82, 181n34, 182n35, 184n51
Oxford, 118

P
papacy, 41–42, 149n1, 162n78, 197n8, 199n35, 201n53
  Act of Succession and, 88, 109, 111
  Henry VIII and, 19, 25, 34–41, 112, 116, 128–31, 134, 149n1, 159n44, 162n75, 162n77, 163nn81–82, 166n14
  martyrdom and, 125, 127, 134, 140
  More's support of, 5–7, 18–20, 22–26, 39–40, 60–61, 110, 141, 155n41, 160nn52–53, 162n72, 162n75, 162n79, 163nn83–85, 211n19
Parliament (England), 6, 15, 36, 60, 104–5, 108, 111–13, 137, 196n83, 201n57
  papacy and, 166n17
Passion, of Christ, 14–16, 32, 49, 51, 53, 62, 108, 117, 125–26, 128, 131–34, 179n12, 179n14, 203n72
  Dialogue of Comfort on, 198n10
  See also *De tristitia Christi*; *Treatise upon the Passion of Christ, A*
Passover, 21, 160n56. *See also* Feast of Unleavened Bread
Patenson, Henry, 38, 103
Paul, Joanne, 153n31, 162n72
Paul the Apostle, 64, 82, 132, 141–42, 172n72
peace, 22, 61, 98–99, 127, 170n61
Peter, saint, 24, 71, 120, 128, 163nn83–85, 184n55
Petrarch, 92
philosophers, political role of, 85, 95, 97–99
philosophy, 77–78, 82, 95, 97–98, 186n76, 186n78, 194n65, 203n74
Plato, 85, 97–98, 119
Pole, Reginald, cardinal, 156n6
polemics, 101, 156n6
  De tristitia Christi as, 129–30, 132–34
  Dialogue of Comfort as, 59, 82–83, 154n36
  Letter to Alington as, 89, 91, 96
  More and, 2–3, 11–13, 18, 23, 43–44, 58, 107, 136, 140–42, 150n9, 151n13, 155n2
  Tower Works and, 7, 9, 24, 31, 51, 57, 153n32
  Treatise upon the Passion as, 22, 29, 34, 42, 46–47, 49, 54
  See also controversial literature
politics, 1, 34–37, 60, 67, 85, 95, 97–99, 169n48
  De tristitia Christi and, 124, 127
Prada, Andrés Vázquez de, 157n19
prayer, 10, 28, 65, 74, 125, 128, 132, 142, 152n19, 171n66, 207n117
  Dialogue of Comfort on, 82
  Erasmus on, 46
  reading and, 43, 175n94, 183n50

Tower Works and, 3, 26
Treatise upon the Passion and, 6, 39, 45
Privy Council (England), 99, 113
Protestantism, 151n16, 153n32, 155n4, 197n9, 205n93, 209n138. *See also* England, Church of; Evangelical Christianity; Lutheranism; Reformation

Q
Quintilian, 76, 81, 192n44, 195n76

R
Rastell, William
  on the Act of Succession, 111
  on Anne Boleyn, 179n6
  Barton and, 169n45
  editing of More's works, 4–5, 12, 26–28, 33, 39–40, 58, 60–61, 86, 164n91
  interpretation of the Tower Works, 8–9, 12–16, 18, 23, 26–33, 153n31
  Letter to Alington and, 7, 86–87, 89, 190n25
  Margaret More Roper and, 72, 83–84, 86, 90, 187n82, 190n24
  modern scholarship and, 4, 136, 152n21, 156n6, 165n5
  on More's martyrdom, 128–29, 152n29
  publication of More's works, 2–3, 9–11, 17–19, 34–35, 42, 67–68, 133, 152n19
  Reed on, 152n22, 152n27
  on the translation of *De tristitia Christi*, 16–18
  Treatise upon the Passion and, 57–58
Reed, A.W., 152n22, 152n27
Reformation, 88, 150n6, 153nn32–33, 155n4, 168n36, 197n9
  martyrdom and, 7, 207n116

theology of, 10, 51
Tower Works and, 6, 136, 154n36
Treatise upon the Passion on, 44, 55
See also England, Church of; Evangelical Christianity; Lutheranism; Protestantism
Responsio ad Lutherum (Response to Luther) (More), 19–20, 58, 115, 160n52, 162nn78–79, 163n85
Resurrection, of Christ, 48–50
Rex, Richard, 167n35, 168n36
Reynolds, E. E., 29–30, 91, 190n25
Reynolds, Richard, 114
Rhenanus, Beatus, 188n8
rhetoric
  Erasmus on, 92–95, 191n40, 192n44, 193n52, 193n59
  of the *Letter to Alington*, 85–86, 89, 92–96, 101–2, 136, 192n51, 195n76
  of More, 74–82, 86, 92–96, 101–5, 136, 188nn4–5, 193n60, 195n76
Rhetorica ad Herennium (book), 63, 75–76, 78, 81, 93–94, 191n38, 192nn50–51
Rich, Hugh, 167n31, 168n39
Rich, Richard, 135–40, 199n22, 200n38, 211n18
Ridley, Jasper, 210n3
Risby, Richard, 167n31
Rodgers, Katherine Gardiner, 205n92, 206n101
Roman Catholicism. *See* Catholicism; Latin Church
Roman Empire, 76
Rome, 19–20, 23–24, 26
Roper, Margaret More
  biographies of, 29
  family of, 16–17, 180n17
  letters from, 6, 62–63, 83–84, 89–90, 114, 180n18, 180n24, 187n82

Roper, Margaret More (*continued*)
  letters to, 18, 62–63, 66, 72–74, 89–91, 109, 113, 117, 125, 131, 151n16
  Letter to Alington and, 7, 85–91, 94–97, 102–5, 188n7, 188n9, 189n10
  More's advice to, 59, 62–65, 70–74, 78, 83, 90, 103–4, 111
  on the oath to the Act of Succession, 62, 72–73, 83–84, 88, 102–3, 196n83
  scholarship of, 191n36
  visits to Thomas More, 12, 73, 75, 84, 89, 91, 114–15, 159n40, 190n24
Roper, William, 10, 30, 88, 110, 133, 156n6, 156n11, 211n18
  Life of Sir Thomas More, The, 12–13, 24, 111, 150n11

S
Sacramentarians, 6, 43, 45, 50, 54, 181n33
sacraments, 41–42, 114, 127–28, 152n19, 153n33, 169n44, 172n75, 174n87
  Confutation of Tyndale's Answer on, 49
  in England, 176n102
  Letter against Frith on, 173n80
  theology of, 172n72
  Treatise upon the Passion on, 6, 27–28, 43–47, 49–51, 56–57
  Tyndale on, 47–49, 51, 57, 173n77, 173n81
  See also Eucharist
sainthood, of More, 5, 13, 136, 152n29, 154n37
saints, 42, 57, 105, 127–28, 141–42
schism
  between Anglicanism and Catholicism, 1–2, 6–7, 19, 22–26, 34, 42, 77, 149n4, 209n129

  Antony on, 69, 77
  between Catholic and Orthodox Churches, 22–23, 139
  De tristitia Christi on, 107, 125, 130, 133
  Dialogue of Comfort on, 6–7
  heresy and, 61, 69, 126, 155n39, 206n105
  More's views of, 19, 22–26, 39–40, 61–62, 77, 115–16, 126–28, 139, 155n39, 206n105
  Treatise upon the Passion on, 22–23, 35, 37 42, 47, 105, 139
Scholasticism, 50, 119, 202n70, 204n81
Scotland, 99
Scott, Alison V., 154n37, 184n53
Seneca, 81–82
Sherborne, Robert, 131
slavery, 67, 81–82
Spain, 37, 40, 100, 207n115
Standish, Henry, 41, 131
Stapleton, Thomas, 14, 27–28, 90, 106, 157n26, 164n95, 181n33
  on Harris, 157n27, 203n72
  on the *Treatise upon the Passion*, 28, 164n92
Stephen, saint, 141–42
St. German, Christopher, 11, 73, 149n4, 208n122
Stoicism, 81–82, 187n79
St. Peter's Basilica, 152n29
Submission of the Clergy (law), 1, 130
Suleiman the Magnificent, 184n51
Supper of the Lord, The (anonymous), 11, 33, 48, 50, 57, 173n81, 174n86
Supremacy Act, 35, 107, 112–13, 116, 211n11
Switzerland, 98
Synoptic Gospels, 21, 175n97
Syon Abbey, 38

T
Tenebrae Wednesday, 20
Tertullian (Church Father), 57
Theophylactus, 121–22, 203n79
Thomas of Canterbury, saint. *See* Beckett, Thomas
Tottell, Richard, 3
Tower of London
  Barton in, 37
  Margaret More Roper's visits to, 12, 73, 75, 84, 89, 91, 114–15, 159n40, 190n24
  More in, 2, 5, 11–16, 27–30, 32, 84–85, 87, 107–8, 111, 123–25, 134, 137
"Tower Works" (More), 2–8, 26–31, 140, 142, 157n25, 165n5
  date of, 10–11, 27
  definition of, 15–16, 27
  on Henry VIII, 19, 139
  historiography of, 60, 135–36, 151n16
  Treatise upon the Passion and, 9, 33, 57–58, 153n31, 158n28, 164n92
Tracy, James D., 120
Treasons Act, 38, 112–13, 117, 138–39, 168n36, 200n38, 200n40, 200n44
Treatise upon the Passion of Christ, A (More), 3–5, 13, 26–27, 51–55, 153n31, 165n3, 166n9, 172n74
  on Christ, 44, 56–57, 165n100
  as controversial literature, 43–44, 46–47, 51–52, 56, 58
  date of, 15–16, 27–29, 32–33, 158nn28–29, 164n92
  on the Eucharist, 5–6, 32, 42–44, 46–47, 49–51, 54, 56
  Haupt on, 171n67
  on the Last Supper, 20–22, 49–50
  Rastell and, 9, 57–58
  on schism, 22–23, 35, 37, 42, 47, 105, 139
  writing of, 32–34, 42–45, 57–58, 106–7, 152n21, 158nn28–29, 165n100, 171n67, 174n90
Tunstall, Cuthbert, 131, 199n35, 209n137
Tyndale, William, 20, 33, 52, 55, 127, 172n74, 173n77, 206n106
  Answer to More, 47–49
  on the Eucharist, 47–49, 51, 57, 173n81
  on obedience, 160n49
  translation of the Bible, 43, 130–31

U
United Kingdom. *See* Britain; England; Scotland; Wales
Utopia (More), 2, 67, 85–88, 101–2, 136, 188n5, 193n60, 210n2
  on royal service, 96–100, 132
  theology and, 187n1, 188n8

V
Valencia, Spain, 157n19
Venice, 98, 192n50
Vincent (*Dialogue of Comfort* character), 59, 63–65, 67–75, 77–83, 88, 116, 182n39, 183n50, 184nn55–56
  Margaret More Roper and, 180n18, 180n23
Virgin Mary, 103, 121

W
Wales, 135
Waley, John, 3
Walker, Greg, 140–41, 151n12, 211n25
war, 98–100
Warham, William, 41–42, 110, 149n1, 167n31
Watt, Diane, 168n43
Whitford, Richard, 170n62
Wilsdon (parish), 15, 157n27

Wolsey, Thomas, cardinal, 25, 93, 98–101, 162n77
women, public role of, 191n36
Worde, Wynkyn de, 44
Works of Sir Thomas More, The, 2–3, 10, 13, 17, 28–29, 33, 60–61, 152n27
Wriothesley, Charles, 37–38, 40

Y
Yale University, 4, 26–28, 149n2, 157n19, 164n92, 177n112

Z
Zim, Rivka, 180n20
Zinneman, Fred, 135
Zwingli, Huldrych, 35, 173n81

TRAVIS CURTRIGHT is professor of humanities and literature at Ave Maria University. He is the author or editor of four previous books, including *The One Thomas More*, and is the editor-in-chief of *Moreana: Thomas More and Renaissance Studies*.

www.ingramcontent.com/pod-product-compliance
Lightning Source LLC
Chambersburg PA
CBHW050137240426
43673CB00043B/1699